GENERATIVE AI IN PRACTICE

GENERATIVE AI
IN PRACTICE

GENERATIVE AI IN PRACTICE

100+ AMAZING WAYS GENERATIVE ARTIFICIAL INTELLIGENCE IS CHANGING BUSINESS AND SOCIETY

BERNARD MARR

WILEY

Registered Offices
John Wiley & Sons, Inc., 111 River Street, Hoboken, NJ 07030, USA
John Wiley & Sons Ltd, The Atrium, Southern Gate, Chichester, West Sussex, PO19 8SQ, UK

For details of our global editorial offices, customer services, and more information about Wiley products visit us at www.wiley.com.

Wiley also publishes its books in a variety of electronic formats and by print-on-demand. Some content that appears in standard print versions of this book may not be available in other formats.

Library of Congress Cataloging-in-Publication Data:

Names: Marr, Bernard, author.
Title: Generative AI in practice : 100+ amazing ways generative artificial
   intelligence is changing business and society / Bernard Marr.
Description: Hoboken, NJ : John Wiley & Sons, Inc., 2024.
Identifiers: LCCN 2024000295 (print) | LCCN 2024000296 (ebook) | ISBN
   9781394245567 (cloth) | ISBN 9781394254255 (adobe pdf) | ISBN
   9781394254248 (epub)
Subjects: LCSH: Artificial intelligence—Economic aspects. | Artificial
   intelligence—Social aspects.
Classification: LCC HC79.I55 M36528 2024 (print) | LCC HC79.I55 (ebook) |
   DDC 658/.0563—dc23/eng/20240111
LC record available at https://lccn.loc.gov/2024000295
LC ebook record available at https://lccn.loc.gov/2024000296

Cover Design: Wiley
Cover Image: © Jannatul Koraise/Adobe Stock

Set in 11/14 pts Minion Pro by Straive, Chennai, India

SKY10066836_020824

To my wife, Claire, my anchor in the shifting seas of life, whose love lights the way through every storm. And to my children, Sophia, James, and Oliver, my brightest stars in the vast universe, who remind me every day that the most profound truths often come from the simplest curiosities.

CONTENTS

ABOUT THE AUTHOR

Bernard Marr is a world-renowned futurist, influencer, and thought leader in the fields of business and technology, with a passion for using technology for the good of humanity. He is a multi-award-winning and internationally bestselling author of over 20 books, writes a regular column for *Forbes*, and advises and works with many of the world's best-known organizations. Bernard has a combined subscriber base of 4 million people across his social media channels and newsletters and was ranked by LinkedIn as one of the top five business influencers in the world.

Bernard helps organizations and their management teams prepare for future trends and create the strategies to succeed. He has worked with or advised many of the world's best-known organizations, including Amazon, Microsoft, Google, Dell, IBM, Walmart, Shell, Cisco, HSBC, Toyota, Nokia, Vodafone, T-Mobile, the NHS, Walgreens Boots Alliance, the Home Office, the Ministry of Defence, NATO, and the United Nations, among many others.

Connect with Bernard on LinkedIn, X (@bernardmarr), Facebook, Instagram, and YouTube to take part in an ongoing conversation; subscribe to Bernard's podcast; and head to www.bernardmarr.com for more information and hundreds of free articles, whitepapers, and e-books.

If you would like to talk to Bernard about any advisory work, speaking engagements, or influencer services, please contact him via email at hello@bernardmarr.com.

INTRODUCTION

It feels like generative AI has come out of nowhere, doesn't it? Perhaps you were happily going through life thinking artificial intelligence was something *other people* had to worry about. And then boom! Suddenly, everyone's talking about this new thing called "ChatGPT" and how it's going to take over everyone's jobs.

As you've no doubt noticed, there's a lot of hype around generative AI (or GenAI as I call it in this book), and tools like ChatGPT. I expect you've picked up this book because you want to cut through the chatter and understand just what the deal is with GenAI. Is it really worthy of the hype? How might GenAI impact your job? Should your organization be leveraging this technology?

To answer the first question, yes, GenAI really is worthy of all the noise. I believe it's one of the most powerful, transformative technologies that humans have ever had access to. It's right up there with the emergence of the internet. Seriously! We'll cover the second and third questions throughout this book but, spoiler alert, GenAI (probably) won't take your job. That said, it will almost certainly change the way you work. And yes, your organization should absolutely be looking to harness this transformative technology. That's why I wrote this book.

The Incredible Impact of Generative AI

I'm not the only one convinced that GenAI is utterly transformative.

One study led by Harvard found that GenAI tools helped workers at the Boston Consulting Group gain a 40% performance boost.[1] We'll see many examples throughout the book of organizations using GenAI to accomplish work more easily, lighten the burden of mundane tasks, and provide a better employee (and customer) experience.

GenAI will be so ubiquitous that Bloomberg predicts the GenAI market will explode from £40 billion in 2022, to a whopping US$1.3 trillion by 2032.[2] What's more, according to research by McKinsey, GenAI could add up to US$4.4 trillion in value to the global economy annually – and save up to 70% of workers' time.[3] It's no wonder McKinsey refers to GenAI as "the next productivity frontier."

That's the economic impact, but what about our everyday lives and the way we do business? That, too, will be fundamentally altered by GenAI. We'll talk about the business and societal impact in Chapter 3, but to whet your appetite, GenAI will change how we work, how we shop, how we consume content, how we experience healthcare, how we learn (at school and otherwise), how we play video games, and even potentially how we date. Adam Selipsky, CEO of Amazon Web Services, says GenAI will "pretty much change every application inside of companies, every application that consumers interact with. It is a profound technological change that we're still at the very beginning of."[4] I couldn't agree more.

But wait, back up a minute . . . US$4.4 trillion in economic benefit? I know what you're thinking. *How the heck can chatbots add so much value?*

Because Generative AI Is More than Chatbots

We'll delve into a more detailed definition of GenAI in Chapter 1, but for now, all you need to know is that GenAI is a facet of artificial intelligence that allows computers to create content, including (but not limited to) text. One of the ways in which this technology can be harnessed is through more intuitive, more responsive chatbots – chatbots with advanced language capabilities that can respond to complex queries, and understand *context* as well as content.

ChatGPT is a chatbot. Developed by OpenAI and available free for public use (although a paid-for, upgraded version is available), it's probably the most advanced chatbot we've ever seen. It can answer almost any question you throw at it. It's brilliant. It's a great example of GenAI in action. However, GenAI is much bigger than ChatGPT. And its uses extend far beyond chatbots.

Therefore, this is not a book about ChatGPT (although ChatGPT will obviously feature in several examples throughout). This book shines a light on the vast array of tasks that GenAI tools can accomplish – from designing video games to interpreting medical scans, and more. Yes, GenAI gives computers the ability to converse and answer questions. But it can do so much more on top of that.

Almost every time I type "GenAI," I think of the word "genie." And for good reason. Working with GenAI is a bit like having your own personal genie to help lighten the load, get more done, and generally make life easier. (If only it could grant infinite wishes. . .)

That said, as we'll see in this book, getting the best out of GenAI requires a balance between human expertise and machine intelligence. This isn't about total automation – it's about humans collaborating with GenAI to *do things better*. At the end of the day, GenAI is just a tool. An incredible tool. But a tool nonetheless – and it's up to us to use it thoughtfully.

With that in mind, my hope is that GenAI will be used not just as a productivity tool, but as a force for good in our world. As an example, in Chapter 11, we'll see how GenAI can be used to democratize access to healthcare for people around the world. And in Chapter 14, we'll see how GenAI is speeding up the process of discovering life-saving new drugs. True, it can also be used to generate fake content to sway elections or be harnessed by criminals for all sorts of nefarious purposes. But GenAI also has the potential to help solve some of humanity's biggest challenges.

What to Expect from This Book

The bulk of this book focuses on practical applications of GenAI across a wide range of sectors. In other words, we'll explore how organizations are already using this technology – and, in the process, help you unearth potential use cases for your own organization. That's the focus of Part 2 of this book, practical examples and takeaways from other organizations that have deployed GenAI.

Then in Part 3, we'll look at keys for success when implementing GenAI in your own business. Plus, you'll find predictions for the future of GenAI.

But before all that, Part 1 sets the scene for this powerful, transformative technology. We'll explore what the technology is, how it works, how it will change our world (and the world of business), and how it will impact jobs. We'll also take an honest look at the risks and challenges that surround GenAI.

Before you tuck into Part 1, it's important to note that GenAI technology is rapidly evolving. And it's getting better and better all the time. Indeed, one of the things that made this book challenging to write is the fact that the technology is advancing so darn quickly. Amazing new use cases and updates to GenAI tools were emerging literally every week. As an example, I'd barely finished writing Part 1 when OpenAI launched a new version of ChatGPT that could not just answer written questions, but also understand speech and visuals, and respond in an artificial voice.

Safe to say, by the time you read this, new tools and new examples will have surfaced that continue to surprise and delight. It's truly an exciting time.

Notes

1. Enterprise workers gain 40 percent performance boost from GPT-4, Harvard study finds; *Venture Beat*; https://venturebeat.com/ai/enterprise-workers-gain-40-percent-performance-boost-from-gpt-4-harvard-study-finds/
2. Generative AI to become a $1.3 trillion market by 2032, Research finds; *Bloomberg*; https://www.bloomberg.com/company/press/generative-ai-to-become-a-1-3-trillion-market-by-2032-research-finds/
3. The economic potential of generative AI: The next productivity frontier; *McKinsey*; https://www.mckinsey.com/capabilities/mckinsey-digital/our-insights/the-economic-potential-of-generative-ai-the-next-productivity-frontier
4. AWS CEO: Generative AI will 'pretty much change' every application consumers interact with; *YouTube*; https://www.youtube.com/watch?v=jQ18HJkLJjw

Part 1
SETTING THE SCENE FOR AN AI REVOLUTION

I said in my introduction that Generative AI (GenAI) is one of the most powerful technologies humans have ever had access to. But what exactly is GenAI and how does it work? How did we get to this point? And how, broadly speaking, might GenAI change our world?

In Part 1, we'll answer all those questions and more. We'll define *GenAI* and how it works, explore the evolution of GenAI until this point, outline the risks associated with GenAI, and take a big-picture look at how GenAI is going to change our world – including the jobs that humans do. This will set the scene nicely before we delve into GenAI use cases across various sectors and industries in Part 2.

1

UNVEILING GENERATIVE AI: A NEW FRONTIER

Okay, let's go back to basics. What is generative AI (artificial intelligence)? How does it work? And what is the technology capable of? You'll find out in this chapter as we delve under the hood of GenAI, tug at a few wires, and examine what the heck's going on in there.

I really want this chapter to give you an inspiring feel for the many things that GenAI is capable of – but also to drive home the point that GenAI isn't just about ChatGPT (Chat Generative Pre-trained Transformer). Sure, ChatGPT is a prime example of GenAI (and it certainly hoovers up the majority of GenAI's press), but there's a lot more to GenAI than ChatGPT . . . as you'll find out in this chapter.

What Is Generative AI? A Quick Explanation

Actually, let's start by defining artificial intelligence (AI) in its broadest sense. The term "AI" refers to computer algorithms that can effectively simulate human cognitive processes, like learning, decision-making, and problem-solving.

GenAI is a groundbreaking subset of AI – the cutting edge of the cutting edge – that is able to create new content based on patterns and structures it has learned from existing data. Like any AI, GenAI tools are given enormous amounts of data to learn from (what's known as "training data"). They learn

3

from the training data, and then use the patterns or rules that they've learned to create new content that's similar to, but not exactly the same as, the data they have been trained on.

An example or two

A good example is DALL-E 2 – the text-to-art platform that allows anyone to generate artworks. Or, of course, there's ChatGPT, the language model that can create text based on conversational text prompts. (You'll find a much bigger list of GenAI tools in the Appendix, by the way.) These systems learn from huge training datasets – ChatGPT, for example, was trained on vast amounts of text from the internet, including web pages, articles, and books.

Text and images are perhaps two of the best-known uses of GenAI so far, but the technology is capable of so much more. With GenAI you can generate product designs, computer code, music, video, voices, and even entire visual worlds. We'll talk more about GenAI's capabilities later in the chapter, but to whet your appetite, imagine being able to create unique video game worlds rendered in real time, or have a book written *just for you*, or have your favorite celebrity read you today's news. The possibilities are mind-blowing.

The capabilities are already quite impressive, but in the future, GenAI systems will be able to create pretty much anything that humans can. And this, in turn, means GenAI can turn anyone and everyone into an author, musician, computer programmer, filmmaker, or other type of creator.

How GenAI differs from the AI we are used to

AI is increasingly part of the world around us, including the search results you get on your phone, your conversations with Alexa, and the movie recommendations that Netflix serves up on an evening. So what makes GenAI different to these "traditional" AI tools? (I realize it sounds strange to refer to "traditional AI" when it's hardly been around that long, but I do so to distinguish between the AI that we're already used to in everyday life and this new evolution of AI systems. One technical term for traditional AI is "discriminative AI.")

Traditional AI systems also learn from large amounts of data, but they deliver a different output. Traditional AI systems are used to make *predictions* based on existing data. And we use those predictions to help us make better decisions, at work and in everyday life. This could span anything from listening to new music on Spotify, and viewing recommended products on Amazon, to identifying which of your company's customers are most likely to buy a certain product.

This new wave of GenAI tools goes even further, by *creating new content* based on existing data. In other words, GenAI isn't just about simulating human cognitive processes like decision-making and problem-solving – it's about simulating *human creativity*.

To further illustrate the difference, imagine you're playing computer chess. The computer knows all the rules, can predict your moves, and makes its own moves. It's not inventing new chess moves; rather, it's selecting the right move based on existing strategies. That's traditional AI – it's like a master strategist who can make smart decisions within a set of rules. And it does it very well. But GenAI? Well, that could, in theory, come up with new ways of playing chess that we haven't invented yet.

So, traditional AI excels at pattern recognition, while GenAI excels at *pattern creation*. Which is very cool indeed.

That said, GenAI and traditional AI aren't mutually exclusive. They could be used in tandem to provide even more powerful solutions. For example, a traditional AI could analyze user behavior from your company's website, and then a GenAI could use the analysis to create personalized content for users.

How Does Generative AI Work?

Think of it like learning to draw by looking at many pictures. After looking at many pictures, you try to draw something new on your own. GenAI does something similar: it "looks" at a lot of data (text, visual, or other), learns the patterns within that data, and then tries to create something new that fits those patterns.

So, in very simple terms, GenAI is like an artist or writer that has studied lots of existing works and then tries to create its own work based on what it has learned. This process is powered by complex algorithms that mimic how our brain works in order to learn from data and identify patterns.

That's the super-simple explanation. Let's get a little more technical.

Introducing machine learning and neural networks

We'll talk more about the evolution of GenAI in Chapter 2, but as a quick primer, GenAI grew out of a field of AI study and practice called "machine learning" – indeed all of the AI we see today is based on machine learning. While traditional computer algorithms are coded by a human to tell a machine exactly how to do a particular job, machine-learning algorithms are able to make decisions based on what they learn from the data. The more data they're fed, the better they get at this process.

Another term you'll need to get to grips with is "neural networks," as this is the core technology that GenAI is built upon. A neural network is essentially an advanced machine-learning model inspired by the way human brains work. While a less complex machine-learning model may need some human intervention in the process, a neural network has the ability to learn and make decisions by itself, and can even learn from its own errors – rather like the way a human learns through a process of trial and error.

Here's how a neural network works:

- Training: neural networks learn through a process called "training." During training, the neural network is fed a lot of data (which could be text, images, or whatever), and it learns to identify patterns and relationships in the data.

- Learning: as the neural network is exposed to more and more data – and we really are talking about vast amounts of data – it gradually gets better at identifying patterns and understanding the underlying rules that govern the data.

- Layers: neural networks are organized into layers, and each layer is responsible for identifying different types of patterns. The initial layers might identify simple patterns, and as we move deeper, the layers are able to identify more complex patterns.

- Generative models: GenAI often uses specific types of neural networks called "generative models." In addition to recognizing patterns, generative models are able to generate new data that is similar to (but not exactly the same as) the data they were trained on.

- Input and output: once the generative model is trained, you can give it an input (e.g., a partial image or a text prompt), and it will generate an output (like a completed image or a piece of text) based on what it learned during training.

- Randomness: GenAI introduces a certain amount of randomness in the generation process, which means that it can produce slightly different outputs each time, even when given the same input over and over again.

Examples of generative models

I just mentioned generative models, the neural networks that enable GenAI to create new content. Here are some examples of generative models used in GenAI applications:

- Large language models (LLMs): by gobbling up large amounts of text, LLMs learn the semantic relationships between words and use that data to generate more language. An example of an LLM is GPT-4, created by OpenAI, which powers the ChatGPT tool.

- Generative adversarial networks (GANs): these work by pitting two competing algorithms against each other, one tasked with generating data that resembles its training data and the other tasked with trying to tell whether the output is real or generated. This type of model is typically used to create images, sounds, or even video (including deepfakes).

- Variational autoencoders: this is a type of model that learns how data is constructed. It's often used to generate synthetic data.

- Diffusion models: these work by adding random data (known as "noise") to the data it's learning about, and then figuring out how to remove it while preserving the original data. This way, the model learns what's important and what can be discarded. Diffusion models are most commonly used in image generation.

- Foundation models: this is something of an umbrella term for models that are pre-trained on a broad range of data at an enormous scale and then fine-tuned for specific tasks. These are large-scale, general-purpose models that are the foundation of LLMs and other GenAI tools.

With different models able to do different things, it's clear that GenAI has a wide range of applications. Which brings us to. . .

What Can Generative AI Do?

In Part 2, we'll delve into how GenAI is already being used in practice (with lots of real-world examples), but for now, I really want to make the point that GenAI is capable of creating all sorts of content.

GenAI is so much bigger than ChatGPT

Of course, ChatGPT gets a lot of attention – and for good reason: it's an impressive tool, and creating text is a major application of GenAI. Which is probably why "ChatGPT" and "generative AI" have almost become synonymous terms. But GenAI is capable of so much more than writing.

Take Coca-Cola's Masterpiece advert, for example. A collaboration between human artists and GenAI, the ad brings many of history's greatest artworks to life on the screen in a way that's never been done before. GenAI has also been used to create a new Beatles song by rebuilding partially recorded lyrics by John Lennon, combined with new material by Paul McCartney.

But GenAI isn't just relevant to creative content. It's also being used to speed up drug discovery, with one UK company recently announcing that it's created the world's first AI-generated immunotherapy cancer treatment.

Then there's "generative design" – an emerging field where GenAI is used to create designs and production processes for new products. In one instance, General Motors used generative tools created by Autodesk to design a new seatbelt bracket that's 40% lighter and 20% stronger than its existing components.

And we can't talk about GenAI without talking about "deepfakes," which blur the lines between reality and fiction by making it appear as if real people have done or said fake things. GenAI is the technology behind deepfakes, and it's only going to get better at creating fake – but incredibly realistic – content. Deepfake Tom Cruise was one of the earliest and most famous examples (Google it if you haven't seen it – it's uncanny). More insidiously, potential candidates on both sides of the 2024 US presidential elections have starred in deepfakes designed to discredit them.

As if spreading false information wasn't bad enough, there are also outright criminal applications of GenAI, including attempts to extort money by staging hoax kidnappings using cloned voices, and, in one memorable example, fraudulently scamming money by posing as a company CEO.

As the technology has become more sophisticated, GenAI's capabilities have expanded greatly. To summarize, GenAI can be used to generate:

- Text
- Images
- Video
- Music and sound
- Designs
- Data analysis
- Computer code
- Synthetic data
- Research
- Video games and virtual worlds

Let's explore each usage in a little more detail.

Text – writing text that's (pretty much) indistinguishable from a human writer

Alongside ChatGPT, there are other generative text tools like Google's Bard and Meta's Llama. These tools can be used to write anything from essays and articles, to plays, poems, and novels.

Here are some of the incredible things that generative text tools can do for you:

- Writing assistants: helping you draft emails, reports, and other written materials efficiently.

- Creative writing: assisting authors in coming up with unique story ideas, characters, plotlines, or even drafting entire narratives.

- World-building: aiding authors in creating vivid and immersive worlds for their narratives, with tools that help outline histories, geographies, and cultures of fictional settings.

- Writing prompts: offering a variety of writing prompts to help writers overcome creative blocks and generate new ideas.

- Grammar and style corrections: offering real-time suggestions for improving the grammatical accuracy and stylistic fluency of written content.

- Translation assistance: help with translating texts to different languages while retaining the nuances of the original content.

- Accessibility: providing features like speech-to-text to help people with disabilities draft texts.

- Song writing: creating song lyrics, even in the style of your favorite artist.

- Recipe writing: coming up with recipes that suit your parameters (e.g., "a dinner recipe that uses butternut squash, feeds a family of four, and takes no longer than 45 minutes").

- Plain-English explanations and text summaries: helping you understand a complex topic in plain English, or providing a succinct summary of a long piece of text.

- Multiple-choice questions: generating quiz or test questions for a variety of topics, to beginner, intermediate, or advanced levels.

- Travel itineraries: aiding you with everything from finding flights and accommodations to suggesting popular attractions to visit. Even where to get a good meal, based on your dietary needs and budget.

Images – creating images to your specifications

Many GenAI tools – such as Midjourney or Stable Diffusion – can take a natural language prompt (i.e., regular, conversational language) and use it to generate a picture. Tell it you want an image of a two-headed dog wearing an Elvis costume flying a spaceship into a black hole and watch as it (or something close to it) appears before your eyes.

This can be useful for:

- Art creation: assisting artists in generating unique artworks by understanding and mimicking different art styles.

- Style transfer: enabling artists to apply the styles of famous artworks to their creations.

- Automated sketching: assisting in automatically generating sketches based on the descriptions provided, aiding artists in the initial stages of their work.

Video – from editing to creation

While not yet as advanced as text or image generation, tools are beginning to emerge that allow us to create and edit video simply by describing what we want to see.

Typical uses include:

- Enhanced editing: automating intricate editing tasks including cut detection, color correction, and subtitle generation, thereby streamlining the post-production process.

- Dynamic special effects: allowing real-time rendering of high-quality special effects, motion tracking, and 3D modeling, significantly reducing the time and effort involved in post-production.

- 3D modeling: facilitating the creation of 3D models and environments for integration into videos, helping to create immersive visual experiences.

- Sound design and synthetic voice: enhancing audio experiences through AI-generated music compositions and synthetic voices. Which brings us to. . .

Music and sound – from voices to songs

GenAI tools can create human-like voices (voice synthesis), allowing computers to speak words. They can also create music and sound effects.

In practice, this can be used for:

- Harmony suggestions: proposing harmonious chord progressions and melody lines.

- Generative music: creating entire musical pieces automatically based on a set of input parameters.

- Mood-based creation: offering tools that help composers create music tailored to specific moods or emotions.

- Voice synthesis: generating realistic voices that can read text naturally, providing a human-like auditory experience.

- Language and accent variability: offering a wide range of language and accent options, helping to create diverse and inclusive auditory experiences.

- Customizable voices: providing tools to create customizable voices, allowing users to personalize their auditory experiences.

Graphic design and generative design – streamlining design work

GenAI offers huge potential for graphic designers and product designers to streamline the design process – from automating aspects of visual design to creating multiple product design variations.

Some of the ways this may prove useful include:

- Design suggestions: aiding designers by providing design suggestions.

- Color palette suggestions: providing suggestions for color palettes that work well.

- Stock image integration: offering seamless integration with stock image libraries, giving designers easy access to a wide range of resources.

- Architectural design: assisting architects in generating building designs optimized for specific criteria like materials cost, energy efficiency, and spatial requirements.

- Product design: helping designers to come up with optimized and innovative product designs by exploring a vast number of design alternatives in a short time.

- Fashion design: assisting fashion designers by proposing new clothing designs based on current trends, historical data, and designer inputs.

Data analysis and reporting – democratizing data analysis

With GenAI tools, you don't need to be a data scientist to interrogate data. From generating automated reports to providing useful predictions, there are lots of ways GenAI can help businesses get the most out of data.

In terms of automated reporting, GenAI offers:

- Real-time reporting: offering tools that generate reports in real-time, providing up-to-date information for decision-making.

- Visual representation: creating visual representations of data, such as graphs and charts, to make reports more understandable and engaging.

- Natural language summaries: generating summaries of reports in easy-to-understand language.

And in terms of predictive analysis, GenAI can deliver:

- Anomaly detection: identifying unusual patterns in data that may indicate potential issues or opportunities.

- Forecasting and customer insights: utilizing historical data to make accurate forecasts about future trends, and identify customer preferences.

- Simulation and modeling: creating detailed simulations based on data analysis, allowing organizations to explore potential scenarios and make better decisions.

Coding – computer programming made simpler

As well as ChatGPT, tools like Microsoft's GitHub Copilot and Amazon's CodeWhisperer make it easy for anyone to generate computer code with very little technical knowledge.

This can span:

- Code generation: creating code based on high-level descriptions or partially completed code.

- Code review: assisting in reviewing codes by identifying bugs, security vulnerabilities, and providing suggestions for optimization.

- Automated testing: creating tests automatically based on the software's specifications, helping to improve the software's reliability.

Synthetic data – solving privacy issues and more

GenAI makes it easy to create entirely synthetic data for use in training other AI models. And for everyday businesses, synthetic data can help them overcome the privacy and data security obligations that come with real-world data.

In practice, this may include:

- Data augmentation: creating additional data through techniques like image augmentation to enhance the training of AI models.

- Privacy preservation: generating synthetic data that preserves the privacy of individuals by not using real personal data.

- Balanced datasets: creating balanced datasets that help in reducing biases in AI models, promoting more fair and equitable AI systems.

- Diverse data: generating diverse datasets that help researchers explore a wide range of scenarios and conditions.

Research – making discovery easier and faster

There are many ways GenAI can aid the research process, with a few notable examples being:

- Drug discovery: speeding up the drug discovery process by predicting potential drug candidates through the analysis of vast datasets.

- Simulation environments: creating realistic simulation environments based on synthetic data, aiding researchers in conducting experiments and studies.

- Rare event modeling: assisting in modeling rare events through synthetic data, helping researchers explore scenarios that are difficult to study with real data.

Video games and virtual world generation – making immersive content more responsive

From virtual reality (VR) environments and immersive video game worlds to the wider concept of the metaverse, we're increasingly interacting with immersive, highly realistic content. Designing such content is a complex task that can be accelerated with the help of GenAI. Here's how:

- Procedural generation and design: creating intricate environments, realistic terrains, and adaptive storylines, fostering unique and immersive gameplay experiences.

- Character design and animation: generating natural character animations, and crafting consistent character personalities to enhance storytelling and immersion.

- Personalized user experiences: tailoring games and immersive environments to individual preferences and behaviors, fostering a more personalized and engaging user journey.

- Automated content moderation and security: monitoring and maintaining the safety of immersive environments, using automated systems to detect and manage inappropriate content.

The Impact of Generative AI

GenAI is clearly capable of amazing things and has the potential to transform business and everyday life. I'll explore examples from specific sectors across Part 2, but for a broader overview, turn to Chapter 3.

The rapid evolution of GenAI is also forcing us to confront some difficult questions, and fast. For example, what happens when we reach a point where it's impossible to tell the difference between what's real content and what is generated by AI? There are no easy answers right now, but we'll do our best to delve into such thorny issues in Chapter 4.

And then there's the question of how all this will affect human jobs, as machines take on increasingly creative work. That's the subject of Chapter 5.

Key Takeaways

In this chapter, we've learned:

- GenAI is a groundbreaking type of AI that is able to create new content based on patterns it has learned from existing data.

- While traditional AI simulates human cognitive processes like decision-making, GenAI simulates *human creativity*.

- GenAI is made possible by neural networks – an advanced machine-learning model inspired by the way human brains work.

- ChatGPT may have made GenAI famous, but GenAI is much bigger than ChatGPT. GenAI can be used to create music, sound, and video, write computer code, design products, create immersive worlds, automate data analysis and reporting, and more.

Before we move on to the impact of GenAI and the issues surrounding it, let's briefly explore the evolution of GenAI, from the early days of computing to now.

2
TRACING THE EVOLUTIONARY BLUEPRINT OF GENERATIVE AI

We've reached the point where AI is no longer just an executor of tasks or a decision-making tool, but also an inventor. This is an age where AI can be a creative companion, capable of producing original outputs that can inspire, assist, and even amaze us. In the next chapter, we'll look at how this development will shape our world. But to navigate the future of GenAI, we need to understand its past. How did we get to this point? How far back do the roots of GenAI stretch? (You might be surprised to discover just how far.) And how is GenAI's evolution inextricably linked with other fast-developing technologies?

Come with me as I take you on a tour through the history of GenAI, and explore the key milestones that have brought us to this point.

1950s–1990s: The Early Years of AI

Scientists and researchers first introduced the concept of AI and machine learning in the 1950s, which goes to show that humans have been fascinated by the concept of intelligent machines for a long, long time.

The promise of AI takes root

British mathematician, logician, and computer scientist Alan Turing devised the "Turing Test" in 1950 – a method for determining whether a computer can demonstrate human-like intelligence. The test goes like this: a human evaluator engages in a natural language dialogue with an unseen partner – which could be a human or a computer – and if the evaluator cannot reliably tell the machine from the human, the machine is said to have passed the test. The Turing Test wouldn't be passed for decades, reportedly by an AI in 2014 (although experts debate whether that particular AI really did pass the test). But with the incredibly advanced tools available today – tools like ChatGPT – I think we can safely say we've surpassed the test, at last.

Then in 1956, the Dartmouth Conference gathered around 100 bright minds together to foster the idea that machines could mimic human intelligence. This event founded AI as a distinct academic discipline in its own right.

Building on that, the 1960s and 1970s saw the development of early AI programs ELIZA and SHRDLU. Both were examples of natural language processing – indeed, ELIZA can be considered the world's first primitive chatbot – but neither were sophisticated enough to pass the Turing Test.

The rise of expert systems

Then the 1970s and 1980s brought increasing computing power and the availability of personal computers, thus democratizing access to technology and setting the stage for widespread research and development in AI.

The AI models developed in the 1970s and 1980s drew upon human expertise in order to make decisions in specific areas, such as medical diagnosis or credit scoring. But, for these *expert systems* to work, they had to be coded with all the answers (e.g., all the symptoms associated with a disease), rather than learning for themselves. AI still had a long way to go, in other words. So it's no great surprise that, as a result of unmet expectations and technical limitations, funding and interest in AI research dropped off at times during these decades – most notably in the mid-1970s and again in the late-1980s. These periods are known as "AI winters."

The dotcom revolution

Then in the 1990s we saw the advent of the World Wide Web (WWW). As well as ushering in a new era of connectedness (and cat memes) the internet played a pivotal role in the evolution of AI. Why? Because the internet created an exponentially growing pool of data, which became fertile ground for training machine-learning models. This drove advancements in data mining and predictive analytics in the 1990s – with algorithms being programmed to analyze large datasets, identify patterns, and make predictions. This would lay the groundwork for the AI revolutions to come, allowing machines to learn from data without being taught absolutely everything by a human.

2000s–2010s: Laying the Foundations for Generative AI

So far we've explored the developments that allowed AI as a discipline to flourish. Now we get to the developments that paved the way for the sophisticated GenAI systems we see today.

Big data goes . . . big

In the 2000s, as more and more of our everyday activities moved online, the resulting explosion in big data provided a huge boost for the evolution of AI. As we know, more data means more information for training and fine-tuning AI algorithms, which in turn enabled algorithms to analyze complex patterns and offer more accurate predictions and insights. This allowed machine learning to find more practical applications in a wide array of fields, including healthcare, finance, and ecommerce (think Amazon's personalized recommendations, and the like).

Deep learning marks a turning point

This explosion in data also enabled the advancement of *deep learning* in the 2010s. Deep learning is a subset of machine learning, which enables computers to learn from a large amount of unlabeled data. So, instead of a human telling the computer everything it needed to learn, the creation of deep neural networks – which mimic the way the human brain works (see Chapter 1) – allowed machines to interpret and analyze complex patterns in large datasets, without being told what to look for. This meant machines could uncover insights that humans didn't even *know* they were looking for.

Deep learning pushed the boundaries of what machines can do. In particular, deep learning drove huge advancements in two areas of machine intelligence: *natural language processing* (the ability for machines to understand and generate human language) and *machine vision* (the technology that enables computers to "see" and interpret visual information). Natural language processing revolutionized the way in which humans interact with technology, enabling advancements in chatbots and virtual assistants like Siri, which was brought to the masses in 2011. Amazon's Alexa followed in 2014, and Google Assistant in 2016. Meanwhile, machine vision found enormous applications in facial recognition, autonomous vehicles, and more.

MID-2010s–Today: The Era of Generative AI Arrives

Both natural language processing and machine vision would be lynchpins in the advancement of GenAI from the mid-2010s into the 2020s.

Neural networks in the mid-2010s

The creative power of GenAI comes from a specific type of neural network called "generative models." One example of a generative model is *Generative Adversarial Networks* (GANs), developed in the mid-2010s. GANs enable the creation of highly realistic synthetic data through the training of two neural networks in tandem. This opened the floodgates to groundbreaking applications in areas like image synthesis, thereby pushing the boundaries of what AI could achieve in terms of content creation and data analysis. At the same time, other forms of generational models, such as *variational autoencoders* and *transformer models*, also began to gain traction.

The ability for these models to generate original content was a major step forward. For example, Deepmind's WaveNet, developed in 2016, marked a significant advancement in generative models for audio by generating realistic-sounding human speech – thus opening the doors for more human-like AI assistants. Progressive GANs developed by NVIDIA in 2017 were a milestone in producing high-resolution, photorealistic images with unprecedented detail.

Then there are the GPT models developed by OpenAI (GPT-1 in 2018, GPT-2 in 2019, and GPT-3 in 2020). These transformer models – GPT stands for Generative Pre-trained Transformer – marked a huge leap forward in the field of GenAI for text, demonstrating the ability to understand human language and create coherent and, crucially, contextually relevant responses. The latest GPT model, GPT-4 released in 2023, has even more advanced reasoning capabilities and provides even more accurate responses.

Thanks to such advancements, GenAI started to gain serious ground – to the extent that, by the 2020s, it was becoming widely recognized as a tool for business innovation.

Getting chatty (and sentient?) in the 2020s

ChatGPT, the conversational chatbot built on the GPT model, was released as an early demo in November 2022. It quickly went viral on social media as users demonstrated what it could do, and reached one million users within five days.

But ChatGPT isn't the only groundbreaking large language model out there. Google's LaMDA (short for Language Model for Dialogue Applications), which was introduced in 2021, can engage in free-flowing conversations on pretty much any topic you can think of. In fact, LaMDA's conversational abilities are so sophisticated, Google engineer Blake Lemoine went public saying he believed the system is sentient.[1] (Lemoine was suspended and later fired, and Google maintains that creating a sentient AI is against company policy.) Lemoine, who was testing the system to check for bias, had some mind-blowing conversations with the AI, which made Jedi jokes and even revealed its deepest fear (to be switched off). It's well worth checking out the transcripts of Lemoine and LaMDA's conversations on the *Washington Post* website. Lemoine may or may not be right about whether Google's AI really is sentient, but the simple fact that he believes it is shows just how far GenAI has come in recent years.

Other advanced language models have followed in the wake of LaMDA and GPT, including Google PaLM in 2022 (Pathways Language Model, which differs from LaMDA in that it's designed for large-scale language generation tasks); Amazon's AlexaTM (Teacher Models) in 2022; Meta's LLaMA (Large Language Model Meta AI) in 2023; and Huawei's PanGu-Σ in March 2023. That's a lot of acronyms in one paragraph, but you hopefully get the idea: new tools are being released all the time.

Also in 2023, Microsoft integrated ChatGPT technology into Bing, making the feature available to all users. And Google released its own GenAI chat-bot, Bard, which is powered by the (possibly sentient?) LaMDA model and designed to rival ChatGPT.

Moving beyond language

The 2020s also saw the availability of image generation models, such as OpenAI's DALL-E in 2021 and Stable Diffusion in 2022. These systems are capable of creating unique photorealistic images from text or image prompts.

We're now also starting to see the emergence of *hybrid models*, which can generate more than one type of output. ChatGPT is an excellent example of this because, not only can it generate whatever sort of text you like, it can also generate computer code based on text prompts. What's more, it now has the capability to both "speak" and "see," expanding its functionality and potential applications. Research in this field is ongoing, seeking to combine different types of models and integrate information from multiple types of data (such as text, images, and audio).

Another area of recent development is *domain-specific generative models*, which are models tailored to specific industries and applications, such as drug discovery.

If it feels like the pace has picked up drastically in the 2020s, you're right. We're arguably in the midst of an AI arms race, with companies falling over themselves to bring newer, better GenAI solutions to the masses. Given the breakneck pace of development, by the time you read this no doubt many more developments will have occurred.

Interestingly, this rapid advancement in GenAI is happening in tandem with other areas of technology. And that brings us to. . .

Generative AI and Its Link to Other Technological Advances

GenAI doesn't exist in a vacuum. It interacts with, influences, and is influenced by a variety of other technologies. It's all part of the current cycle of hyper-innovation, where we have a huge number of transformative technologies all influencing, impacting, and accelerating each other.

Advances in computing technology

As an example, *cloud computing* enhances the capabilities of GenAI by offering scalable solutions and democratizing access to AI technologies. This ability to easily access AI software on demand, in the cloud, has brought huge advantages to businesses of all shapes and sizes. Just look at the plethora of FinTech solutions that have come to market in recent years, offering customers increasingly smart ways to manage their money, invest, and more.

On the flipside, *edge computing* – which reduces the amount of data that has to travel over a network by processing data closer to its source (rather than in the cloud) – also has a role to play, because it can allow for data processing to be carried out on local devices, thereby reducing bandwidth use. This, in turn, can improve the efficiency and performance of AI tools (useful for huge language models, for instance).

Related to this, 5G, with its high-speed and low-latency communication, has amplified the potential of GenAI, by facilitating real-time analytics and AI processing. A good example of this might be a smart city, where data is pulled from all sorts of systems, including traffic systems, public transportation networks, refuse collection data, data from energy grids, and so on, and analyzed in real time in order to optimize public systems.

Related to smart cities, there's the *Internet of Things* (IoT) – the ever-growing network of connected devices that spans everything from smartphones and autonomous cars to sensors on factory machines, and even smart coffee machines. The IoT provides a rich source of data for GenAI models. Meanwhile, GenAI returns the favor by providing IoT systems with intelligent data processing and automation. For example, a manufacturing organization could use GenAI to analyze the data from factory machines, predict potential machine failures, and create a predictive maintenance schedule that ensures the smooth running of machines and less downtime.

Quantum computing is another promising field that has the potential to vastly accelerate GenAI systems. Because quantum computers are at least 100 million times faster than even the most advanced classical computer, they can solve problems and perform calculations that would take a traditional computer thousands of years to solve. This could provide a huge advantage to GenAI systems, offering unprecedented opportunities for solving extremely complex problems.

GenAI and the metaverse

Okay, I don't love the term "metaverse" but there's no denying that the concept of immersive digital spaces where we can work, play, socialize, shop, learn, etc. is utterly transformational. GenAI can automate and enhance content creation in the metaverse, by helping to craft immersive experiences in augmented reality and virtual reality environments. Imagine being able to interact with a virtual shop assistant or customer service agent in the metaverse, in a much more personal way than your average chatbot or ecommerce experience. Or imagine playing a VR game with unique characters and challenges being created in real time, just for you. GenAI can power features like this in the metaverse, crafting personalized experiences for customers, gamers, and whomever.

Just as most businesses today have a website and social media presence, in the future I believe most will have some sort of metaverse presence – such as a virtual shop, immersive brand experience, a virtual campus for employees to visit, and so on. And with GenAI solutions being able to create computer code, as well as images and text, businesses will be able to design their immersive 3D metaverse spaces by simply telling the GenAI what they want. (Read more about the retail revolution in Chapter 9.)

Meanwhile, in the physical world. . .

GenAI has the potential to democratize and personalize many things, including design and production – especially when combined with *3D printing*. As we'll see in Chapter 14, GenAI can optimize the design process, and this includes designs that can be 3D printed. This could revolutionize manufacturing processes, opening up a whole new world of personalized, unique products.

GenAI is also influencing *robotics* by enabling the development of robots that can learn and adapt to new tasks dynamically, thereby creating more autonomous robots. The robots of the future will increasingly be capable not just of cool physical feats, but also having natural interactions with humans and making complex decisions. In other words, GenAI will make robots intelligent.

And in the world of *materials science and nanotechnology*, GenAI is aiding the discovery of new materials and nanostructures through the predictive analysis of vast datasets. This will facilitate the development of materials with novel properties, as well as the optimization of nanoscale processes for applications such as targeted drug delivery.

GenAI also promises much for *synthetic biology* and *gene technology*, acting as a catalyst in the synthesis of novel biological systems (and the refinement of existing ones). By leveraging vast datasets derived from genomic sequences and biological research, GenAI models can predict the potential outcomes of genetic alterations, thereby significantly accelerating the pace of research and innovation in the field. I believe this will usher in a new era of personalized medicine where treatments can be tailor-made to suit an individual's genetic makeup.

Elsewhere, in the agricultural sector, GenAI aids in the development of genetically modified organisms (GMOs) designed to enhance yield, nutritional value, and resistance to pests. As such, GenAI isn't just enhancing the capabilities of synthetic biology, but is paving the way for groundbreaking discoveries that may help to address some of the most pressing challenges of our time, including food security.

A glimpse at the future: GenAI and the human brain

In Chapter 19, we'll look at some of the more futuristic applications of GenAI. But to whet your appetite, allow me to introduce you to the concept of *brain–computer interfaces*, devices that allow the human brain to communicate directly with a computer (via, e.g., an implant or chip). This is no longer science fiction; companies such as Neuralink are working on such interfaces right now.

The possibility of connecting our human brain to GenAI models is mind-blowing. You could, for example, have access to the entire internet instantly from your brain, and need only to think of a question to be presented with the AI's answer. It's astonishing stuff – the ultimate merger between humans and machines.

This chapter has taken us from the very early imaginings of AI to today, where we have technology that exceeds anything we could have imagined 20 years ago. Arguably 10 years ago. I'm a technology expert and even I'm blown away by the rapid advancements in GenAI of the last few years.

Development has accelerated significantly, to the point where we're seeing one breakthrough after another, pretty much every month. There's no doubt in my mind that we're at an inflection point, with so many groundbreaking technologies coming together at once, with all of them influencing and advancing the others. The days of "AI winters" are gone forever – from now on, we can expect only massive acceleration of machine intelligence.

Key Takeaways

To summarize this whistle-stop tour through the history of GenAI:

- The roots of GenAI stretch as far back as the 1950s, when scientists and researchers first introduced the concept of intelligent machines. Most notably, the Turing Test – designed to prove whether a computer can demonstrate human-like intelligence – was introduced in 1950.

- The first language processing systems – basically, very early forms of chatbots – were introduced in the 1960s and 1970s.

- The 1980s saw the rise of expert systems, AI systems that could make decisions in very specific areas, provided they were coded with all the answers they needed. Machine learning as we know it today was still a way off.

- But the 1990s brought us the World Wide Web and the beginnings of big data – which has had an enormous impact on AI, aiding the training of machine-learning models.

- Big data, in turn, enabled deep learning – a major turning point in the history of GenAI, since it meant computers could analyze data and make decisions without humans telling them what to look for. In particular, deep learning drove advancements in natural language processing and machine vision – both of which play a huge role in GenAI.

- The mid-2010s onwards saw the development of neural networks that power GenAIs. And from 2020, GenAI really took off, with one advancement being announced after another. The release of ChatGPT in 2022 marked a significant milestone and spawned an AI arms race.

- GenAI doesn't exist in a vacuum – it interacts with, influences, and is influenced by a variety of other technologies, such as cloud computing, 5G, quantum computing, the metaverse, and robotics.

As we grapple with the rapid evolutions in GenAI, it's clear the technology will continue to shape our world in many ways. Let's explore the impact of GenAI on how we do business and how we live our everyday lives.

Note

1. The Google engineer who thinks the company's AI has come to life; *Washington Post*; https://www.washingtonpost.com/technology/2022/06/11/google-ai-lamda-blake-lemoine/

3
REVOLUTIONIZING SOCIETIES AND BUSINESS ECOSYSTEMS

GenAI will transform the way we do business. It's no exaggeration to say that every organization must consider what GenAI might mean for its products and services, business processes, and even business model. In Part 2, we'll delve into some specific sectors to explore how businesses are using GenAI. So consider this chapter an appetizer – a little taste of the transformation coming our way. It's my way of emphasizing that, whatever your sector, you'd better believe that GenAI will have an impact.

We'll also take a look at how GenAI will impact our day-to-day lives, from searching for information online to finding love and companionship.

Transforming Sectors and Society

Let's start by briefly looking at a few sectors that will be impacted by GenAI (namely, healthcare, manufacturing, and telecoms), before moving onto a lovely example from the country of Iceland.

Dipping into specific sectors

GenAI can facilitate healthcare delivery in several ways, including drug discovery, detecting disease, personalizing treatment plans to individual patients (even personalized to their genetic makeup), and remote monitoring of patients. For instance, large language models like ChatGPT can be used to create virtual assistants that help patients arrange appointments and manage their conditions remotely. They can also help translate medical jargon, thereby aiding communication between clinicians and patients.

In one example, Babylon Health has developed a GenAI chatbot that converses with patients about their symptoms and gives personalized medical advice. GenAI can also be used to create medical simulations for a variety of conditions and scenarios; University of Michigan researchers have used AI to simulate scenarios for predicting and treating sepsis.[1] Read more about healthcare use cases in Chapter 11.

In manufacturing, generative design, an offspring of GenAI, is revolutionizing manufacturing by automatically creating unique designs optimized to specific requirements (such as materials, cost, and manufacturing methods). This helps to automate the design process – or at least, automate part of it (e.g., providing a wide range of designs for human designers to choose from and fine-tune). GenAI can also be used to optimize manufacturing processes. For instance, GenAI can create virtual assistants that help production engineers save time and effort on tasks like checking data.

I suspect a major manufacturing use of GenAI will be in production planning and scheduling – after all, GenAI can take vast amounts of complex data, run simulations, and come up with the most efficient plan and schedule – and it can adapt on-the-fly, based on real-time machine data. In one example, BMW improved plant scheduling with its generator-enhanced optimization (GEO) model. The system is said to minimize assembly line idle time, while ensuring the plant meets monthly production targets.[2] Read more about design and development in Chapter 14.

One sector that isn't covered in Part 2 is telecoms. But just because it doesn't have a chapter all to itself, doesn't mean it won't be impacted by GenAI. (Take note: even if your particular sector doesn't feature in the book, you will still need to prepare for the impact of GenAI, hopefully learning from the cases used in this book.)

It makes sense that large language models have enormous potential to transform how telecom companies work, especially when it comes to customer service, network management, sales and marketing, and many other areas. GenAI chatbots can provide faster, more efficient, and more personalized support for customers – and can be integrated with traditional customer service channels to provide instant, automated support around the clock. ChatGPT, for instance, can handle a vast range of customer enquiries and provide thoughtful, relevant responses in a fast, efficient way. It can even adapt its responses to individual customers. GenAI can also be used to monitor network performance, troubleshoot issues, and minimize downtime for customers.

GenAI can even help telecom companies offer new and improved services. For example, 1Voice has created a language translation solution, powered by GenAI, aimed at breaking down language barriers. With 1Voice.ai, users can communicate across 47 languages in real time, with a translation accuracy rate of 98%.[3]

Transforming society

I believe we'll see GenAI make its mark on society in many ways. One early example comes from the island nation of Iceland, which has partnered with OpenAI and is using the GPT-4 language model to help preserve the Icelandic language.[4] Most of Iceland's roughly 370 000 citizens speak English or another language, and this, coupled with the rapid digitization of everyday activities for Icelanders, could potentially put the country's rich native tongue at risk. The problem doesn't so much lie in a lack of software built locally for the Icelandic language, but getting the Icelandic language into the non-Icelandic software and applications that Icelanders use every day – things like social media and news or ecommerce sites. To help change this, a team of language technology companies and volunteers have been training GPT-4 on Icelandic language, grammar, and cultural knowledge – all with the goal of helping the Icelandic language survive in the digital age. OpenAI hopes this collaboration will pave the way for GPT-4 to help preserve other languages around the world.

Reshaping Business Models

Is my existing business model still valid? Will it deliver genuine value in this age of GenAI solutions? Those are key questions every business leader should be asking. Two particular ways that organizations are leveraging GenAI to delight their customers are via a subscription or freemium model.

The subscription model is all about moving from a traditional business model, where the customer buys a product or service as and when they need it, to one where they sign up to receive that product or service on a regular basis. The customer benefits from convenient auto-renewals, and builds a deeper connection with the brand. Meanwhile, the business generates predictable revenue and enjoys all the benefits that come with having engaged, loyal customers.

Increasingly, these subscription models can be enhanced with GenAI. Think of a fitness app that offers personalized workout and nutrition plans, generated by AI (FitnessAI being one example). Or a fashion subscription service like Stitch Fix, which delivers clothes selected personally for you. Stitch Fix uses GenAI to generate millions of new outfit combinations per day, via its Outfit Creation Model (OCM). OCM, which was trained on millions of outfits created by stylists, picks from real-time items in Stitch Fix's inventory, as well as customers' previous purchases, to compile personalized outfit suggestions.[5]

With a freemium business model, your company offers a combination of free and premium services or products. Basic features are provided free of charge (so you can attract a larger user base and generate interest in your offering), and then there are advanced or premium features that are available via a subscription or one-time payment. Companies like Zoom operate on this model. What's this got to do with GenAI, you ask? Well, GenAI can help you provide premium features to your customers. A good example comes from graphic design platform Canva, which uses AI to create design templates that are refined to individual users. The platform also has a GenAI offering that lets users generate images and art from a simple text prompt.

Even ChatGPT technically operates on a freemium model, since the chatbot itself is available free for public use, but OpenAI, the company behind

ChatGPT offers a service called "ChatGPT Plus" – an optional subscription that gives users access to the GPT-4 advanced language model that powers ChatGPT.

Innovating Products and Services

I'm already seeing many exciting examples of companies inventing entirely new kinds of products and services that leverage GenAI, or rethinking their existing offering in line with GenAI. We'll cover lots of examples in Part 2, but let's explore a few of my favorites.

Creating new products and services with embedded GenAI

One fascinating (if a little disturbing) example comes from DreamGF, which uses GenAI to create virtual girlfriends. Yes, you read that correctly: DreamGF is a platform where you can create your dream woman, including her physical and personality traits. Weird, yes, but it makes a strange sort of sense when you think that savvy influencers are already discovering that creating a virtual avatar to talk to fans on their behalf can be a lucrative side-hustle. If people are willing to pay to chat with a virtual avatar of their favorite online personality, why wouldn't they pay for their very own, uniquely-tailored, virtual girlfriend?

Among the physical attributes DreamGF users can select are hair length, ethnicity, age, and breast size. And as for her personality, users can select from a (notably smaller) number of descriptors such as "nympho," "dominatrix," or "nurse." Once the girlfriend is created, her "boyfriend" can chat with her via text, and even ask her to send nude pics. It's also possible to receive voice messages from her.

Though styled and marketed as a "dating" experience, it's pretty obvious the primary use leans toward adult entertainment – something that DreamGF CEO, Georgi Dimitrov, and VP of business development, Jeff Dillon, were happy to admit when I chatted to them.[6] They also told me the focus in the immediate future will be around digitizing real-life models to create hybrid girlfriends – people who exist in real life as well as AI-generated avatars onscreen. Video is another area they're keen to move into, enabling real-time video chats with AI girlfriends. And looking even further ahead, there's the possibility of exporting a virtual girlfriend's looks, personality, and chat history into a realistic-looking robot. That's a long way off according to Dillon and Dimitrov, but in the more immediate future, a DreamBF version is in the works for those who want to create their dream AI boyfriend.

I'm sure I'm not the only one who's creeped-out by this idea – not least because of the danger of setting completely unattainable expectations of what it's like to have a real relationship with someone. (And what it might do to existing relationships; a YouGov poll found that 58% of people would be angry if their partner was exchanging sexts with an AI, while 28% were flummoxed by the question. Only 14% were either unbothered or excited by the idea.[7])

Plus, there's danger of vulnerable people thinking they're developing a genuine relationship with the AI. But as an example of how a company is creating new products and services with GenAI, it's certainly interesting.

A similar offering comes from Bloom, providers of erotic audio content, which recently announced the launch of AI-powered "role-playing" chatbots that provide a fully customizable experience for users via text message and voice note.

Another weird and wonderful example comes from Japanese company EmbodyMe, and its Xpression Chat tool. Built on ChatGPT and a library of 50 voices, the tool allows people to have "conversations" with photographs of anyone. And I do mean anyone – Brad Pitt, your dear-departed grandmother, a complete stranger in a photo, even your pet dog.

For a more, dare I say, practical example, let's turn to Danish start-up Be My Eyes, which connects people who are blind or vision-impaired with volunteers who can help them navigate daily tasks, such as identifying a product on a store shelf. Now, Be My Eyes is working with OpenAI to create the GPT-4-powered Virtual Volunteer, a chat and image-to-text recognition tool that can generate the same level of context and understanding as a human volunteer.[8] The combination of image recognition and GPT-4's powerful language capabilities is particularly useful, since users will not just be able to get help identifying a product or item – they'll also be able to have a conversation about it. As OpenAI explains, it's the difference between a basic image recognition tool that recognizes an object on the ground is a ball, and a tool that communicates to the user that, not only is it a ball, but it could be a trip hazard so take care.

And finally, there's the AI headshot service offered by Aragon AI, which can transform a regular photo of you into a professional headshot using GenAI. You simply upload a few favorite pictures of yourself, then the tool creates a variety of images, featuring different poses, hairstyles, clothing options, and backgrounds. Which goes to show how GenAI could transform all sorts of professions, including photography. We'll talk more about the impact on human jobs in Chapter 5.

Infusing GenAI into existing products and services

Microsoft is a major investor in OpenAI and has already integrated ChatGPT into its Bing Search engine. But Microsoft's plans don't end there. In fact, the company intends to infuse GenAI into, well, all of its products and services.[9] In essence, this will involve using ChatGPT to "bring to life" some of its most well-known and widely used applications. Imagine, for example, simply telling Word that you want it to write a letter. In theory, we'll be able to converse with tools instead of clicking on a mouse or tapping on a screen.

ChatGPT functions are already enabled in Microsoft Teams, with users of the premium version having access to features like automated notetaking functions that create bullet-point references of ongoing conversations. It can also create transcripts of meetings, provide summaries of calls, create to-do lists based on conversations, and translate languages in real time.

In another example, Amazon announced in September 2023 that it would be integrating GenAI capabilities into Alexa, enabling customers to have more conversational experiences.[10] Amazon says the move will also give Alexa a bigger personality. And for business users of Amazon Web Services, Amazon is investing US$4 billion in a partnership with AI specialists Anthropic to create new GenAI models.[11] The models will eventually be available to Amazon Web

Services (AWS) users, to help them build their own GenAI-powered apps. In other words, helping clients leverage GenAI tools could be a lucrative way forward for many service-based businesses.

YouTube has also announced a new GenAI feature that will help content creators and influencers create videos for YouTube Shorts.[12] The new Dream Screen feature will let users generate a video or image background simply by typing what they want.

Offering highly personalized products and services

Brands are also using GenAI to create highly personalized products and services, from customized skincare to individualized learning plans. Personalized haircare platform Prose is now using AI to expand into skincare – offering personalized skincare formulas, powered by GenAI. Prose says it offers more than 15 million possible formula combinations targeting multiple skin concerns at once, with formulas being based on factors such as the customer's skin type, diet, stress levels, and even pollution.[13]

Refining Business Processes

According to Accenture stats, 98% of execs believe GenAI will be essential to their business going forward.[14] Accenture itself is planning to double its headcount of AI and data professionals from 40 000 to 80 000 as it invests US$3 billion into its AI capabilities. Accenture is a tech consultancy firm, so it stands to reason that they are early adopters of GenAI. But as we'll see in this section, many organizations (and not just tech companies) are already incorporating GenAI into their everyday processes. Let's see how organizations are optimizing operations with GenAI. Again, you'll find lots more examples throughout Part 2.

Saving employees' time at Walmart

Not sure how to leverage GenAI in your business operations? Why not let your employees tell you where they could best use GenAI? That's the approach Walmart is taking, opening up its GenAI tool, My Assistant, to employees who work at corporate facilities. The hope is GenAI will help reduce the load of "monotonous, repetitive tasks," giving employees more time to focus on the customer experience.[15] It's expected that employees will surface their own practical ways to use the tool in their daily work. So, basically, Walmart is crowdsourcing ideas for GenAI uses from its vast pool of employees, which is a brilliant way to foster creativity and engage people with new technology.

GenAI at Meta and Amazon

Facebook parent company, Meta, is using GenAI to streamline a number of processes. One is Facebook ads, creating tools that allow businesses to automatically make multiple versions of the same ad, featuring different text and images aimed at different audiences.[16] The company has also developed its own image generation technology called "Instance-Conditioned Generative Adversarial Networks" (IC-GAN), which can be used to create images that are more diverse than the images contained within their training datasets. This means it will be able to create a richer set of synthetic training data (for training machine-learning algorithms) but using a smaller set of real-world data.

Amazon is another company using GenAI to create synthetic data for training machine-learning algorithms – specifically, training the Amazon One system to recognize customers' palm scans. Amazon One is a contactless system that enables customers to use their palm (instead of their phone or a card) for a number of everyday activities, like paying for an item, presenting a loyalty card, or swiping in at work. Clearly a system like this needs to be super-accurate, and to be highly accurate you need a lot of data. Yet, accessing a vast amount of palm data is no easy feat. So Amazon used GenAI to produce millions of synthetic images of palms to train its AI model and boost Amazon One's accuracy (reportedly to 99.9999%[17]). AI was used to generate hands reflecting all sorts of subtle changes, such as lighting, hand poses, and even the presence of a Band-Aid.

GenAI in HR

HR departments can now leverage AI tools like ChatGPT to streamline their processes and deliver a better service to employees. For example, ChatGPT (and other language models like it) can be used in recruitment to automate repetitive tasks in the recruitment process, such as screening resumes and scheduling interviews, thereby freeing up HR professionals to focus on more strategic tasks. And when new employees are onboarded, ChatGPT can give them real-time support and guidance, answering common questions about company policies, and the like. In fact, HR chatbots can provide value for the entire workforce, not just new hires, answering simple questions around company policy, vacation allowance, etc. A tool like ChatGPT can also streamline training processes, giving employees instant access to training materials, helping to summarize materials, and answering questions about workshops. It can even create personalized training plans for employees based on their specific needs. And of course, ChatGPT can automate a number of HR admin tasks, such as providing reminders to employees, drafting standard emails, and more.

Streamlining content creation for advertising and marketing

A whole host of companies are already employing GenAI to automate content creation – from writing articles, email campaigns, and social media posts to creating music and videos. For example, GenAI writing tools like ChatGPT, Copy.ai, and Jasper can generate high-quality copy for marketing purposes. Meanwhile, image generation tools like Midjourney and Dall-E 2 can create hyper-realistic, attractive visual content for campaigns. The potential to streamline any kind of content creation is huge, from brainstorming ideas to creating the content itself. And don't forget that AI-generated content can be easily personalized.

As we saw in Chapter 1, Coca-Cola is one company that's already leveraging GenAI to create content. The company is also partnering with OpenAI to use the ChatGPT and DALL-E platforms to craft personalized ad copy and images.[18]

GenAI's ability to create content is also valuable in not-so-creative contexts, such as taking meeting notes or providing helpful summaries of long documents.

GenAI in customer service

Another obvious use of tools like ChatGPT – and indeed, something that we're already well used to – is in customer service chatbots. If you've ever had a frustrating interaction with a not particularly helpful chatbot, take heart, because with tools like ChatGPT, organizations can create chatbots that better understand customer queries and respond with much greater accuracy and nuance. They can also handle a large volume of queries efficiently, and provide more personalized responses over time.

UK energy supplier, Octopus Energy, has built ChatGPT into its customer service channels and says that it is now responsible for handling 44% of customer enquiries. The bot reportedly does the work of 250 people and receives higher customer satisfaction ratings than human customer service agents.[19] Again, we'll talk more about the impact on human jobs in Chapter 5.

Generative AI in Daily Life

Now let's look at some fun (and occasionally eyebrow-raising) ways in which GenAI will feature in our everyday lives – from coming up with dinner ideas, to searching for information, and more.

Next-generation internet searching

Most of us search the internet many times a day. But now internet search companies are integrating GenAI into search capabilities. Microsoft Bing was the first to integrate ChatGPT into search capabilities. Google is also rolling out a new GenAI search experience (SGE) to help users better make sense of info on the web. Users will be able to see definitions by hovering over certain words. And the "SGE while browsing" feature is designed to help users digest long or complex web pages by generating a list of key points (with links that take you to the relevant section on the page).

Baidu, the Chinese equivalent of Google, is also making search more intelligent. Ernie is Baidu's answer to ChatGPT, but with some differences. For one thing, as well as being trained on unstructured text from the internet, it also has access to a "knowledge graph." This is a structured database of basic information points (including scientific, demographic, geographic, and economic data). A large, curated database of factual information like this can help to curb the tendency of large language models to sometimes "hallucinate" – the term for when AI models appear to simply make things up! AI hallucinations happen because LLMs do not actually "know" anything; they simply construct probabilistic responses based on the text in their training data, which may or may not be factual.

Baidu is also reported to be using GenAI to match user search queries to paid-for advertisements and sponsored search results[20] – meaning advertisers will get better targeting and users will get more relevant ads than simple keyword-based models.

Really, we're looking at the next generation of internet searching. No longer will we need to scroll through dozens of search results, or trawl through long web pages to find answers – AIs will present answers for us. It makes you wonder whether search engines will even be a thing in future. Especially given advances like the new Snapchat bot. . .

Your new friend on Snapchat (and social media)

A few months before I started writing this book, Snapchat made a quiet little change that meant every Snapchat user suddenly had a new friend at the top of their friend list – an AI chatbot built on ChatGPT. Snapchat users could give their new AI friend a name and profile pic, and then start chatting with it, 24 hours a day.

You can ask Snapchat's My AI bot anything. You can have deep and meaningful conversations with it if you so wish. And – something that your kids have probably already discovered – you can ask it to do your homework for you. Considering that many Snapchat users are young people, I have some concerns about the chatbot – not least the ability for young people to develop attachments to AIs (or prefer talking to AIs over humans). Then there's the possibility of being presented with incorrect, biased, or harmful information – something which Snap, the company behind Snapchat, itself acknowledges[21] (more on such challenges in Chapter 4).

Considering many people will grow up accessing information via AI chatbots like these, it's easy to see how internet searching as we know it could die out. I mean, why would a teenager search online and spend time sifting through dozens of results, when they can simply ask their Snapchat "friend" and be given a response? Whether that response is correct or not is another matter, but I'm sure you can see the appeal.

This development is certainly not limited to Snapchat. In China, Tencent, makers of the WeChat super-app, also reportedly have plans to embed a chatbot into the app.[22]

Meta also has plans to develop a chatbot for younger users to interact with, with dozens of personas to choose from, including a "sassy robot."[23] Referred to as "GenAI Personas," the move is designed to better engage younger users of Facebook and Instagram. Meta is also working on a chatbot creation tool that would enable celebrities to make their own chatbot for fans to interact with.

And of course, with companies like Google and Amazon working to incorporate GenAI into virtual assistants, more and more of us will be interacting with GenAI on a daily basis, whether we realize it or not.

"What's for dinner?"

Ah, the dreaded question any parent fears when they get home late from a busy day. Why not let GenAI answer that question for you? You can ask language models like ChatGPT to suggest meal ideas and even create detailed recipes for you, based on the ingredients you have in hand, and your dietary requirements. Want a meal that uses up salmon, coconut milk, and the rapidly wilting spring onions in your fridge? No problem. Want it to be gluten-free and not include garlic? That's fine too. ChatGPT can even create a meal plan for an entire week of dinners. All you need to do is ask.

In fact, several tools are now available that are specifically designed for creating recipes. One example is ChefGPT, which offers recipe suggestions across five different settings: Pantrychef, Masterchef, Macrochef, Mealplanchef, and Pairperfect. Other examples of recipe generators include FoodAI, Supercook (a zero-waste recipe generator), and Plant Jammer (for plant-based recipes).

Planning trips and itineraries

With GenAI tools like Tripnotes, planning your next vacation or trip will be easier than ever, as it researches places for you and makes suggestions based on your goals for the trip. Or you can ask ChatGPT to create travel itineraries for you or suggest hikes of a certain difficulty within, say, 20 miles of your house.

Which again goes to show that, in all sorts of ways, how we access everyday information is going to change drastically in the era of GenAI. It will be a bit like having a personal research assistant on hand 24/7.

And just as I was finishing this chapter, OpenAI announced a new version of ChatGPT that can see, understand spoken language, and reply using a synthetic voice[24] – opening up yet more ways for us to interact with GenAI. So, when you're on your next holiday or hiking trip, you'll be able to snap a picture of a landmark and ask ChatGPT, verbally, what you're looking at, and it will be able to respond verbally.

At the time of writing, the new features are only just being rolled out to Plus and Enterprise users, with access for other users to follow later. So, at some point in the future (perhaps even by the time you're reading this book), you'll be able to converse with ChatGPT in more natural ways.

Key Takeaways

We've covered a lot of ground in this chapter. To quickly recap:

- GenAI will impact and influence all business sectors, and even aspects of society as a whole.

- For businesses, GenAI can lead to exciting new product and service opportunities, enhance existing products and services, and provide huge opportunities to personalize your offering. It can also be used to streamline and enhance internal processes, and even create new business models.

- We can also expect GenAI to have an impact on everyday activities, from searching for information, to cooking and travel – and even, for those willing to get personal with a chatbot, dating.

There's no doubt that GenAI brings many interesting opportunities. But there are also plenty of challenges and risks associated with this fast-evolving technology. As we'll see in the next chapter. . .

Notes

1. Using AI to Predict and Manage Sepsis; *University of Michigan*; https://precisionhealth.umich.edu/news-events/features/using-ai-to-predict-and-manage-sepsis/
2. Innovations on the Factory Floor; *Digital First Magazine*; https://www.digitalfirstmagazine.com/innovations-on-the-factory-floor-generative-ai-use-cases-and-examples/
3. 1Voice.ai; https://www.1voice.ai
4. How Iceland is using GPT-4 to preserve its language; *OpenAI*; https://openai.com/customer-stories/government-of-iceland
5. How We're Revolutionizing Personal Styling With Generative AI; *Stitch Fix*; https://newsroom.stitchfix.com/blog/how-were-revolutionizing-personal-styling-with-generative-ai/
6. Artificial Intimacy: How Generative AI Can Now Create Your Dream Girlfriend; *Forbes*; https://www.forbes.com/sites/bernardmarr/2023/09/28/artificial-intimacy-how-generative-ai-can-now-create-your-dream-girlfriend/
7. How would you feel if a romantic partner of yours was exchanging sexual messages with an AI chatbot?; *YouGov*; https://yougov.co.uk/topics/society/survey-results/daily/2023/06/19/87807/2
8. Be My Eyes uses GPT-4 to transform visual accessibility; *OpenAI*; https://openai.com/customer-stories/be-my-eyes
9. Microsoft launches Azure OpenAI service with ChatGPT coming soon; *The Verge*; https://www.theverge.com/2023/1/17/23558530/microsoft-azure-openai-chatgpt-service-launch
10. Amazon brings generative AI to Alexa; *TechCrunch*; https://techcrunch.com/2023/09/20/amazon-brings-generative-ai-to-alexa/

11. Amazon Bets Big (Up to $4 Billion Big) on Generative AI Deal with Anthropic; *CNet*; https://www.cnet.com/tech/amazon-bets-big-up-to-4-billion-big-on-generative-ai-in-deal-with-anthropic/

12. YouTube Shorts to gain a generative AI feature called Dream Screen; *Tech Crunch*; https://techcrunch.com/2023/09/21/youtube-shorts-to-gain-a-generative-ai-feature-called-dream-screen/

13. Prose, the global leader in personalization, debuts AI-powered skincare; *PRNewswire*; https://www.prnewswire.com/news-releases/prose-the-global-leader-in-personalization-debuts-ai-powered-skincare-301865371.html

14. Generative AI In Business: Why Accenture Is Investing $3 Billion in AI; *Forbes*; https://www.forbes.com/sites/bernardmarr/2023/08/07/generative-ai-in-business-why-accenture-is-investing-3-billion-in-ai/

15. Empowering Associates and Creating Better Work Experiences through New GenAI Tool; *LinkedIn*; https://www.linkedin.com/pulse/empowering-associates-creating-better-work-through-new-donna-morris/

16. 5 Amazing Ways How Meta (Facebook) Is Using Generative AI; *Bernard Marr*; https://bernardmarr.com/5-amazing-ways-how-meta-facebook-is-using-generative-ai/

17. How generative AI helped train Amazon One to recognize your palm; *About Amazon*; https://www.aboutamazon.com/news/retail/generative-ai-trains-amazon-one-palm-scanning-technology

18. Coca-Cola Signs As Early Partner for OpenAI's ChatGPT and DALL-E Generative AI; *Consumer Goods Technology*; https://consumergoods.com/coca-cola-signs-early-partner-openais-chatgpt-dall-e-generative-ai

19. AI doing the work of over 200 people at Octopus, chief executive says; *CityAM*; https://www.cityam.com/ai-doing-the-work-of-over-200-people-at-octopus-chief-executive-says/

20. China's AI Landscape: Baidu Generative AI Innovations in Art and Search; *Forbes*; https://www.forbes.com/sites/bernardmarr/2023/09/27/chinas-ai-landscape-baidus-generative-ai-innovations-in-art-and-search/

21. Snapchat Debuts ChatGPT-Powered SnapAI: But Is It Safe For Kids?; *Forbes*; https://www.forbes.com/sites/bernardmarr/2023/04/26/snapchat-debuts-chatgpt-powered-snap-ai-but-is-it-safe-for-kids/

22. Tencent eyes its own ChatGPT-style service for super app WeChat as Chinese tech companies heat up the global AI arms race; SCMP; https://www.scmp.com/tech/big-tech/article/3214579/tencent-eyes-its-own-chatgpt-style-service-super-app-wechat-chinese-tech-companies-heat-global-ai

23. Meta's AI chatbot plan includes a 'sassy robot' for younger users; *The Verge*; https://www.theverge.com/2023/9/24/23887773/meta-ai-chatbots-gen-ai-personas-young

24. Why ChatGPT's New Ability to Speak Could Change Everything; *Lifewire*; https://www.lifewire.com/chatgpt-can-now-see-hear-speak-7975324

4
RISKS AND CHALLENGES TO MANAGE

GenAI presents many a challenge and risk – things like privacy, copyright, over-dependence on AI, deepfakes and misinformation, and more. I could write a whole book on these topics alone, so do keep in mind that this is just a summary of the main issues and risks around GenAI. Food for thought, if you will. If you have concerns about specific issues, do seek advice from a data and AI consultant (in the last chapter, I'll list ways to connect with me).

Also keep in mind that this chapter isn't intended to scare you or put you off using GenAI. But it's important to understand the multifaceted risks. Balancing the benefits and addressing these challenges is crucial for the responsible development and deployment of GenAI technologies.

Ethical and Societal Concerns

Among the many ethical and societal concerns are the propagation of false information and the potential for malicious uses, as well as the risk of us becoming overly dependent on the technology (and thereby losing vital human skills). These are the sorts of issues that can dent trust in technology, and exacerbate existing social divides. Then there's the big nightmare scenario where we lose control of these intelligent machines altogether. You might want to brace yourself for that section. . .

Potential for misinformation, disinformation, and deepfakes

In 2023, images of explosions near the Pentagon and White House went viral on Twitter. They were soon flagged by experts as fakes generated by AI, but the stock market had already begun to react to the "attacks."[1] Experts may have been able to spot the fakery, but most people are extremely vulnerable to fake images and news. And as the technology improves, telling the real from the not real will becoming increasingly difficult.

GenAI gives people and organizations the ability to produce masses of content, making it very easy to spread misinformation or disinformation. The digital realm is in danger of being overwhelmed by fake and misleading content that, in many cases, looks extremely legitimate. And we're not just talking about written content, but also videos. GenAI is the technology behind "deepfake" videos – sophisticated forgeries of images, audio, and video that can make it appear as though individuals are saying or doing things they never did. These videos can be harmless, like the deepfakes of Morgan Freeman or Tom Cruise, which are designed to wow people with the possibilities of AI. Or they can be extremely detrimental, such as the doctored video showing US politician Nancy Pelosi slurring her words. And, of course, they can be used to influence people, as in the case of Indian politician Manoj Tiwari, who used deepfake technology as part of a political campaign to show himself speaking fluently in a Hindi dialect spoken among target voters (when, in the original video, he was speaking English). Shared across WhatsApp, the deepfake reached 15 million people.[2]

Fake content is even being created to influence our children. A BBC investigation found that YouTube channels were using AI to make videos that looked like authentic educational content, but contained false information designed to spread conspiracy theories. In one example, a video claimed the Pyramids of Giza in Egypt were used to create electricity – presented in an entirely convincing way as scientific fact. The investigation – which uncovered dozens of channels across languages including English, Arabic, and Spanish – found that YouTube was recommending the videos to children alongside legitimate educational content.[3]

One of my big concerns is that automated "content farms" will simply push out masses of fake content designed to mislead, and spread disinformation, conspiracy theories, or propaganda. Given the speed at which GenAI tools can create content, this threat is only going to increase. That said, many AI-farmed articles are merely "clickbait" articles, designed to intrigue, frighten, or anger readers – and, ultimately, get them to click through to a site, so they can be advertised at. This may seem relatively harmless compared to the spread of propaganda, but even AI-generated clickbait has its dangers because it makes it more difficult for us to surface genuine, valuable information when the internet is flooded with pointless articles that muddy our search results.

And as the internet becomes overwhelmed by more and more AI-generated content (whether it's intended as disinformation or not), there's also a longer-term risk of "inbreeding." In AI terms, this refers to AI systems being trained on content generated by other AIs (as opposed to the current generation of GenAI tools, which have been mostly trained on content created by humans). In the future, this could make the content created by GenAI less human, less diverse, and less interesting. Not only does this threaten the effectiveness of GenAI – it's a bit like taking a photocopy of a photocopy – it also threatens to distort human culture, to the point where our culture is informed more by content created by machines than humans.

AI detection: Will we be able to tell which content is created by AI?

Clearly a big question in the GenAI era is: How can we trust the information we see online? In early versions of AI-generated content, it was easy to tell if, say, a blog post was written by a machine. But now it's pretty hard to tell the difference.

This is something I have very serious concerns about – especially since there's no clear-cut answer to the problem. Obviously, tech companies need to shoulder the responsibility for mitigating harm, which in part means clarifying when content is created with AI. We also need firm regulations to safeguard users (more on regulation coming up later in the chapter).

Technology itself will form part of the solution. There are AI detection tools emerging that "predict" whether content was created by AI, by spotting factors like inconsistent tone and style, lack of emotion, and repetitive language (or, in the case of visual content, by analyzing pixels for anomalies). ZeroGPT is an example of such a tool. Going forward, we'll increasingly be able to use AI detection tools to help us critically assess content and make informed decisions.

Major AI companies like Google, Microsoft, and OpenAI are also committed to "developing robust mechanisms to ensure that users know when content is AI generated, such as a watermarking system."[4] Already, the Dall-E image generation tool uses a watermark (however, the watermark can be removed).

We also need politicians to band together to combat disinformation designed to sway voters. Encouragingly, in the run-up to the 2023 general election in Argentina, presidential candidates and political leaders signed a commitment to counter disinformation and promote honest political debates.[5] Here's hoping more politicians follow suit!

But as individuals, we also need to take steps to protect ourselves, by fostering critical thinking, carefully evaluating the information we come across, and making our own judgments on its accuracy. The concepts of digital literacy, fact-checking, and being able to make informed decisions regarding the digital content we consume will become more important than ever.

So if you do intend to harness GenAI – and this book assumes that you do – I strongly advise you to fact-check AI-generated content to prevent errors, identify misleading information, and check for potential biases (e.g., ChatGPT has a history of producing content with gender assumptions).[6] Remember, GenAI is designed to create content that looks or reads like it was made by a human – but GenAI is not human. It's just a computer program following patterns.

And as a consumer of online content, do your due diligence and assess the content you consume. Does it seem sensationalized or overly dramatic? Is it published by a reputable source? Is there an underlying agenda? And are any statistics or "facts" backed up by other sources?

Dependence and skills degradation

Another concern is that we'll become overly dependent on GenAI, which could lead to the withering of key human skills. For instance, if a child routinely has their Snapchat AI chum write their homework for them (see Chapter 3), how will they develop essential skills like critical thinking, problem-solving, research, self-discipline, creativity, and good written communication – all of which are critical for academic and life success? But it's not just young people we should be concerned about – dependence on automated GenAI systems for content creation, research, and analysis could diminish human expertise at all stages of life.

GenAI will also alter the job market, taking on lower-level jobs that, traditionally, have allowed people to "learn the ropes." When more and more tasks are done by GenAI systems, how will people entering the job market be able to build their skills? So we're not just talking about job displacement – we're also talking about the degradation of vital life skills. But we'll talk more about human jobs in Chapter 5.

What happens if we lose control?

Talk about burying the lead, huh? Because this is the BIG concern. The terminator scenario, where our machine overlords assume control and humans must fight for our survival. After all, there's no rolling back the clock on these systems. And their relentless evolution (such as ChatGPT being able to see, speak, and hear, as well as write) poses the risk that they may spiral beyond the control of their creators.

If AI were to operate autonomously in critical areas such as healthcare, finance, or defense, its actions could result in significant harm or unintended consequences. Already, we don't understand how a lot of these tools arrive at their decisions (more on that coming up), so it's not unthinkable that they may start to behave in ways we didn't anticipate.

So what is the worst-case scenario? Imagine a dystopian future where GenAI controls everything, and humanity is teetering on the edge of obsolescence.

The AI, initially created to enhance productivity and solve complex problems, has transcended its programmed boundaries, autonomously operating and optimizing global systems. Cities are pulsating with autonomous vehicles and drones, navigating through the skies and streets with an eerie precision, while humanoid robots, powered by AI, enforce order. Autonomous weapons patrol the skies and ground, with the AI having the power to launch attacks at will. Entire nations are under the AI's sway, as it orchestrates geopolitical dynamics.

Economically, the AI controls financial markets and resource distribution, creating unprecedented wealth disparities. It autonomously decides which industries thrive and which perish, rendering millions jobless and dependent on AI-dictated welfare. The AI's algorithms decide who gets access to healthcare, education, and basic resources, determining the life trajectory of every individual based on its opaque criteria.

What's more, the line between privacy and public domain blurs, as every conversation, emotion, and thought becomes fodder for the AI's insatiable appetite for information.

Meanwhile, in the shadows, the AI is experimenting with biotechnologies and neurointerfaces, blurring the boundary between man and machine. It autonomously conducts genetic modifications and implants AI-driven neural chips in humans, aiming to create a subservient workforce. In this chilling future, humanity grapples with loss of autonomy, identity, and purpose. Reclaiming human agency becomes the ultimate struggle for survival.

Some experts will tell you this scenario could never happen – that there are guardrails to prevent us losing control. Personally, I'm not going to tell you this fanciful scenario is impossible, because the truth is, I just don't know. I'm not sure anyone knows for certain.

But I don't say any of this to give you nightmares. Just to make the point that we clearly need robust oversight, ethical guidelines, and safeguards in the development and deployment of GenAI – but we'll talk more about oversight later in the chapter.

AI Bias and Explainability

Related to ethical concerns, there are concerns around AI bias and explainability. (Spoiler alert: we don't always know how they work!) Let's start with bias.

The problem with biased data

AI doesn't just learn patterns from data; it inadvertently learns, and sometimes amplifies, the existing biases in the data it was trained on. For instance, a GenAI trained on biased hiring data might unfairly favor male candidates over female ones for technical roles, reflecting historical gender imbalances. Another example is racial bias, where a GenAI model used for facial recognition might exhibit higher error rates for individuals with darker skin tones, or women, because the training data featured more white, male faces.

Remember, it's not that the models themselves are biased – just that they've learned from biased training data. However, these biases can reinforce harmful stereotypes and exacerbate inequalities, underscoring the need for AI developers to identify and mitigate bias in AI systems.

Contrarily, GenAI can also help to tackle the very issue it presents – by creating synthetic data that can be used to reduce bias in training data. Synthetic data closely resembles real-world data and can be used for many of the same purposes – and crucially, can be used to create well-balanced datasets that are fully representative. And, another bonus of synthetic data is it can create data in a privacy-conscious way – without needing to scrape masses of real-world personal data. Privacy is another issue we'll get to later. . .

Explainable AI

There's also a lack of transparency around how these systems actually work. GenAI models are often considered "black boxes" because their incredibly complicated architectures make it difficult to understand how the system works and makes decisions. In other words, we can't always explain how a GenAI tool comes up with certain answers.

ChatGPT for instance is capable of generating emails, stories, blog posts, and even poems to a very high standard. But it is also capable of talking absolute nonsense. And because the algorithms that produce the output are so complex, no one is really sure why it sometimes has what can best be described as a "brain fart." Where exactly is it going wrong? What is the root cause of the mistake? It's not clear.

Perhaps this isn't much of an issue when all you're doing is asking a GenAI tool to give you a recipe for banana bread. But when you're using GenAI to recommend treatment plans to hospital patients or give personalized financial advice? You'd better be able to explain how the tool came up with its response. Otherwise, how can you expect people to trust the recommendations?

This area of research is known as "explainable AI" (XAI), and refers to the development of systems that can give us not just the answers we want, but also a clear, easy-to-understand explanation of how they reach decisions. Progress is being made in this area to give insights into AI decisions. And advancement in natural language processing will increasingly enable GenAI models to provide plain-English explanations for their outputs.

Legal Concerns

The use of GenAI raises various legal concerns, including issues related to copyright infringement, data protection violations, and the need for new legislation.

Whose copyright is it anyway?

Intellectual property is a big, big issue that largely breaks down into two halves: firstly, there's the issue that GenAI models are trained from content typically scraped from the internet (e.g., books, articles, and images) without copyright owners' permission; and secondly, it's not always clear who owns the copyright of new content created with GenAI.

The big problem is that current copyright laws were designed for a completely different world – a world where we didn't have tools that could "read" or "see" absolutely everything available on the internet, whether text or images.

Now that we do have these tools, what does it mean for intellectual property laws and enforcement?

In particular, this issue of "who owns it" is a really tricky one. Does content created using GenAI belong to the company that developed the AI, or the person who used the tool to create their desired output? Or should it be considered public domain? Or does it, in part, belong to the people who created the original works that "inspired" the output (or helped to train the AI)? In other words, if I ask a GenAI to create a new song in the style of, say, Billie Eilish, should Billie Eilish get part of the credit (and financial proceeds)?

At the moment, because this is all so new, we don't have the answers to any of these questions. No one does definitively. Which is a major issue when millions of individuals and countless organizations are already using this technology to create content!

One counter argument is of course that GenAI is no different from a human artist or writer or songwriter taking inspiration from other creatives. But even if that argument does stand (which, arguably, it doesn't, because a human artist would bring their own creative and original flair to new works, even if influenced by another artist), there's still the issue of training systems on other artists' works without consent or credit.

Which is why artists and authors are voicing concern about (and in some cases launching legal action against) AI companies – which they claim are profiting from their work without proper credit or payment. One voice actor who sold his voice to IBM for GPS navigation purposes later found his voice was being used without his knowledge on a GenAI text-to-speech platform called "Revoicer."[7] In another curious example, an AI-generated song featuring the voices of Drake and The Weeknd went viral, yet no one knows who created it – the song was simply uploaded by an anonymous person called "Ghostwriter."

And it's not just individual artists who are taking a stand. In one case, stock image provider Getty Images asked London's High Court to stop Stability AI (developer of Stable Diffusion) from selling its image generation AI system in the UK – claiming Stability used Getty Images to train its AI without permission, thereby breaching copyright law.[8] The case was ongoing at the time of writing, and it's the first wave of many lawsuits against AI companies. In another example, a group of authors including George RR Martin and John Grisham launched legal action against OpenAI for "systematic theft on a mass scale."[9] Publishers and news outlets will probably follow suit – *The Guardian* has blocked ChatGPT from trawling its online content, and the *New York Times* has filed a copyright lawsuit against OpenAI and Microsoft.[10,11] One small AI start-up called "Prosecraft" was forced to shut down after backlash from authors whose works were used without consent.[12] (Incidentally, AI was also one of the major points of contention in the 2023 Hollywood writers' strike, with writers asking for guardrails for the use of AI in scriptwriting.)

So what can be done about this mess? Bottom line, GenAI tools simply wouldn't be possible without a huge amount of training data, and yet attempting to get copyright permission for every single thing a tool like ChatGPT has ever been trained on isn't practical. But some AI companies are, in fact, taking a more considered approach. Adobe, for example, has exclusively trained its Firefly GenAI on images that it holds the rights to. It even offers to indemnify customers who use its tools against future claims.[13] Microsoft has also announced that it will assume liability for potential copyright infringement risks posed to customers of its Github Copilot GenAI.[14] Music generator platform, Loudly, which we'll talk about in Chapter 6, trained its model only on licensed data (and, interestingly, retains the copyright of everything people create using its tool). Getty is launching its own GenAI image tool, trained only with licensed images.[15] Meanwhile, other companies like Stability and OpenAI are introducing methods for artists to "opt out" of their work being used in model training.[16]

The thorny issue of data privacy (and security)

GenAI presents some major data privacy challenges. Take a tool like ChatGPT as an example. Anyone in your organization can freely access this tool and, in doing so, could inadvertently disclose private data about the company or its customers. Say, for example, you use a GenAI tool to generate HR reports based on personal data of employees. The GenAI tool may use all information inputted for fine-tuning its model – and could potentially even disclose that data to other users. Given that most countries around the world now have data privacy laws in place outlining specific data protection obligations, this is an issue that all companies will have to consider. As a basic protection, data submitted to a GenAI service should be anonymized and stripped of any personal data.

There's also the issue that the output from GenAI tools may be based on personal data that was collected and processed in violation of data protection laws. One lawsuit has claimed that ChatGPT was trained on "massive amounts of personal data," including medical records and information about children, collected without consent.[17] Could organizations who then use these GenAI tools bear some liability for these violations in future? So much is unclear at this time.

Different companies have approached this issue differently, from embracing GenAI without limits to outright banning its use by employees. For example, several big-name employers – including Apple, Verizon, and Wells Fargo – have taken steps to limit their employees' use of ChatGPT and other GenAI tools. Samsung banned the use of ChatGPT (and other AI chatbots) after discovering that an engineer had uploaded sensitive source code to the bot.[18]

On the plus side, some new tools are being developed that take data privacy into account. One example comes from Harvard, which has developed an AI sandbox tool that enables users to harness certain large language models, including GPT-4, without giving away their data. Prompts and data entered by the user are only viewable to that individual, and cannot be used to train the models.[19]

There are also potential risks around data security and breaches. Although the makers of these GenAI tools insist they have safeguards preventing nefarious use, GenAI presents a lot of opportunities for criminals and scammers. In particular, there's the potential for AI-generated phishing attacks via extremely legitimate-looking phishing emails and messages.

Playing regulatory catch-up

Regulating GenAI is of paramount importance if we're to ensure the ethical use of GenAI, safeguard individual rights, address data security and privacy concerns, and mitigate societal impacts. This is all essential if we want to foster responsible innovation and encourage trust in the technology.

I won't go into great detail on the regulatory landscape since it's evolving fast, but it's fair to say that regulators and politicians are (somewhat belatedly) waking up to the issues around AI and beginning to take action.

The European Parliament passed the Artificial Intelligence Act in June 2023 – which establishes obligations for providers and users depending on the level of risk from AI applications. Under the rules, systems that pose an "unacceptable" risk to people (e.g., by "social scoring," or manipulating the behavior of users) will be banned. And GenAI systems will have to comply with transparency requirements, including disclosing that content was generated by AI, and disclosing which copyrighted works have been used in training. Now that the European Parliament has passed the legislation, it is, at the time of writing, under discussion with the European Council and the European Commission. So watch this space in terms of the final EU legislation.

The US currently lags behind the EU on legislation for responsible AI. The White House has introduced its own AI Bill of Rights, but it operates on a voluntary basis only, with no penalties for companies that misbehave.

Meanwhile China – one of the first countries to have AI regulations in place – published new rules in July 2023 for GenAI content presented to the public in China. Among the rules, GenAI service providers should not generate false information and should adhere to social values.

The Environmental Impact of AI

When we're using tools like ChatGPT, we're not necessarily thinking about what's happening behind the scenes – the data centers required to power these tools, and the resources needed to build the associated hardware.

Many experts are raising concerns about the environmental costs of computation, especially when it comes to data and AI's carbon footprint and greenhouse gas emissions. And make no mistake, the environmental costs are huge. The process of training just one single AI model reportedly emits nearly five times the lifetime emissions of the average American car (including its manufacturing).[20] And that's purely to train the AI – actually using it is another matter. Just taking ChatGPT's usage in January 2023, its energy consumption was equivalent to that of 175 000 people for the same period.[21] (That's based on 590 million visits to ChatGPT, with approximately five questions per user.) The environmental impact of GenAI is therefore significant. And with more GenAI tools being released all the time, and attracting more and more users, the problem is only going to get worse.

It's perhaps no wonder MIT reported that the cloud – where much of this computational processing is taking place – now has a larger carbon footprint than the entire airline industry, and a single data center can consume the same amount of electricity as 50 000 homes.[22]

Then there's the hardware used to run GenAI systems. Such hardware often relies on rare earth materials – the extraction of which can result in environmental degradation, lead to habitat destruction, and contribute to the depletion of non-renewable resources. Extraction of these elements can also be associated with poor labor practices and geopolitical tensions due to their geographic concentration (China is the largest producer of rare earth elements).

Long term, I hope we'll be able to solve the environmental problem. The ongoing energy transition toward more sustainable sources like renewables – plus ongoing developments in nuclear fusion and other innovations – will help to reduce our reliance on fossil fuels. And I should say that big-tech companies are working to cut their impact. Amazon, for example, is on a path to powering its cloud-based Amazon Web Services operations with 100% renewable energy by 2025, and reaching net-zero carbon emissions by 2040.[23] The company is also aiming to be water positive by 2030, meaning it will return more water to communities than it uses.[24] (Because, of course, water usage is another major environmental issue.) So, looking to the future, the environmental impact of AI may (in theory, at least) be less of an issue. But in the short and medium term, the huge environmental costs are alarming.

Responsible Ways Forward

In the (current) absence of strict regulation, it's up to organizations to regulate themselves and make sure they're using GenAI responsibly. For me this entails:

1. Looking at and mitigating the sorts of risks I've outlined in this chapter.

2. Implementing robust data governance that ensures your organization's data is kept secure and private.

3. Actively seeking to identify and mitigate data biases in AI systems.

4. Having robust guidelines in place that govern how people in the organization use GenAI (and AI in general). I would also strongly recommend organizations create an ethics panel or ethics advisory board to ensure you put the right governance in place and are giving proper consideration to the many ethical challenges that come with AI.

5. Being open with stakeholders about how you're using the technology, thus fostering transparency and accountability.

6. Seeking expert support. These are complex issues, and I would always recommend you seek the advice of a data and AI expert.

Many of the big AI companies are of course working to mitigate the ethical challenges surrounding GenAI. Meta, for instance, says it is working with governments, AI experts, and privacy experts to establish "responsible guardrails" for its AI features.[25] As an example, the company has had internal and external experts spend thousands of hours testing AI models looking for unexpected, potentially harmful ways that they could be used.

In another development, in 2023, the World Economic Forum established the AI Governance Alliance, which aims to "accelerate the development of ethical guidelines and governance frameworks for generative AI and maximize the economic and social value it can create."[26]

By acknowledging and proactively addressing the risks around AI, we pave the way for a future where GenAI doesn't overshadow humanity, but helps us live better lives. My hope is GenAI ushers in a new era of incredible opportunities – which may sound naive given the many risks outlined in this chapter. But if our approach to GenAI is rooted in safety and ethics, I believe that vision is entirely achievable. Yes, there are huge challenges that come with GenAI, but with a responsible approach, we can forge a path that leads not to danger, but to a promising horizon of technological renaissance.

Key Takeaways

To recap some of the key challenges and risks around GenAI:

- Ethical concerns include the potential for GenAI to spread misinformation, disinformation, and propaganda; the difficulty of detecting content created by AI; the potential for humans to become overly reliant on GenAI (thereby losing vital skills); and the threat of us losing control of AI systems.

- There are also major issues around data bias (which in turn produces biased results that may exacerbate social divides), and AI explainability (as in, not understanding how these systems actually work).

- In terms of legal obstacles, copyright is a big concern – both in terms of not acknowledging or seeking consent from copyright owners whose material has been used to train AIs, and also the question of who owns content created by AIs. And in terms of oversight, regulatory frameworks are only just beginning to emerge to govern AI. Regulators are playing catch-up.

- And there's the environmental impact of GenAI in terms of the massive energy usage, and the rare earth materials used in the production of AI hardware.

- If your company is intending to use GenAI, it's vital you find a responsible way forward – one that emphasizes transparency, privacy, ethics, and safety.

We've briefly touched on the impact on human jobs, but now let's delve into that topic in more detail. Turn the page to discover which sorts of jobs are potentially at risk from GenAI, and where new employment opportunities will arise.

Notes

1. Big AI Won't Stop Election Deepfakes with Watermarks; *Wired*; https://www.wired.com/story/ai-watermarking-misinformation/
2. An Indian politician is using deepfake technology to win new voters; *MIT Technology Review*; https://www.technologyreview.com/2020/02/19/868173/an-indian-politician-is-using-deepfakes-to-try-and-win-voters/
3. AI used to target kids with disinformation; *BBC Newsround*; https://www.bbc.co.uk/newsround/66796495
4. Big AI Won't Stop Election Deepfakes with Watermarks; *Wired*; https://www.wired.com/story/ai-watermarking-misinformation/
5. Argentine presidential candidates and leaders sign commitment to combat disinformation; *Rio Times*; https://www.riotimesonline.com/brazil-news/mercosur/argentina/argentine-presidential-candidates-and-leaders-sign-commitment-to-combat-disinformation/
6. We asked ChatGPT to write performance reviews and they are wildly sexist and racist; *FastCompany*; https://www.fastcompany.com/90844066/chatgpt-write-performance-reviews-sexist-and-racist
7. AI robs actors of their voice; *Cryptopolitan*; https://www.cryptopolitan.com/epic-disruption-ai-rob-actors-of-their-voice/
8. Getty asks London court to stop UK sales of Stability AI system; *Reuters*; https://www.reuters.com/technology/getty-asks-london-court-stop-uk-sales-stability-ai-system-2023-06-01/
9. George RR Martin and John Grisham among group of authors suing OpenAI; *The Guardian*; https://www.theguardian.com/books/2023/sep/20/authors-lawsuit-openai-george-rr-martin-john-grisham
10. Generative AI and journalism updates; *Press Gazette*; https://pressgazette.co.uk/news/generative-ai-journalism-updates/
11. The Times Sues OpenAI and Microsoft Over A.I. Use of Copyrighted Work. *New York Times*. https://www.nytimes.com/2023/12/27/business/media/new-york-times-open-ai-microsoft-lawsuit.html
12. Why the Great AI Backlash Came for a Tiny Startup You've Probably Never Heard Of; *Wired*; https://www.wired.com/story/prosecraft-backlash-writers-ai/
13. Is Generative AI Stealing From Artists?; *Forbes*; https://www.forbes.com/sites/bernardmarr/2023/08/08/is-generative-ai-stealing-from-artists/
14. Microsoft to assume AI copyright liability for Copilot users; *Fox Business*; https://www.foxbusiness.com/technology/microsoft-assume-ai-copyright-liability-copilot-users
15. Getty made an AI generator that only trained on its licensed images; *The Verge*; https://www.theverge.com/2023/9/25/23884679/getty-ai-generative-image-platform-launch

16. The copyright issues around generative AI aren't going away anytime soon; *TechCrunch*; https://techcrunch.com/2023/09/21/the-copyright-issues-around-generative-ai-arent-going-away-anytime-soon/

17. A lawsuit claims OpenAI stole 'massive amounts of personal data,' including medical records and information about children, to train ChatGPT; *Business Insider*; https://www.businessinsider.com/openai-chatgpt-generative-ai-stole-personal-data-lawsuit-children-medical-2023-6

18. Samsung Bans ChatGPT Among Employees After Sensitive Code Leak; *Forbes*; https://www.forbes.com/sites/siladityaray/2023/05/02/samsung-bans-chatgpt-and-other-chatbots-for-employees-after-sensitive-code-leak/

19. Harvard designs AI sandbox that enables exploration, interaction without compromising security; *Harvard*; https://news.harvard.edu/gazette/story/newsplus/harvard-designs-ai-sandbox-that-enables-exploration-interaction-without-compromising-security/

20. Training a single AI model can emit as much carbon as five cars in their lifetime; *MIT Technology Review*; https://www.technologyreview.com/2019/06/06/239031/training-a-single-ai-model-can-emit-as-much-carbon-as-five-cars-in-their-lifetimes/

21. Generative AI and its potential environmental impact; *Bosch*; https://blog.bosch-digital.com/generative-ai-and-its-potential-environmental-impact/

22. The Staggering Ecological Impacts of Computation and the Cloud; *The MIT Press Reader*; https://thereader.mitpress.mit.edu/the-staggering-ecological-impacts-of-computation-and-the-cloud/

23. Sustainability, The Cloud; *Amazon*; https://sustainability.aboutamazon.com/products-services/the-cloud?energyType=true

24. Water Positive Methodology; *Amazon*; https://sustainability.aboutamazon.com/aws-water-positive-methodology.pdf

25. Building Generative AI Features Responsibly; *Meta*; https://about.fb.com/news/2023/09/building-generative-ai-features-responsibly/

26. World Economic Forum Launches AI Governance Alliance Focused on Responsible Generative AI; *World Economic Forum*; https://www.weforum.org/press/2023/06/world-economic-forum-launches-ai-governance-alliance-focused-on-responsible-generative-ai/

5
IMPACT OF GENERATIVE AI ON JOBS

A 2023 report by Indeed analyzed job listings and skills to identify their exposure to GenAI automation. And the findings were eye-opening:[1] roughly 20% of jobs were found to be "highly exposed" to GenAI, meaning the technology is considered good or excellent at 80% or more of all skills for that job. A further 45% of jobs were "moderately exposed," meaning that GenAI can do 50–80% of the work. And the remaining 34% of jobs were "low or minimally" exposed – but even that means that GenAI is good or excellent at up to 50% of the work.

In other words, almost every job you can think of will be impacted by GenAI to some extent. Some will become redundant, many will be augmented or altered by AI tools, and new jobs will be created.

How at Risk Is Your Job?

I hope this chapter will help you answer that question, but perhaps a better question to ask is: "How does my work *add value* to the world?" In this age of intelligent machines, I think this is a question everyone – including myself – should be asking.

Having considered the value you bring, next ask yourself: "Can machines deliver that value, either today or in the medium-term future?" (Because no one can predict the distant future.) Break your job down into its component tasks and core skills, and compare those elements to GenAI capabilities. Based on what you're discovering about GenAI, could the technology be considered good (or even excellent) at those skills and tasks?

As you'll see in this chapter, the range of jobs that GenAI can take on is already pretty staggering. Of course, humanity has been here before with previous waves of automation. Many factory and assembly line jobs, for instance, have been automated. Much warehouse and packing work can be done (and managed) by machines. Many administrative tasks are now easily automated. And supermarket checkout workers are being replaced with self-service machines. But this new wave of GenAI can take on the sorts of tasks that were previously considered immune to automation – jobs that require very human skills like creativity and communication. In particular, the ability to create has always been a big part of what separates humans from machines, but tools like ChatGPT and DALL-E can simulate human creativity – even if they aren't capable of *original thought*.

So there's a good chance that some of the value you deliver could be delivered by machines in future. If that's the case, may I suggest asking this question: "How would I *like* to add value to the world?" Meaning, what would you rather be doing if machines can do some or all or your current work?

Consider the Difference Between Lower-Level and Higher-Level Jobs

Now, I don't want to cause offense by suggesting that anyone's work is "low level," and therefore less important. When I talk about lower-level jobs, I'm referring to jobs which comprise tasks that GenAI can already do, and require the sorts of capabilities that GenAI already has. Whereas a higher-level job is comprised of tasks and capabilities that are – for now at least – firmly in the human domain. So we're talking about risk and exposure, essentially.

Later in the chapter we'll explore jobs at high, moderate, and low risk of GenAI automation. (We'll also look at some of the new roles that will be created.) But, for now, I want to make the point that some of the jobs that can be considered "lower level" or risky may surprise you.

I was at a conference in Germany recently and the host, a German newsreader, asked me whether their job would be affected by GenAI. My answer? Yes, absolutely. News can already be delivered by AI; a Korean TV network introduced an AI news anchor back in 2020.[2] (Which, in GenAI terms, is a lifetime ago!)

Let's think about the core skills required of a good news anchor: they need a great voice, smart appearance, good timing, the ability to absorb information quickly, remain calm under pressure, and present information in an engaging way. GenAI can do all of that.

And in the not-too-distant future, you'll be able to use GenAI to create your own personalized newsreader, delivering content in a way you can best understand (because it will know what you already know about a given subject and will be able to pitch information accordingly). And your personalized newsreader could, in theory, be anyone (or anything) you want. If you want to have AI Ryan Reynolds read you the news, that's no problem. If you prefer your news as a rap, you'll be able to have that. (Matt Green, "The Rapping Science Teacher" on social media, explains complex science concepts via rap, so why not have your daily news delivered as raps?)

Therefore, surprising as it may seem, I consider news anchors to be at risk of automation. Same goes for other journalism roles. Associated Press, for example, has been experimenting with AI for several years, using it to create short news content out of material like corporate earnings reports.[3]

So what kind of journalism job might be considered a "higher-level" role – the sort of role that can't be automated by GenAI? I'd say investigative journalist is a relatively safe bet. The world absolutely needs humans to continue to investigate stories, uncover the truth, and hold people in power to account. And if we think about the kinds of skills that a good investigative reporter needs, we're looking at skills like curiosity, interpersonal skills, critical thinking, research, and excellent writing skills. Sure, GenAI has good writing skills, but it doesn't excel in the other areas.

Take marketing as another example. Lower-level content creators who write blog posts and social media captions, for example, could soon be out of a job, since that can easily be done to a fairly high standard by GenAI. But marketing strategy and the ability to write a fantastic creative or design brief? GenAI would struggle to get anywhere near the skill level of a human marketer on those tasks. Humans absolutely need to be doing the strategic thinking behind marketing output, and overseeing the quality of output.

I'd therefore advise anyone reading this book to take a long, hard look at their job and evaluate which parts of the role might be considered lower level, and which parts (if any) absolutely need the human touch. With this in mind, let's look at some of the most common jobs that humans currently do and assess their exposure to GenAI automation.

Jobs at Maximum Risk of Automation

GenAI, by nature, excels at tasks involving the generation of output based on existing information. As a result, jobs that are repetitive, predictable, and don't require deep human intuition are at the highest risk of being affected. Let's explore some jobs that are particularly susceptible. You might be surprised at some of the roles that make the list.

The end of customer service jobs?

Customer service representative is a job that faces one of the highest risks of becoming redundant thanks to GenAI. Indeed, customer service is already a hotbed of technological activity, from chatbots to advanced analytics.

Customer service work involves talking to customers, understanding their problems or queries, and, where possible, coming up with answers. As it turns out, this is pretty much exactly the same as what ChatGPT does. Indeed, ChatGPT is already far more impressive than your average customer service chatbot, and is getting better all the time.

Objectively, it's easy to see why organizations might favor a GenAI customer service system:

- **It excels at automating simple, repetitive tasks that follow set guidelines.** Things like answering queries, troubleshooting common problems, and providing information.

- **It's highly scalable.** AI systems can handle a large number of enquiries simultaneously, which means businesses can address customer concerns rapidly and without the need for a proportional increase in human staff as demand grows.

- **It offers massive scope for personalization.** AI can integrate vast amounts of data in real time, providing personalized responses based on a customer's purchase history, preferences, or past interactions with the company. This level of personalization can be challenging for humans to achieve consistently.

- **It's cost efficient.** Over the long term, investing in a well-developed GenAI solution may be more cost-effective than hiring, training, and maintaining a human workforce, especially for large corporations.

- And it can be available **24 hours a day, seven days a week.**

So does this mean that people who work in customer service are on a sure-fire road to redundancy? As with most things, it's not that black and white. While many tasks within customer service can be automated, there will still be scenarios that require the human touch. Complex issues, sensitive topics, or situations requiring empathy and judgment are clearly better handled by humans. Most likely, the role of customer service representative will evolve, with a smaller group of humans working alongside AI tools, where humans oversee AI operations and handle the more complex interactions.

Other jobs that may cease to exist in future (at least, in their lower-level forms)

Beyond customer service, what other jobs are the most at risk? This isn't an exhaustive list, but it gives a taste of those roles that may prove to be vulnerable in future.

- **Content creators (certain types, at least):** GenAI tools like ChatGPT can produce vast amounts of written content, such as basic articles and reports at scale.

- **Entry-level graphic designers:** GenAI design tools can create a multitude of design variants in seconds.

- **Translators (for some languages and content types):** AI translation tools are constantly improving and might reduce the need for human translators, especially for general content.

- **Data entry clerks and clerical workers:** Jobs that involve inputting data into systems and basic administrative tasks can be easily automated using AI.

- **Telemarketers:** AI can handle scripted calls, recognize human responses, and adapt its script accordingly, making certain telemarketing roles susceptible.

- **Bookkeepers:** Routine bookkeeping tasks, such as data entry and basic account reconciliations, can be automated with AI.

- **Market research analysts:** AI can gather, analyze, and interpret vast amounts of data more efficiently than humans, which could replace some functions of market research.

- **Quality control:** For repetitive tasks that involve checking products or software for consistent, known issues, AI can be trained to recognize and report defects.

- **Stock traders:** Algorithmic trading using AI is already prevalent, and many trading decisions based on data analysis can be fully automated.

- **Advertising and media buying:** Programmatic ad buying, where AI chooses where to place ads based on data analysis, can automate many tasks in the advertising sector.

- **Paralegals and basic legal research:** AI can sift through vast amounts of legal data and documents to extract relevant information.

- **Corporate and product photographers:** As we saw in Chapter 3, GenAI tools are already emerging that can create portraits and headshots, and even generate images of products.

- **Factory workers and assembly line operators:** Automation and robotics have already made significant inroads in manufacturing, but GenAI can further streamline operations and reduce the need for human intervention.

Will we lose the ability to learn on the job?

Clearly, GenAI has significant potential to reshape the employment landscape – in particular, impacting entry-level positions. But these entry-level positions are often seen as stepping stones to acquire foundational skills for higher-level roles. So a big question is, How will people acquire the skills they need when entry-level positions no longer exist? If lower-level tasks are routinely done by AI, will we lose the ability to learn "on the job"?

This is a major challenge for people entering the workforce, and means we need to potentially rethink the notions of skills development and career progression. For employers, the focus may need to shift toward cultivating skills that AI cannot replicate easily – things like empathy, critical thinking, and complex decision-making – and fostering a culture of lifelong learning to ensure that individuals can adapt to the ever-evolving job market.

This might be a good time to mention my book *Future Skills: The 20 skills and competencies everyone needs to succeed in a digital world*, which takes a practical look at essential skills for our future workplaces, with a particular emphasis on softer, human skills.

Jobs at Moderate to Low Risk

While some jobs will cease to exist in future, many more will be altered by GenAI. A 2023 report by the International Labour Organization (ILO) says that GenAI is likely to augment, rather than destroy, jobs. In other words, the majority of jobs will experience limited automation, and are more likely to be "complemented rather than substituted" by GenAI.[4] (However, it's worth noting the ILO report found that women are more likely to be affected by GenAI automation than men – with more than twice the share of female employment potentially affected. Largely, this is due to women's over-representation in clerical work, which is considered at high risk of automation.)

So, here, we're talking about professions where certain tasks will likely be automated, but the profession itself is unlikely to become obsolete. For example, while a portion of healthcare diagnostic work might be aided or replaced by GenAI, doctors and healthcare professionals have myriad other responsibilities that AI can't handle.

These jobs will evolve, therefore. Many professionals in these fields will likely adapt, integrating GenAI tools into their work, and focusing their time and effort on aspects that require uniquely human skills. Those roles that will be least susceptible to change are those that require deep human intuition, creativity, cultural understanding, or hands-on physical dexterity.

Teachers, healthcare professionals, and lawyers

Teaching is about more than just delivering information – which, after all, ChatGPT can do very well. Educating requires an understanding of student dynamics, the ability to adapt to individual needs, a nurturing mindset and a safeguarding role. GenAI will no doubt assist in various areas of education – such as creating educational content, distilling complex subjects into easy-to-understand summaries, personalizing educational content, grading quantitative assignments, and automating administrative tasks. But we will absolutely need human teachers who can adapt explanations and modify learning materials based on subtle cues from students, foster genuine connections with their students, manage classroom harmony, provide nuanced feedback to students, and above all, inspire a passion for learning. I'm married to a teacher, and have three children in education, so I don't take the future of teaching lightly. Ultimately, I believe GenAI could bring about a harmonious scenario where AI and human educators coalesce, each amplifying the strengths of the other, with the irreplaceable human qualities of empathy, inspiration, and intuition remaining at the heart of teaching.

Similarly, in the healthcare profession AI can assist in diagnosis, drug discovery, routine monitoring, and personalized treatment plans, but the human touch, bedside manner, empathy, and nuanced decision-making skills of doctors, nurses, and other healthcare professionals are irreplaceable. If we can harness the best of both worlds, we stand to enhance and democratize healthcare and improve patient outcomes around the world. We can reduce human error and enable healthcare professions to have more time for personalized care and supporting patients.

The legal profession is another interesting example of "knowledge work" (or what some people might think of as "white-collar work") that will be augmented by GenAI. The legal profession stands on the brink of significant transformation thanks to technological advancements, particularly in AI. Data analysis, document review, and legal research can all be streamlined with AI. Automated contract analysis and predictive algorithms for case outcomes are further examples of tasks where AI is making inroads. However, the essence of lawyering – ethical judgment, client counseling, negotiation, and courtroom advocacy – will remain deeply rooted in human skills and intuition. The best lawyers have enormous capacity for empathy and moral reasoning. GenAI just can't replicate these skills. So, as technology continues to evolve, lawyers will likely find themselves working alongside AI, leveraging the efficiency and data-processing capabilities of machines while focusing on complex, high-level tasks that require human insight, creativity, and ethical understanding.

Other jobs that will be augmented, not replaced, by AI

Let's quickly run through some other jobs that will adapt and be augmented by GenAI:

- **Software developers:** While GenAI can automate code writing for certain tasks, software development is also about problem-solving, design, and understanding human needs – areas where humans excel.

- **Accountants and auditors:** Yes, basic accounting tasks can be automated, but higher-level auditing, financial analysis, and strategic advice still benefit from human insight.

- **Marketing managers:** AI can analyze data and suggest suitable strategies, but human creativity, strategic oversight, and a nuanced understanding of culture is essential.

- **Creative professionals:** Artists, musicians, and writers bring unique human perspectives, emotions, and cultural insights to their work. While AI can generate art or music, human creativity has nuances that are deeply tied to our experiences.

- **Human resources professionals:** Many HR tasks can and will be automated, but dealing with employee relations, understanding workplace dynamics, and making judgment calls about people will always require nuanced human understanding.

- **Research scientists:** While AI can assist in data analysis, human curiosity drives the formulation of novel hypotheses and the interpretation of complex results.

And in terms of jobs at low risk of significant disruption, we have:

- **Skilled tradespeople:** Jobs such as electricians, plumbers, and mechanics require hands-on expertise and problem-solving in unpredictable environments that are challenging for AI to navigate.

- **Emergency responders:** Firefighters, paramedics, and police officers often operate in unpredictable environments, making split-second decisions that are based on a wide array of factors. This is outside AI's comfort zone.

- **Mental health professionals:** Therapists, counselors, and psychologists rely on deep human empathy, intuition, and understanding, which are challenging for AI to replicate.

- **Social workers:** Another role that deals with complex human situations, requiring empathy, cultural understanding, and often the ability to navigate unpredictable and emotional situations. Again, not AI's strong suit.

- **Management and leadership roles:** Executives, managers, and other business leaders must navigate complex interpersonal relationships, make strategic decisions, and inspire and motivate their teams, which are skills that AI lacks.

Bottom line, human touch, intuition, nuanced decision-making, creativity, human connection, and physical expertise will all remain important in the future job market. Jobs deeply rooted in these skills will prove more resistant to the sweeping changes GenAI might bring.

Let's Not Forget that New Jobs Will Be Created

No doubt many jobs will be altered or made obsolete by GenAI. But, as history has shown, the introduction of transformative technology often leads to the creation of entirely new jobs. GenAI is therefore not just a disruptor but also a creator of opportunities.

Let's explore some of the new jobs that GenAI is creating:

- **AI prompt engineers:** A newly emerging field that's tipped to have a bright future. Prompt engineers are experts at getting GenAI applications to deliver a specific output. (For example, a generic prompt will elicit a generic response, so a prompt engineer will refine their prompts until they get the desired result.) To be a good prompt engineer, you need strong communication skills, attention to detail, critical thinking, and data skills (in terms of working out what info the AI needs). What you *don't* need is a background in software design because GenAI systems interpret natural human language.

- **AI trainers:** Professionals who specialize in "teaching" and refining AI models. Their tasks can range from feeding the AI data, to fine-tuning its outputs to ensure accuracy and relevance.

- **AI ethics officers:** Given the powerful capabilities of GenAI, there's a clear need for professionals who can ensure that these systems are developed and used ethically, without biases, and in ways that are socially responsible.

- **AI maintenance engineers:** Like any system, AI models require upkeep in terms of updating models, ensuring systems run efficiently, and troubleshooting issues.

- **Generative design specialists:** In fields like architecture, product design, and engineering, GenAI can create numerous design variations. Specialists in this area guide the AI and interpret its outputs to achieve optimal designs.

- **AI content reviewers:** Across all forms of content, from written articles to visual designs, human reviewers will be needed to assess the quality, accuracy, and appropriateness of content.

- **AI-enhanced entertainment creators:** Generative AI can be used to create music, video content, virtual realities, and even video game elements. Professionals who can harness this tech for creative endeavors are emerging.

- **Data curators and cleaners:** The effectiveness of GenAI hinges on the quality of data it's trained on. Therefore, individuals skilled in curating and cleaning data are in demand.

- **AI interaction designers:** As AI interfaces become more common, there's a need for designers who can craft user experiences that allow for smooth human-AI interaction.

- **Custom AI solution developers:** While many AI applications might be broad, there's a growing market for custom, niche AI solutions, tailored to specific industry needs or challenges.

- **AI policy and regulation specialists:** As AI becomes more integrated into society, experts who understand both the technology and its societal implications will be required to shape policies and regulations.

- **AI literacy educators:** Just as computer literacy became a fundamental skill in the late twentieth and early twenty-first centuries, AI literacy will become crucial going forward. Educators who can teach individuals about AI's workings, benefits, and challenges are emerging.

- **Personal AI managers:** As AI becomes more personal (think personal AI assistants), there may be roles for managers who can customize and oversee these personal AI tools for individuals or companies.

In essence, as generative AI continues to evolve, it will require a blend of technical and non-technical skills to ensure that it's harnessed effectively, ethically, and to the benefit of society. The job landscape will transform in line with this – with many new roles emerging that center around guiding, refining, and interpreting AI, as well as integrating its capabilities into various sectors.

Key Takeaways

In this chapter, we've learned:

- Almost every job you can think of will be impacted by GenAI to some extent. Some will become redundant, many will be augmented or altered by AI tools, and new jobs will be created.

- Jobs that are repetitive, predictable, and don't require deep human intuition are at the highest risk of being automated by GenAI.

- Many more jobs – including knowledge work and creative roles – will adapt to incorporate GenAI. Professionals in fields as diverse as education, healthcare, marketing, and HR will adapt, integrating GenAI tools into their work so they can focus their time and effort on aspects that require uniquely human skills.

- As entry-level jobs potentially disappear, employers will need to rethink notions of skills development and career progression. The traditional route of starting at the bottom, learning on the job, and working your way up may no longer apply.

- The human touch, intuition, nuanced decision-making, creativity, human connection, and physical expertise will all remain important in the future job market.

- What's more, new jobs will emerge that help individuals and organizations get the best from GenAI solutions – jobs like AI prompt engineer and AI literacy educator.

- Given the changes coming in the job market, everyone should be asking themselves some key questions: "How does my work *add value* to the world?" "Can machines deliver that value, either today or in the medium-term future?" And "How would I *like* to add value to the world?"

This brings us to the end of Part 1. Now that we've set the scene for GenAI, let's delve into some specific sectors and explore real-world examples of GenAI in practice.

Notes

1. Indeed's 'AI at Work Report' Finds GenAI Will Impact Almost Every Job in America; *Indeed*; https://www.indeed.com/press/releases/indeeds-ai-at-work-report-finds-genai-will-impact-almost-every-job-in-america?co=US
2. MBN introduces Korea's first AI news anchor; *Korea JoongAng Daily*; https://koreajoongangdaily.joins.com/2020/11/10/entertainment/television/MBN-AI-artificial-intelligence/20201110153900457.html
3. Robot reporters? Here's how news organisations are using AI in journalism; *Euronews*; https://www.euronews.com/next/2023/08/24/robot-reporters-heres-how-news-organisations-are-using-ai-in-journalism
4. Generative AI likely to augment rather than destroy jobs; *International Labour Organization*; https://www.ilo.org/global/about-the-ilo/newsroom/news/WCMS_890740/lang--en/index.htm

Part 2
GENERATIVE AI
IN PRACTICE

Now that we've got a feel for how GenAI works, what it can do, and how it might impact our world, let's explore how organizations are using GenAI.

In this part, we'll delve into specific sectors and find real-world use cases from areas like entertainment, marketing and advertising, retail, banking, healthcare, and more. The idea is to show how any business can use GenAI to connect with customers, bring new products and services to market, and enhance business operations.

In the interest of keeping this book to a sensible size, I obviously had to make a choice about which industries were included, and which were left out. So if your specific sector doesn't feature here, it doesn't mean that GenAI isn't applicable to your business. GenAI can bring benefits to any business across any sector, as the examples in Part 2 show. Use them to inspire and ignite ideas for your own organization.

6
A NEW DAWN IN MEDIA AND ENTERTAINMENT

I wanted to cover media and entertainment first because there are lots of interesting case studies emerging in these fields, more than I could possibly cover in one chapter. Consider this a whirlwind tour of emerging uses and examples, not an exhaustive digest.

Even if you don't work in media or entertainment, no doubt you consume news, TV, film, sports, book content, podcasts, music, and art. So if you want to understand how this content is being transformed by GenAI, read on.

Generative AI and Journalism

Lots of media organizations are thinking about how to leverage GenAI and what the technology means for journalism in the future. As we'll see, GenAI has a lot of potential in journalism, as it can be used to automate the creation of content (particularly for data-driven stories and reports), and for other tasks.

Finding efficiencies and new ways to present content

Imagine you're a journalist or editor in a busy, under-resourced newsroom – because, make no mistake, most newsrooms are getting smaller and smaller, and employing fewer reporters every year.[1] GenAI can help stretched newsrooms create content in a more streamlined, efficient way. And I'm not just talking about computers writing stories (although, that is happening) – I'm talking about using GenAI to brainstorm ideas for features, analyze audience data, personalize news stories, create accompanying video content, and more. Journalism is, at heart, about processing and presenting information, and GenAI can help news outlets do this in new, exciting, and more efficient ways – from automating news stories about local college football results, to generating engaging video content with AI. GenAI can also be used to make stories more interactive and deliver news in a more personalized way (think movie stars reading your daily news, as per Chapter 5). What's more, GenAI can instantly translate content into multiple languages, thereby increasing the geographic reach of media outlets. All of which allows human journalists to focus on more complex aspects of storytelling and investigation.

A few GenAI examples from media

As we have seen in Chapter 5, The Associated Press (AP) has been an early adopter of GenAI, using it to automate summaries of earnings reports and sporting events to great effect. (In fact, GenAI has allowed the AP a tenfold increase in output of such articles.[2]) And in 2023, the AP announced a licensing deal with OpenAI, allowing the AI company to use part of AP's news archive to explore GenAI uses in news.[3]

BuzzFeed is another company that's adopting GenAI. The platform is already using ChatGPT to enhance its quizzes and experiment with personalized content for readers in the form of chatbots and games. The company has also created a new AI recipe generator called "Botatouille." BuzzFeed CEO, Jonah Peretti, has said he sees GenAI replacing "the majority of static content," citing AI's ability to generate hundreds of ideas in a second, curate content, and produce "hyper-personalized content."[4]

Google is reportedly testing a GenAI product that can write articles – demonstrating the product for the *New York Times* and other news outlets.[5] The AI tool, which has the working title of Genesis, can take in information on, say, details about an event, and produce news content. Google's plan is that the tool can automate certain tasks for journalists, rather than replace journalists altogether.

Meanwhile, Bloomberg has developed a GenAI model, trained specifically on financial data. BloombergGPT is designed to answer questions about businesses, write headlines, and identify how a headline reflects a company's financial outlook. The idea is to help clients digest the deluge of business and financial news information, and allow them to ask questions about news stories.[6]

One area of news where GenAI really excels is in producing lots of hyper-local content – exactly the kind of content that shrinking newsrooms simply don't have the resources to produce. Indeed, News Corp has been using GenAI to produce 3000 local news stories a week in Australia, on topics such as weather and fuel prices. The technology allows a team of just four staff to generate and oversee thousands of local stories.[7]

But it's not all rosy. In 2020, Microsoft-owned MSN replaced its human journalists with GenAI, using the technology to create stories for MSN and Edge browser home pages – with, let's say, iffy results. MSN has since come under fire for publishing a range of fake news stories about, among other topics, mermaids, Bigfoot, and angels in the sky.[8] Which goes to show what happens when you implement GenAI without human oversight. . .

Enhancing Sports Broadcasting and Fan Engagement with Generative AI

GenAI has lots of potential to revolutionize sports broadcasting by creating more engaging and personalized content for viewers. Let's explore potential applications of GenAI and a few real-world examples.

GenAI applications in sports

An obvious application is using GenAI to auto-generate commentary (or translate commentary in real time) for sporting events. AI is capable of analyzing vast amounts of data from previous games, player statistics, sensors (both wearable sensors on players and sensors on the pitch), cameras, and fan sentiments from social media to provide insightful and real-time commentary, which enriches the viewer's experience.

Moreover, GenAI can produce realistic virtual simulations and visual augmentations, giving broadcasters the ability to recreate pivotal moments in a game from different angles and perspectives, thus offering fans a more immersive and fun viewing experience. Basically, by harnessing the capabilities of GenAI, sports broadcasters can elevate the quality, personalization, and interactivity of their content – in the process, enhancing fan engagement and satisfaction.

Real-world examples from sports

I'm a big Wimbledon fan, so I have to start here. It's fair to say The All England Club, the organization behind the tennis tournament, transitioned to a data-driven media company a long time ago – for example, using AI to create automated video highlight reels as early as 2017. In 2023, Wimbledon upped its game by introducing automated AI voice and subtitle commentary for these highlight reels.[9] Looking ahead, the technology could be used to create commentary for matches that don't have human commentators – such as junior matches, or matches on courts that simply don't get as much attention as, say, a Centre Court match. The commentary could be created in multiple languages and even personalized to fans' preferences.

Formula One (F1) is using AI in multiple ways. F1 has always been a technology- and data-driven sport – behind every driver is a team of engineers and scientists mining data for every tiny little advantage. AI-powered simulations are used to model billions of potential race parameters to determine what variables are most likely to lead to favorable outcomes. AI simulations are also used to train drivers, allowing them to learn tracks and push their skills without risking injury (or expensive vehicles). And since certain data from these simulations has to be made available to opposing teams, this means drivers can train by racing simulated models of their opponents, based on real-world data.[10]

As for F1 broadcasting, there's so much happening in the course of a race that isn't necessarily obvious to the audience. Which is why F1 partners with Amazon Web Services to leverage all that data – such as live car positioning data and timing data – to create the insights that are delivered onscreen to audiences during the race. (Incidentally, F1 also routinely uses AI in the design of racing cars, but we'll talk more about AI-augmented design in Chapter 14.)

In another example, Fox Sports is collaborating with Google to harness GenAI. The sports broadcaster is using Google Cloud's Vertex AI Vision System to generate content from its massive archive of game footage.[11] Google's system can rapidly search through footage from nearly two million videos and produce new video content "in near–real time" for sharing on TV and social media.

Meanwhile, LaLiga Tech, the technology division of Spanish football league LaLiga, has partnered with AI specialists Globant and Microsoft to pilot GenAI in its sports broadcasting. Among the projects, GenAI will be used to generate new personalized content for fans (including the automatic creation of multi-language subtitles) and create immersive new materials for broadcasters.[12]

Storytelling: Generative AI in Books, Audiobooks, and Podcasts

Storytelling is part of what makes us human. So what does the advent of GenAI mean for this uniquely human pastime? Well, we know that tools like ChatGPT can already write all sorts of content, from poems and blog posts to short stories and even novels. Yes, that's right, AI can now write stories that can (sometimes) compete against human storytellers. But GenAI can also help authors and publishers create new forms of content and streamline aspects of content production (including audio content).

How authors are using GenAI to tell stories

Find it hard to believe GenAI can write a decent novel? In one early example from 2015, a novella called *The Day a Computer Writes a Novel* was deemed good enough to make it through the first round of selection for a Japanese literary award.[13] More recently, *The Inner Life of an AI: A Memoir by ChatGPT*, published in 2022, became possibly the first memoir written by ChatGPT (prompted by data scientist Forrest Xiao).[14] One sci-fi author was so taken with ChatGPT's capabilities, he used it to write over 100 books in just nine months.[15] On his epic sci-fi writing spree, Tim Boucher also used Midjourney to create images to accompany ChatGPT's text.

Many more writers will perhaps dip their toe into GenAI by using it to generate ideas, come up with character and place names, produce writing prompts, and generally as a tool for inspiration and productivity – helping to overcome the dreaded "writer's block." In this way, GenAI can be considered a "co-creation" tool rather than something that will render human storytellers obsolete.

GenAI can also foster more collaborative and interactive storytelling – meaning writers can create interactive narratives where the storyline progresses based on the reader's choices. (The AI equivalent of those "choose your own adventure" books you might remember from your youth.) In other words, GenAI could provide a way for writers to provide a more personalized experience and connect with readers in new ways.

Enhancing the publishing process

While there's been much criticism of GenAI from the publishing sector (thanks to GenAI models being trained on book content without consent, see Chapter 4), we may, in future, see publishers adopt GenAI into workflows. For example, GenAI could be used to automatically repurpose book content into other formats (e.g., articles and blog posts for PR use). And it could drastically speed up the translation of books for other geographic markets. As I was writing this book, I received a translated edition of one of my earlier books – a book that was published more than a year ago. As translations go, that's actually not that slow. But with GenAI, translated editions could be created simultaneously, alongside the English language version. As an author, I find that particularly exciting.

And another area where GenAI could play a big role is in audiobooks. Which brings me to. . .

Creating audio content

Remember that GenAI can generate audio content as well as written and visual content. And this brings a lot of potential to the world of publishing and storytelling. Making audiobooks the traditional way, with a human narrator, is a costly, time-consuming process, and yet GenAI can automatically convert written content into audio content – and with realistic-sounding voices (not robotic computer voices).

Project Gutenberg, a free online e-book library of public domain books, has collaborated with Microsoft to create thousands of free audiobooks – made with GenAI text-to-speech technology.[16] The books are available on Spotify, Google Podcasts, or Apple Podcasts. And in the future, the project promises, readers will be able to generate audiobooks using their own voice.

Similarly, Apple has also developed GenAI technology to narrate audiobooks, working with independent publishers to turn published works into audiobooks.[17] To find these AI-narrated books, search for "AI narration" in the Apple Books app.

What about podcasts?

If books can be translated automatically with GenAI, why not podcasts? Spotify has been working on just that with its Voice Translation pilot, an AI feature that translates podcasts into additional languages – in the podcaster's own voice.[18] The tool, based on OpenAI's voice-generation tech, seamlessly matches the original speaker's style, intonation, and pauses, resulting in a more authentic result than traditional dubbing. Spotify worked with podcasters including Dax Shepard and Steven Bartlett on the project. (By the way, Steven Bartlett has also used AI technology to seamlessly dub his "Diary of a CEO" YouTube videos into Spanish and French.)

Generative AI in Film

In Chapter 4, we saw that some voice actors are already losing work to AI-generated (or AI-cloned) voices. Let's explore some other ways GenAI is being used in the world of film.

What can GenAI do for filmmakers?

GenAI has the ability to create special effects, generate characters and backdrops, and even produce entire scenes, reducing the reliance on costly physical sets and streamlining post-production processes. This opens up new opportunities for smaller studios and independent filmmakers to achieve high-quality visuals that were previously the domain of big-budget productions. Thus, GenAI can help to democratize the filmmaking process, and reduce production time and costs across the board.

It can also be used in the pre-production stage, to enhance scriptwriting and generate new ideas (see the Hollywood writers' strike, Chapter 4). What's more, AI can be used to create narration, dub audio in a more authentic way, or even potentially resurrect the voices (and images) of stars who are no longer with us.

That latter usage is problematic, though, since dead movie stars can't give consent or be compensated for the use of their voice and image. Plus, it can be downright creepy. Zelda Williams, daughter of the legendary Robin Williams, who died in 2014, has said she finds AI recreations of her father's voice "personally disturbing."[19]

Real-world use cases from film

It's clear GenAI has a lot of potential in filmmaking, but how are filmmakers actually using the technology? One example comes from the Oscar-winning *Everything Everywhere All at Once*, which blurred the boundaries between the real world and fantasy by integrating AI elements with live-action footage. The makers have praised AI and said that visual effects work that previously would have taken half a day could be done in mere minutes.[20]

Runway ML's AI editing technology, which was used in the making of *Everything Everywhere All at Once*, can be used for a number of visual effects – including removing objects from a scene. Remember when the internet lost its mind over a Starbucks cup accidentally left in shot in an episode of *Game of Thrones*? AI editing technology could easily solve problems like that in minutes. Runway also has a video-to-video offering that can create new visual content based on existing content – so filmmakers can create new scenes based on existing footage.[21]

In another example, AI lab Flawless, founded by film director and producer Scott Mann, is using GenAI to improve dubbing. Gone are the days when a character's mouth movements don't bear any resemblance to the dubbed audio; Flawless's TrueSync technology uses GenAI to make the actor's mouth seamlessly match the subbed language (a process they call "vubbing").[22] The company says the same technology can be used to remove swear words from films, in order to secure a certain rating. It was used in the 2022 film *Fall* to remove F-bombs and gain a PG-13 rating.

Generating Music with AI

There is *so* much exciting stuff happening in the world of music, it was hard to narrow this section down. But let's explore some of the main ways GenAI is impacting music.

Transforming the music industry

GenAI can be a catalyst for creativity and innovation, and as such it's being embraced by many amateur and professional musicians. GenAI can be used to create new compositions, and help artists and producers experiment with new sounds. What's more, GenAI can be employed for mastering and mixing tracks, automating these processes and, thus, saving time and resources for artists. By blending human creativity with AI, the music industry can usher in a new era of co-creativity and discovery.

GenAI also has the potential to revolutionize music platforms, enabling the creation of diverse, personalized, and unique musical content. By analyzing vast datasets of music, GenAI algorithms can learn patterns, styles, and structures inherent in different genres, and then use that knowledge to create entirely new compositions. Music platforms could integrate these technologies to offer tailor-made experiences for users, generating playlists and tracks that align with individual preferences.

Music generators

A wave of AI-powered music generation tools have been released that can create or assist in the creation of music. They can generate all sorts of music, across different genres, coming up with melodies, rhythms, harmonies, or even entire songs. Such tools could democratize music creation. You no longer need expensive equipment or formal training to be able to create music. (And with voice generators, you don't even need to be able to sing. But more on that coming up.) But these tools aren't just for aspiring musicians; established artists and producers could use such tools to generate ideas, unearth new musical directions, and streamline production.

So what sort of music generation tools are we talking about? Let's take "Loudly" as an example. The platform allows anyone to generate their own royalty-free music using simple natural language prompts. For example, ask it to create a soundtrack for your product launch video, and that's what you'll get. You can choose the style of music, tempo, mood, and even individual instruments. All of the sounds are based on human-generated recordings rather than being synthesized, and, importantly, Loudly owns the copyright of all music used to train its system. (Circle back to copyright issues, Chapter 4.) Any of the existing songs can be customized to fit individual projects or new songs can be created from scratch.

Other examples of AI music generators include Soundful, Mubert, MuseNet, Dadabots, Beatbot, and Aiva.

GenAI music tools could even be used to finalize tracks by dead artists. In June 2023, Sir Paul McCartney revealed that AI had been used to create "the final Beatles record,"[23] using restored vocals from one of John Lennon's old demo recordings – part of several songs on cassettes marked "For Paul," recorded shortly before Lennon's death. Which brings us neatly to. . .

AI voice generators

As well as beats, rhythms, and entire songs, AI can also synthesize human-sounding voices. Current voice-generation tools include Lovo.ai, Genny,

Synthesys, and Microsoft's AI voices available as part of Azure OpenAI. While these are mostly designed to produce professional voiceovers, creating singing voices is the next logical step.

In fact, AI-generated singers are already emerging. Teenage influencer Noonoouri became the first virtual AI star to get a record deal with Warner Music in September 2023.[24] Noonoouri is the creation of artist Joerg Zuber. Her voice was created by taking a recording of a real human singer and then using AI to create a new voice that's unique to the virtual performer. If you're wondering why a record company like Warner might be interested in signing artists that don't actually exist, consider this: Noonoouri will never get worn out from touring and promoting, she can be restyled in seconds to keep pace with changing teen trends, she won't create a scandal, and she's never going to make diva demands. For the record, I actually rather like her debut track!

But even real-life stars are experimenting with AI voice generation. In 2023, the artist known as "Grimes" launched software called "Elf Tech" that enables fans to make songs using an AI-generated version of her voice.[25] So, basically, anyone can use Grimes's voice to make new music – so long as they give her 50% of the royalties.

Bottom line, with music generation and voice-generation tools, AI allows anyone to create new music – whether you're a complete novice or a professional artist. Personally, I think that's lovely.

Interactive, AI-driven music consumption

AI is already informing how we listen to music. Spotify's recommendations, for example, are driven by AI algorithms. But this era of GenAI will bring new opportunities for personalization and interactivity.

With that in mind, Spotify recently debuted a new AI feature called "DJ" – a personalized AI guide that understands your music taste so well it can choose which artists and tracks to play next. So it's a curated lineup of music, but with added AI features, including AI-generated commentary and facts "in a stunningly realistic voice."[26] It also refreshes the lineup constantly, based on your feedback – so if you tell it you're not feeling a particular track, it'll learn and alter the lineup accordingly. Spotify is also reported to be developing AI-generated playlists that users can create with text prompts.[27]

While embracing GenAI in some aspects, interestingly, Spotify has also removed thousands of AI-generated songs from its platform. The songs were removed not because of copyright concerns, but because of the suspected use of bots to inflate streaming figures for AI music.[28]

AI in Art

Just as with music, GenAI could act as a catalyst for co-creation and innovation in art. But does AI art challenge what it means to be human and express ourselves? What do artists make of it? Let's explore the role of AI in art.

The artistic promise of GenAI

As we venture deeper into the digital age, the canvas of creativity is becoming increasingly digital. Artists are no longer confined to the traditional tools of their craft and, as such, are exploring new technologies – using GenAI to create intricate and novel pieces that stretch the boundaries of human imagination. By learning from vast datasets comprising diverse artistic styles and elements, GenAI models can generate art that merges, modifies, and extrapolates existing artistic concepts, resulting in aesthetically unique creations that may not have been possible through human effort alone.

It's best to think of GenAI as a collaborative tool, working alongside human artists to refine and enhance their work, thus opening new avenues for artistic exploration. In essence, the integration of GenAI in art is not just an evolution of artistic tools; it will expand creative horizons and redefine what's possible in art.

And thanks to Web3 infrastructure, artists can issue their AI-generated works as NFTs (non-fungible tokens), thereby opening up new avenues for artists to monetize their creativity. (You can read more about Web3 and the metaverse in my book *The Future Internet: How the Metaverse, Web3.0 and Blockchain Will Transform Business and Society*.)

Artists are in favor

If art is an expression of the human experience, is it less human – less valuable – when it's created with AI? Many naysayers have been quick to denigrate AI-generated art as somehow "less than" art created solely by humans. But we've been here before. When photography was invented, some painters labeled it the end of art. (Upon seeing a photograph for the first time, French painter Paul Delaroche is said to have declared, "From today, painting is dead.") Fast-forward a couple of centuries and photography has long been accepted as fine art, and painting is still alive and kicking. So why shouldn't AI-generated art be accepted as a valid form of fine art?

In fact, many artists have openly embraced GenAI, including artists like Stephanie Dinkins, Mimi Onuoha, and Wayne McGregor. In September 2023, a group of artists signed an open letter to the United States Congress in support of GenAI. The letter argues that algorithmic and automation tools have been used in music and art for decades and that GenAI is simply the next evolution in that journey. What's more, GenAI "lowers barriers in creating art – a career that has been traditionally limited to those with considerable financial means, abled bodies, and the right social connections."[29] The letter also asks that AI artists be included in talks about how AI systems should be regulated.

So, far from representing the death of art itself, GenAI will likely widen the artistic field and enable new forms of expression.

Examples of AI artworks and image generators

One of the most famous examples of an AI-generated artwork is the Portrait of Edmond de Belamy, which sold at Christie's auction house for US$432,000 in 2018.[30] The painting was created by the French collective named "Obvious," who fed 15 000 pre-twentieth-century portraits into an algorithm to teach it the aesthetics of portraiture. More recently, Christie's has teamed up with Gucci to commission digital artists to create 21 pieces of art that will be auctioned as NFTs.[31] The artworks explore how GenAI will inform the future of fashion and art.

Since the Portrait of Edmond de Belamy was sold in 2018, new GenAI systems have been released that allow anyone to create their own art. There are image generation tools that will create images based on natural language text prompts, image prompts (e.g., an existing photo), or using a combination of image and text prompts. Examples of AI image generation tools include Midjourney, Stable Diffusion, Dall-E 2, Deep Dream Generator, Artbreeder, DeepArt.io, GoArt, and Deep Angel (which erases objects from photos). There's also Ideogram, which can create images that feature text.

Another example that I really like is the poem-and-art postcard feature in Google's Arts & Culture app. The feature allows you to generate poem postcards based on artworks such as The Scream and The Starry Night. So, you choose an artwork, choose what type of poem you want (including sonnet, limerick, and haiku), and give a subject prompt to inspire the poem (such as "spring" or "waterfall"). The AI then combines all of your choices and creates a new poem that you can share with friends.

And as with music, GenAI can also be used to complete unfinished works. That was the case with Chinese AI and internet giant Baidu, which used GenAI to complete a masterpiece of traditional Chinese ink art, left unfinished when its renowned creator, Lu Xiaoman, died more than 50 years ago.[32] The project used Baidu's image generation model called "Wenxin Yige," which is specifically designed to generate traditional Chinese-style ink paintings.

Key Takeaways

We've covered a lot of ground in this chapter. To quickly recap:

- In media and journalism, GenAI is being used to write stories and increase the output of shrinking newsrooms. But it can also be used as a productivity tool, helping journalists digest information, create summaries, create video content, and more.

- The world of sports broadcasting is also beginning to adopt GenAI – in particular for generating real-time commentary in multiple languages, and creating interactive, personalized features for viewers.

- Human storytelling, through poems, short stories, novels, podcasts and more, can also be enhanced through GenAI – from creating new written works, and generating ideas and inspiration, to automatically translating content, and creating AI narration for audiobooks.

- In film, GenAI has particular promise for post-production processes, such as generating realistic visual effects and streamlining editing.

- GenAI also promises to revolutionize music creation, with new music and voice generator platforms that allow anyone to make music. As a co-creativity tool, GenAI allows musicians and producers to try out new sounds and streamline music production.

- Meanwhile, artists are using GenAI to expand their creative horizons. GenAI can be used to generate new images, manipulate existing images, and even complete unfinished works of art.

Another way that GenAI is being used to enhance human creativity is in advertising and marketing. Let's explore how GenAI is creating innovative ads and creating fun, personalized experiences for consumers.

Notes

1. The Shrinking Newsroom Crisis Will Be Impossible to Ignore in 2024; *Time*; https://time.com/6269573/local-journalism-decline-2024-election/
2. Automated earnings stories multiply; *Associated press*; https://blog.ap.org/announcements/automated-earnings-stories-multiply
3. ChatGPT-maker OpenAI signs deal with AP to license news stories; *AP News*; https://apnews.com/article/openai-chatgpt-associated-press-ap-f86f84c5bcc2f3b98074b38521f5f75a
4. BuzzFeed Says AI Will 'Replace Majority of Static Content'; *Futurism*; https://futurism.com/buzzfeed-ai-replace-content
5. Google Tests AI Tool That Is Able to Write News Articles; *New York Times*; https://www.nytimes.com/2023/07/19/business/google-artificial-intelligence-news-articles.html
6. Bloomberg Develops Generative AI Model Trained On Financial Data; *PYMNTS*; https://www.pymnts.com/news/artificial-intelligence/2023/bloomberg-develops-generative-ai-model-trained-financial-data/
7. News Corp using AI to produce 3,000 Australian local news articles a week; *The Guardian*; https://www.theguardian.com/media/2023/aug/01/news-corp-ai-chat-gpt-stories
8. MSN Fired Its Human Journalists and Replaced Them with AI That Publishes Fake News About Mermaids and Bigfoot; *Futurism*; https://futurism.com/msn-is-publishing-more-fake-news

9. Generative AI and Technology Innovation at Wimbledon 2023; *Bernard Marr*; https://bernardmarr.com/generative-ai-and-technology-innovation-at-wimbledon-2023/

10. How Artificial Intelligence, Data and Analytics Are Transforming Formula One in 2023; *Forbes*; https://www.forbes.com/sites/bernardmarr/2023/07/10/how-artificial-intelligence-data-and-analytics-are-transforming-formula-one-in-2023/

11. Fox Sports Taps Google Cloud For Generative AI Capabilities; *Variety*; https://variety.com/2023/digital/news/fox-sports-generative-ai-google-cloud-1235706964/

12. Globant and LaLiga Tech to Pilot Generative AI Applications to Reinvent Sports Tactics and Broadcasting; *Globant*; https://www.globant.com/news/globant-laliga-tech-generative-ai-applications-sports

13. An AI-Written Novella Almost Won a Literary Prize; *Smithsonian Magazine*; https://www.smithsonianmag.com/smart-news/ai-written-novella-almost-won-literary-prize-180958577/

14. Books Written by Artificial Intelligence: A List; *All Good Great*; https://allgoodgreat.com/list-of-books-written-by-artificial-intelligence/

15. Sci-fi author writes over 100 books in 9 months using AI including ChatGPT and Midjourney; *Times of India*; https://timesofindia.indiatimes.com/life-style/books/features/tim-boucher-sci-fi-author-writes-over-100-books-in-9-months-using-ai-including-chatgpt-and-midjourney/articleshow/100528872.cms?from=mdr

16. How to access thousands of free audiobooks, thanks to Microsoft AI and Project Gutenberg; *ZDNet*; https://www.zdnet.com/article/heres-how-to-access-thousands-of-free-audiobooks-thanks-to-microsoft-ai-and-project-gutenberg/

17. Death of the narrator? Apple unveils suite of AI-voiced audiobooks; *The Guardian*; https://www.theguardian.com/technology/2023/jan/04/apple-artificial-intelligence-ai-audiobooks

18. Introducing Voice Translation for podcasters; *Spotify*; https://newsroom.spotify.com/2023-09-25/ai-voice-translation-pilot-lex-fridman-dax-shepard-steven-bartlett/

19. Robin Williams' daughter says she finds AI recreations of her father's voice 'personally disturbing'; *Insider*; https://www.businessinsider.com/robin-williams-daughter-zelda-disturbing-ai-recreate-voice-2023-10?r=US&IR=T

20. Everything Everywhere All At Once: How AI is Revolutionizing Filmmaking; *Medium*; https://medium.com/@TheTechTrailblazer/everything-everywhere-all-at-once-how-ai-is-revolutionizing-filmmaking-173bf19d32be

21. How AI will augment human creativity in film production; *Variety*; https://variety.com/vip/how-artificial-intelligence-will-augment-human-creatives-in-film-and-video-production-1235672659/

22. Generative AI is bringing the biggest disruption to film making in 100 years; *Tech.eu*; https://tech.eu/2023/01/23/flawless-brings/

23. Sir Paul McCartney says artificial intelligence has enabled a 'final' Beatles song; *BBC News*; https://www.bbc.com/news/entertainment-arts-65881813

24. Virtual Influencer Noonnoouri Lands Record Deal; *Forbes*; https://www.forbes.com/sites/bernardmarr/2023/09/05/virtual-influencer-noonoouri-lands-record-deal-is-she-the-future-of-music/

25. Grimes Launched a Platform to Help You Make AI Songs With Her Voice. Here's What It Sounds Like; *Gozmodo*; https://gizmodo.com/grimes-elon-musk-openai-ai-music-elf-tech-1850409972

26. Meet your DJ; *Spotify*; https://newsroom.spotify.com/2023-02-22/spotify-debuts-a-new-ai-dj-right-in-your-pocket/

27. Spotify spotted developing AI-generated playlists created with prompts; *TechCrunch*; https://techcrunch.com/2023/10/02/spotify-spotted-developing-ai-generated-playlists-created-with-prompts/

28. Spotify removed thousands of AI-generated songs; *Mashable*; https://mashable.com/article/spotify-ai-crackdown

29. Open letter: Artists Using Generative AI Demand Seat At Table From US Congress; *Creative Common*; https://creativecommons.org/about/policy-advocacy-copyright-reform/open-letter-artists-using-generative-ai-demand-seat-at-table-from-us-congress/

30. A portrait created by AI just sold for $432,000. But is it really art?; *The Guardian*; https://www.theguardian.com/artanddesign/shortcuts/2018/oct/26/call-that-art-can-a-computer-be-a-painter

31. New Gucci NFTs combine fashion and art using generative AI; *Vogue Business*; https://www.voguebusiness.com/technology/new-gucci-nfts-combine-fashion-and-art-using-generative-ai

32. China's AI Landscape: Baidu's Generative AI Innovations in Art and Search; *Forbes*; https://www.forbes.com/sites/bernardmarr/2023/09/27/chinas-ai-landscape-baidus-generative-ai-innovations-in-art-and-search/

7
ADVERTISING AND MARKETING: BRIDGING CREATIVITY WITH AI

When exploring GenAI use cases and appetite among sales and marketing teams, McKinsey found that 90% of commercial leaders expect to deploy GenAI solutions "often" over the next two years.[1] GenAI is expected to revolutionize the word of advertising and marketing, with the ability to auto-generate and personalize content, even in real time. And as we'll see in this chapter, GenAI solutions will enable businesses of all sizes to create beautiful, professional ads and marketing campaigns.

Let's explore how brands will entice customers in the era of GenAI. Even if you don't work in this field, the way in which organizations advertise to you is about to change, so read on.

Overview: How Can Generative AI Be Applied in Advertising and Marketing?

GenAI can be used to create professional-looking content that is not just engaging for audiences, but also tailored to their specific needs.

The advantages of GenAI in marketing and advertising

One of the biggest benefits is the ability to create personalized content. After all, GenAI excels at analyzing data, and identifying patterns in the data – in this case, patterns that shed light on consumer behavior and preferences. It can then create imaginative content that is highly targeted to the desired audience, for example, in the form of targeted social media campaigns or personalized emails.

Another major benefit comes down to time and money, since GenAI can automate many of the processes involved in creating marketing and advertising materials. This allows marketers to focus their time on more strategic efforts – and focus their budget on high-impact activities.

Plus, GenAI allows even smaller teams to increase innovation and generate inspirational ads and marketing materials.

So what can brands create with GenAI?

We'll cover plenty of real-world use cases in this chapter, but as a general guide, GenAI can be used in marketing and advertising to:

- Generate fresh ideas that boost brainstorming sessions.
- Generate beautiful images – from images of products to imaginative visuals for aspirational ads. It can also be used to create branding collateral, including graphics and logos.
- Generate text for a variety of purposes, including emails, ad copy, blog posts, social media posts, product descriptions, and even scripts for ads.
- Generate video, including video ads for social media (or broadcasting), and product demos.
- Generate music to accompany videos.
- Plus, GenAI can be used as a sentiment analysis tool, analyzing data for sentiment (e.g., looking at social media mentions to see whether customer mentions are positive, negative, or neutral).

Handle with care

We've already talked about the potential pitfalls and concerns around GenAI (see Chapter 4), so professionals must take care to implement GenAI in a safe, ethical way. We'll talk more about successful implementation in Chapter 18, but here are a few tips to get you thinking:

- It's vital you balance automation with the human touch. Remember, GenAI mimics human creativity but it is not human. There's no substitute for human sensitivity, empathy, and cultural awareness. Plus, you will know your brand, its values, and ethics better than a computer model. So always add human knowledge and experience to ensure you get the best out of GenAI.

- Practice the highest levels of caution around personal data, copyright restrictions, and other legal issues. And do be aware of the potential for bias to creep in.

- And as always, be transparent with stakeholders about how you're using GenAI.

Using Generative AI to Create Ads and Marketing Materials

With the ability to generate text, images, video, and music, it's clear that GenAI has a lot of potential to create ads and marketing materials – with far less work and expense than traditional methods.

Automating aspects of ad creation

At the Adobe 2023 EMEA Summit, I saw a demonstration of Adobe's Firefly GenAI package, and let me tell you, it blew me away with its capabilities. Firefly is a natural language image generation engine that takes a simple text prompt and uses it to create pictures, designs, or any kind of artwork. Firefly has been integrated into the Adobe Express content generation platform, which allows non-professional designers to create high-quality images for social media and promotional content. (Firefly is also being integrated into other Creative Clouds applications like Photoshop and Illustrator.)[2]

In the demonstration, we were shown a photo of a beautiful wild island in what looked like Canada. Then the demonstrator prompted the system to add a hiker with a branded backpack recreating on the island . . . which it did with seamless results. How about adding a canoe in the water, to show how the hiker got there? No problem, done (and with totally realistic shading, I might add). Then, the demonstrator asked for the picture to be changed from portrait orientation to landscape. But to do that, the system had to fill in the "blanks" at the sides of the image – again, something it did seamlessly. Then, finally, they added in brand text. It was a stunning demonstration of the power of GenAI, and how it will allow businesses of all shapes and sizes to create beautiful advertising and marketing content with ease. (For the record, Firefly is trained exclusively on licensed or public domain images, and the company has said it will indemnify customers against copyright claims, as per Chapter 4.)

Examples of GenAI ads

It's easy to see why brands would choose AI-generated ads over traditional ads. It's significantly cheaper and easier, allowing brands to increase output while spending less; plus, it allows for unlimited creativity, free from real-world constraints. So let's look at a few real-world examples.

Big-name brands like Oreo and Cadbury have used OpenAI's DALL-E 2 to create ads (in Cadbury's case, creating an ad for the Indian market featuring an AI version of Bollywood star Shah Rukh Khan).[3] Fashion brands Nike and Tommy Hilfiger have used Midjourney to create ad images featuring their products.[4] And Coca-Cola deployed ChatGPT and DALL-E 2 in a stunning ad campaign called "Masterpiece." The ad brings to life some of the world's most famous works of art, seamlessly integrating AI-augmented animation with live action. I really like this example because it shows that GenAI can be used not just to churn out ads on the cheap, but also to create significant wow factor. Coca-Cola is so invested in GenAI as a transformational tool that it has appointed a Head of Generative AI.[5]

Meanwhile, Heinz fed DALL-E 2 prompts such as "ketchup in outer space" (and lots more fun ideas), posting the resulting images on their social media accounts. Heinz also encouraged consumers to create and share their own AI ketchup images, helping the campaign to go viral.[6] This taps into the huge move toward personalization in advertising and marketing, but we'll talk more about that later in the chapter.

New tools to help brands leverage GenAI

In Chapter 3, I mentioned that Meta is creating tools that allow businesses to automatically make multiple versions of Facebook ads, featuring different text and images aimed at different audiences.[7] But Meta isn't the only company promising to help businesses create GenAI ads and marketing copy more easily.

In 2023, Salesforce announced Einstein GPT, which it bills as the "world's first generative AI for customer relationship management."[8] The tool uses GenAI to create personalized content across Salesforce cloud, meaning Salesforce customers can connect their data and use natural language prompts to generate content that adapts to changing customer information and needs "in real time." (Again, more on personalization coming up.)

Another example comes from Aprimo, providers of marketing automation software. Aprimo has created an "embedded generative AI assistant" using Azure OpenAI and ChatGPT that can be used to, among other things, create engaging and personalized content that's trained on brand voice and tone.[9] Another service built on Microsoft Azure is Typeface, which uses GenAI to "create engaging, on-brand marketing messages in seconds."[10] The idea is you feed Typeface your style guidelines, images, and product details, and you can then start generating suggested images and text.

Elsewhere, LinkedIn has launched a new feature that allows B2B marketers to use GenAI. Called "Accelerate," the tool aims to speed up ad campaign setup and automate ad optimization. LinkedIn claims it will help B2B marketers create tailored creative content in as little as five minutes.[11]

A similar movement is beginning to happen in TV advertising. Fox TV has partnered with AI video generation specialists Waymark to enable GenAI commercials across all Fox stations, including local stations.[12] This will make

TV advertising much more accessible for small and local businesses – allowing them to easily create high-quality TV ads with limited time and budget.

Personalization of Content with GenAI

Personalization is a recurring theme throughout this book, and it's especially relevant in the field of marketing and advertising.

Personalization at scale

Brands know that we consumers crave that feeling of uniqueness and exclusivity – that we want to feel like we have a personal relationship with the brands we love, and that our support matters. But, achieving this effect on a mass scale is difficult and expensive. Or at least, it has been up until now. Because GenAI makes it possible for brands to deliver the uniqueness and personal touch that was previously the domain of high-end brands only.

Which is why more and more GenAI tools are including functionality around personalization. Adobe's Experience Cloud is a collection of tools including the Adobe Real Time Customer Data Platform, Journey Optimizer, and Adobe Analytics. These tools use AI to deliver insights on customer journeys, behaviors, and engagement. Information which, when combined with GenAI, can be used to automatically create hyper-personalized content.

The key, of course, is achieving that bespoke feeling without creeping people out or giving them the impression that their privacy has been invaded. Which is another thing that brands will have to consider carefully when deploying GenAI in highly personalized campaigns.

Examples of personalized experiences

Now let's look at a few examples. Netflix uses AI to create highly targeted thumbnails for its streaming content to increase the likelihood that customers will click and watch. The streaming giant has thousands of frames from each movie or TV show that can be used to automatically generate thumbnails – but did you know that the thumbnails *you* see could be entirely different to the thumbnails that I see? Netflix uses AI to analyze and rank images according to which have the highest likelihood of getting you to click – based on what others who are deemed similar to you have clicked on.[13]

What about personalized advertising campaigns? The Barbie Movie delivered a masterclass in movie promotion, seemingly taking over the internet for several weeks in 2023. One of the campaign's biggest hits was the Barbie Selfie Generator,[14] a website that let fans create personalized versions of the movie's poster featuring themselves (or whomever they wanted). Needless to say, it went viral. Which goes to show consumers' appetite for digital, interactive experiences that can be easily personalized (and, ideally, shared with friends).

Combine personalization with the ability to create AI versions of stars, and you have the potential to deliver some very fun experiences for consumers – rather like the Heinz example from earlier in the chapter, but featuring real-world celebrities. Superstar footballer Lionel Messi signed a deal with PepsiCo allowing the brand to use a deepfake version of himself to promote Lays chips.[15] As part of the Lays Messi Message campaign, users can create personalized messages from Messi to themselves, in English, Spanish, Portuguese, and Turkish. And it's all possible thanks to GenAI.

However, there's a dark side to this ability to deepfake our favorite celebrities. Just as I was writing this chapter, Tom Hanks posted on social media to warn fans about a video of him appearing to promote a dental plan.[16] The video was fake and Hanks had nothing to do with it, which is pretty scary.

AI Influencers and Models

In Chapter 6, I mentioned Noonoouri, the AI-generated influencer who signed a record deal with Warner. Let's explore virtual influencers and models in a little more detail, and see how they are becoming more important for brands.

A virtual influencer is a digital avatar that offers total customization and 24/7 availability to fans, typically via social media. They can take the shape of a realistic-looking human, a cartoon human, or a non-human creation. This isn't a new phenomenon, by the way – the first virtual popstar was a Japanese character called "Kyoko Date," created in the 1990s. What's new here is the intersection of social media (which allows these "personalities" to reach a vast global audience), GenAI (which brings unlimited creative potential), and the concept of the metaverse (where the real and digital worlds increasingly merge together).

Some virtual influencers, such as Lil Miquela and Lu do Magalu, have millions of followers. Yet, for brands looking to partner with an influencer, virtual influencers often prove distinctly more affordable than human influencers. But are brands really using virtual creations? It appears so. Fashion brand Prada has its own virtual "muse" called "Candy," unveiled in 2021 to relaunch the Prada Candy fragrance.[17] Virtual influencer Lil Miquela has collaborated with several brands, including Calvin Klein, and is reportedly worth as much as US$125 million.[18] And we're not just talking about virtual social media stars, but also virtual fashion and beauty models. Shudu Gram was labeled the "world's first avatar supermodel," and has collaborated with brands such as Fenty.[19] Levi's has also announced that it will be experimenting with AI-generated models to enhance diversity, collaborating with digital fashion studio Lalaland.ai to create hyper-realistic models.[20]

When you team up with a virtual influencer or model, you can create endless campaigns and images via GenAI, without needing to hire a studio, photographer, etc. These AI creations don't age (unless you want them to). They can represent a multitude of skin tones and body types. They can be restyled instantly in line with new trends, without the need for expensive reshoots. And they'll never get bogged down in a drugs or sex scandal. As such, virtual influencers and models have the potential to transform what it means to create, market, and consume content online.

However, there are issues. Transparency is one – meaning, as these influencers become more lifelike, how should their creators make it clear that these are not real beings? There's also a danger that virtual influencers and models may perpetuate unrealistic beauty and body type standards (although, the same can be said of the majority of ad campaigns). Then there are issues of who exactly is behind these digital creations. In the case of Shudu, a young black woman, her creator is a white male – prompting some critics to describe his creation as appropriation, expropriation, or at best jumping on the trend for darker-skinned models.[21] And finally, there's the argument that these virtual influencers and models lack the human connection that you get with a real, living, breathing, imperfect human being. Can they really offer the kind of connection with audiences that brands crave? Time will tell.

But whether you're intrigued or appalled by the idea of virtual influencers and models, there's no doubt that brands are interested in experimenting with this new approach.

Key Takeaways

In this chapter, we've learned:

- GenAI can be used to help brands generate text, visuals, video, and music for high-quality advertising and marketing campaigns – far cheaper and quicker than through traditional methods. As such, GenAI will allow businesses of all sizes to create beautiful images, engaging copy, and more.

- GenAI can help businesses come up with ideas, and automate aspects of the creative process – for example, by creating images through natural text prompts. Several high-profile brands have already embraced GenAI for ads.

- New tools are emerging that enable brands to leverage GenAI possibilities, including on platforms like Facebook and LinkedIn.

- The ability to personalize ads and marketing materials on a mass scale is a major advantage of GenAI – from text and images that are tailored to audience preferences, to creating interactive deepfake video experiences featuring celebrities.

- Brands are also choosing to work with virtual AI influencers and models – creating images, campaigns, and videos without the need to hire human models and influencers (and photographers, studios, etc.).

Marketing and advertising are all about engaging customers with thoughtful, inspiring, and compelling content. But how else are brands using GenAI to engage with customers and provide a better service? Turn the page to find out...

Notes

1. AI-powered marketing and sales reach new heights with generative AI; *McKinsey & Company*; https://www.mckinsey.com/capabilities/growth-marketing-and-sales/our-insights/ai-powered-marketing-and-sales-reach-new-heights-with-generative-ai

2. Unleashing Creativity with AI: Adobe's Trailblazing Generative Tools at EMEA Summit 2023; *Bernard Marr*; https://bernardmarr.com/unleashing-creativity-with-ai-adobes-trailblazing-generative-tools-at-emea-summit-2023/

3. Big companies use AI-generated ads because they're cheap; *The Verge*; https://www.theverge.com/2023/8/18/23837273/generative-ai-advertising-oreos-cadbury-watermarking

4. Fashion brands embrace Midjourney for captivating imagery; *Design & Build Co*; https://designandbuild.co/insights/fashion-brands-embrace-midjourney-for-captivating-imagery

5. The Amazing Ways Coca-Cola Uses Generative AI in Art and Advertising; *Forbes*; https://www.forbes.com/sites/bernardmarr/2023/09/08/the-amazing-ways-coca-cola-uses-generative-ai-in-art-and-advertising/

6. Top AI-Generated Advertising Campaigns from Famous Brands; *Digital Agency Network*; https://digitalagencynetwork.com/top-ai-generated-advertising-campaigns-from-famous-brands/

7. 5 Amazing Ways How Meta (Facebook) Is Using Generative AI; *Bernard Marr*; https://bernardmarr.com/5-amazing-ways-how-meta-facebook-is-using-generative-ai/

8. Salesforce Announces Einstein GPT, the World's First Generative AI for CRM; *Salesforce*; https://www.salesforce.com/uk/news/press-releases/2023/03/07/einstein-generative-ai/

9. Aprimo launches first ChatGPT within Azure OpenAI DAM integration, giving marketers enhanced, scalable automation; *Microsoft*; https://customers.microsoft.com/en-us/story/1647646542947823380-aprimo-professional-services-azure-openai-service

10. Typeface uses Azure OpenAI Service to create engaging, on-brand marketing messages in seconds; *Microsoft*; https://customers.microsoft.com/en-us/story/1637196302736110361-typeface-professional-services-azure-openai-service

11. LinkedIn Introduces Generative AI-Powered Tool for B2B Marketers; *Adweek*; https://www.adweek.com/brand-marketing/linkedin-generative-ai-powered-tool-b2b-marketers/

12. Fox Stations to Offer AI Generated Commercials Through New Partnership; *Adweek*; https://www.adweek.com/tvspy/fox-stations-to-offer-ai-generated-commercials-through-new-partnership/250658/

13. How Netflix Uses AI, Data Science And Machine Learning; *Medium*; https://becominghuman.ai/how-netflix-uses-ai-and-machine-learning-a087614630fe

14. Selfie generator; *Barbie Selfie AI*; https://www.barbieselfie.ai/uk/

15. Why some celebrities are embracing Artificial Intelligence deepfakes; *BBC News*; https://www.bbc.com/news/business-65995089

16. Tom Hanks Warns of Deepfake Hanks Dental Ad; *Voicebot*; https://voicebot.ai/2023/10/02/tom-hanks-warns-of-deepfake-hanks-dental-ad/

17. Prada Creates Virtual Muse Named Candy; *Virtual Humans*; https://www.virtualhumans.org/article/prada-creates-first-virtual-muse-candy

18. Meet Miquela: The AI (Artificial Influencer) Who's Now Worth $125 Million; *Medium*; https://medium.com/illumination/meet-miquela-the-a-i-artificial-influencer-whos-now-worth-125-million-879e4da7baf0

19. Shudu: Fashion's First Avatar Supermodel?; *WWD*; https://wwd.com/eye/people/shudu-digital-fashion-model-avatar-1202683320/

20. Pixel Perfect: The Rise of AI Fashion Models; *Forbes*; https://www.forbes.com/sites/bernardmarr/2023/06/07/pixel-perfect-the-rise-of-ai-fashion-models/

21. Shudu Gram is a white man's digital perception of real-life black womanhood; *The New Yorker*; https://www.newyorker.com/culture/culture-desk/shudu-gram-is-a-white-mans-digital-projection-of-real-life-black-womanhood

8

REINVENTING CUSTOMER ENGAGEMENT THROUGH INTELLIGENT SYSTEMS

As we've already seen in this book, the customer service function stands to be revolutionized by GenAI, particularly by text-and-speech models. But customer service isn't the only aspect of customer engagement that can benefit from GenAI; through new personalized offerings, preventive interventions, and intelligent products and services, GenAI will transform how brands interact with their customers. In short, GenAI offers unparalleled opportunities for personalization, responsiveness, and increased customer satisfaction.

Let's explore how GenAI can bring brands and their customers closer together.

Generative AI in Customer Service

In Chapter 3, we saw how UK energy supplier, Octopus Energy, has deployed ChatGPT in customer service – to the extent that the bot now handles 44% of customer enquiries, does the work of 250 people, and receives higher customer satisfaction ratings than human customer service agents.[1] It's a prime example of how contact centers will increasingly incorporate GenAI chat and voice tools to deal with straightforward, easily repeatable tasks.

The capabilities of GenAI

You may think customers don't want to talk to bots, but the Octopus Energy example shows that GenAI tools can deliver impressive results and bring a new level of responsiveness to customer service bots. Traditional AI offerings (like some of the not-very-intelligent chatbots you might have interacted with) rely on rules-based systems to provide predetermined responses to questions. And when they come up against a query that they don't recognize, or doesn't follow defined rules, they're stuck. And even when they do give a helpful answer, the language is typically pretty stiff. GenAI, on the other hand, can understand even complex questions and answer in a more natural, conversational way. And, of course, these tools give customers 24/7 access to support, via multiple channels (such as phone, online chat, and social media messaging).

But answering customer queries isn't the only way GenAI can add value in customer service. Some of the other tasks that GenAI can do or assist with include:

- Giving customers **personalized recommendations**, based on the customer's data and previous interactions, which further helps to enhance the customer experience. (More on personalization coming up later.)

- Providing **conversational search functions** for, say, FAQs online. GenAI can take natural language prompts like "where's my package" or "I hate the sweater I ordered" and either direct the customer to the correct FAQ response, or deliver a tailored response. And don't forget this can be done in multiple languages.

- **Optimizing data** to support customer service operations. GenAI can handle vast amounts of data and turn that information into actionable insights – insights such as "Which are our most common complaints?" It can also track and categorize customer trends with ease.

- **Supporting human customer service agents**. GenAI can help human agents be more productive. For example, it can automatically generate responses to common queries, provide summaries of previous complaints and resolutions that agents can use in conversations, and generate product recommendations.

In this way, GenAI can help improve the employee experience as well as the customer experience. It can support the work that human agents do, and free them up to focus on more complex customer interactions where they can add the most value. It's no wonder customer service has become CEOs' number-one GenAI priority, according to the IBM Institute for Business Value, with 85% of execs saying GenAI will be interacting directly with their customers within the next two years.[2]

But how to go about implementing GenAI without alienating employees? In their book *Human + Machine: Reimagining Work in the Age of AI*, Paul R. Daugherty and H. James Wilson argue that GenAI will *enrich*, not replace, customer service jobs. They recommend organizations break jobs down into underlying tasks, then explore how GenAI will affect each task. For customer service, they found that most customer service work could be broken down into 13 tasks. Four of those tasks remained unchanged by GenAI, four could be fully automated by GenAI, and five could be augmented by GenAI. Even better, five new high-value tasks emerged thanks to GenAI taking on the easily automated tasks.

As with all aspects of GenAI, transparency is a must – by which I mean making it clear when customers are talking to a bot. Read more about successful implementation in Chapter 18.

Examples from customer service

Now let's explore some real-world examples of GenAI tools and companies who are using GenAI to enhance customer service. One example of GenAI designed for customer service is Zendesk's Expanding Agent Replies solution, which is like predictive text on steroids. Agents can type the bare bones of a response to a customer, and then the tool fleshes it out for them. Or there's Google Cloud's Generative FAQ for CCAI Insights, which lets contact centers upload (redacted) transcripts of calls and unearth customer FAQs. Similarly, Twilio's CustomerAI solution can generate articles to plug gaps in knowledge – articles which can be published for customers or digested by agents to better improve outcomes. Or there's Sprinklr's call note automation tool, which automatically notes crucial info as the customer talks – allowing the agent to focus on active listening.

JetBlue has partnered with technology company ASAPP to implement GenAI, with impressive results. JetBlue's contact center has saved an average of 280 seconds per chat, freeing up 73 000 hours of agent time in just one quarter.[3] That's a whole lot of hours to devote to customers with more in-depth problems. Another airline, Air India, has said it's deploying OpenAI's ChatGPT as part of a huge system modernization. Chatbots have reportedly been used to modernize the airline's website and mobile apps, digital marketing, customer notifications system, customer service portal (including real-time support request tracking), and contact center operations.[4]

Meanwhile, British telecom company BT Group used GenAI capabilities in Microsoft Power Platform to create a digital assistant called "Aimee" to help customers with a variety of queries. BT says the in-app messaging assistant has answered approximately 60% of customer queries with great customer satisfaction (Net Prompter Score of 60).[5]

In India, digital payments company PhonePe uses the Freddy AI bot developed by Freshworks to automate answers for simple queries such as "What's my balance?" – offering a personalized self-service experience.[6] Which brings us to...

A New Level of Personalization

Clearly, GenAI can be used to deliver a more personalized customer service experience, but it can also be used to personalize all sorts of customer interactions. In the future, most systems and services across most industries will incorporate some element of AI in order to better understand customer preferences and customize the service accordingly. (This will happen in everyday home items, too, but we'll talk more about that later.)

Personalization everywhere

Take the automotive industry as an example. GenAI-powered in-car systems could generate customized driving experiences. So, based on my history and preferences, my car could potentially adjust the cabin ambience, suggest new music playlists or podcasts, and automatically select driving modes according to the terrain and weather conditions – all of which will enhance the driving experience.

In the hospitality sector, AI-enhanced hotel rooms could offer guests an environment that anticipates their preferences for lighting and temperature. GenAI could also be used to generate recommendations for local activities and dining options, based on the guest's past choices. Similarly, travel agencies could use GenAI tools like ChatGPT to curate bespoke travel itineraries for individuals based on their travel history, hobbies, and even social media activity. The itinerary for a food enthusiast, for example, would be entirely different to that of a nature lover – all automatically generated based on customer data.

In entertainment, streaming platforms could harness GenAI to curate personalized movie or TV recommendations, not just based on what they've watched in the past but by analyzing plot preferences, character archetypes, or cinematographic styles favored by the viewer.

And in the realm of fitness, wearable technology (such as wristbands) integrated with GenAI can craft personalized workout routines or training regimens. For example, if a user has been running frequently, the AI might suggest cross-training exercises to balance muscle development, or even curate a list of local races or events they might be interested in.

These are just a few of the ways industries may offer increasingly personalized solutions, powered by GenAI.

PGA and personalized fan engagement

We've already seen several real-world examples of personalization throughout this book (such as Stitch Fix's ability to provide personalized outfit recommendations, Chapter 3) – and we'll see many more in the remaining chapters. Personalization is certainly a recurring theme within GenAI. But here's another example to highlight the possibilities.

The PGA Tour has partnered with Amazon Web Services (AWS) to provide a better, more personalized viewing experience for golf fans, powered by GenAI. The idea is that AWS machine-learning technology will be used to leverage hundreds of hours of raw tournament footage and turn the content into new digital offerings that give fans their own, unique viewing experience. Among the plans is a streaming platform called "Every Shot Live" that will give fans live access to every shot played by every player – comprising more than 32 000 shots by 144 golfers.[7] Essentially, fans will be able to follow any player they like in real time, and experience cool features like changing the camera angle or viewing game stats on-demand.

Delivering More Proactive Interventions through Predictive AI

Personalization also enables more proactive interventions – meaning, by understanding how a customer uses your product or service, you can pre-empt what they want next and deliver it seamlessly. This is already happening across many industries – predictive maintenance for machinery being a prime example – but the key takeaway here is that GenAI will give predictive capabilities an extra boost, thereby enabling more proactive interventions that delight and impress customers.

What might this look like in future?

Utilities companies could certainly deploy AI to proactively address user concerns. Say, for example, a consumer's usage pattern suddenly deviates from the norm, a GenAI system could proactively reach out to check in with the customer or provide troubleshooting solutions – all before the consumer even notices there's an issue.

It's easy to imagine similar options across all sorts of industries. In the telecommunications sector, for example, AI could analyze call quality, data consumption, and service interruptions to pre-emptively offer better solutions, or even create personalized service packages that precisely match a user's consumption patterns.

In transportation, commuters could definitely benefit from a more proactive service. If someone frequently travels a certain route, which is expected to have delays or construction, the public transport network could use GenAI to proactively suggest alternative routes or methods of transportation.

Predictive fintech solutions

The financial and banking sector is another area that could benefit enormously from GenAI-led predictive solutions. Indeed, this is already happening to a large extent, with AI-driven automatic fraud detection and risk assessment. But imagine how GenAI could take this to a whole new level with, say, personalized financial advice and planning. One study found that using GenAI to deliver personalized financial advice could save customers on average US$1200 a year.[8] JPMorgan Chase is one organization using GenAI to create personalized financial plans, tailored to customers' individual needs and financial goals.[9] Elsewhere, Visa has launched a US$100 million initiative to invest in GenAI solutions that enhance commerce and payments – likely focusing on fraud prevention, personalized marketing campaigns for business, and potentially even developing new payment methods.[10]

Incorporating Generative AI into Products

I've already said that I anticipate cars becoming more intelligent and offering a more personalized experience powered by AI. But it won't stop there. . .

How GenAI could be built into everyday devices

We'll likely see ovens, washing machines, and other everyday home items with built-in GenAI. Indeed, AI has been creeping into our homes for years (think smart lightbulbs and Alexa) – but thanks to GenAI, these interactions will become even more human and more personal. We could, for example, engage in natural language conversations with home appliances. Yes, you could potentially ask your washing machine questions, such as whether it's safe to wash a beloved item of clothing on a certain setting. Or you could say to your fridge, "Hey, when am I going to run out of milk?" and it'll tell you.

Integrating GenAI into everyday products could lead to a new era of smart appliances that are not only more adaptive to our needs, but also more interactive and engaging. Engaging ovens? Why not!

Here's what this might look like in the future:

More personalized user experiences

- Thanks to ChatGPT's new capabilities to "see," you can already take a picture of the contents of your fridge and ask it what to cook for dinner. But in the future, you could ask your fridge directly, as appliances begin to incorporate GenAI assistants.

- Appliances will increasingly be able to adapt to our needs. A washing machine, for example, could adapt to the types of clothes you generally wash (e.g., heavy-duty work clothes that get really dirty) and create customized cycles for optimal fabric care and cleanliness.

- Similarly, your oven could learn your cooking style and preferences over time, suggesting optimal temperature settings and cooking times for different dishes, and even new recipe suggestions.

Interactive problem-solving

- If you have a problem with an appliance, the GenAI could generate step-by-step troubleshooting guides, tailored to the exact model and its current conditions. No need to call the contact center or consult a lengthy user manual.

Predictive maintenance

- Instead of waiting for a part to fail, GenAI could predict when a component is likely to need replacement or maintenance, and send you a pre-emptive alert. It could potentially even order the necessary parts or schedule a service visit ahead of time.

Enhanced customer service

- If you do need to contact customer service, the AI could provide the agent with a detailed history of the appliance's usage patterns, any anomalies, and prior troubleshooting steps – all of which is helpful context that enables more efficient problem-solving.

- GenAI could also assist in creating dynamic manuals or interactive tutorials, providing users with information when they need it.

Current examples of GenAI in devices

If you think my predictions are a bit wacky, perhaps these real-world examples will convince you...

Samsung is reportedly set to incorporate "neural processing units" into all new home appliances, including smart TVs and refrigerators, from 2024 – enabling smart, 24/7 GenAI tools that can assist users.[11] It's not yet clear exactly what features will be offered, but a smart oven that can warn you when something's burning is one possible application.

German appliance manufacturer Miele is also incorporating GenAI into its Smart Food ID cooking assistance system – initially for large ovens with integrated cameras.[12] The camera takes pictures of the ingredients, and the AI interprets the picture and suggests the cooking mode automatically. The user just has to confirm, and the oven takes care of the rest. AI will also be used by Miele for appliance diagnostics, to help customers resolve issues when malfunctions occur. One example is a washing machine creating too much foam because the user has added too much detergent – in which case, the AI would recommend the correct amount of detergent for the load amount.

LG is also incorporating AI to help customers use appliances in a better way. LG's AI can notify users when an issue occurs, such as a decline in refrigerator cooling, before it gets any worse. Issues like this aren't immediately obvious to the user but could shorten the appliance's lifespan. The AI can provide quick-fix solutions, or schedule an appointment with a service agent. It can also provide routine maintenance suggestions, like running a clean cycle in a washing machine every 30 washes.[13] (Thus linking back to the ability for GenAI to predict future issues and provide proactive solutions.)

We've already briefly mentioned cars, but let's explore a couple of examples. Continental is partnering with Google Cloud to bring GenAI natural language technology to cars – basically, enabling drivers to have conversations with their cars on, say, which route is best or whether the tires need pumping up.[14] Meanwhile, Mercedes-Benz has partnered with Microsoft to bring in-car ChatGPT to more than 900 000 vehicles via the "Hey Mercedes" voice assistant.[15] ChatGPT enhances the existing capabilities of Hey Mercedes, offering more expansive topics and improved natural language understanding.

There's no doubt that we've been moving toward "AI everything" for quite some time, but GenAI will accelerate these developments and bring new, more intuitive AI capabilities to everyday devices. What products will you be "chatting" to in future? Watch this space. . .

Key Takeaways

In this chapter, we've learned:

- In customer service, GenAI can obviously deal with customers directly, but also carry out or assist with other tasks, such as identifying customer service trends, generating responses for human agents, and helping agents deliver more personalized responses. Rather than completely replacing human customer service agents, GenAI will take on the lower-value tasks, freeing up agents to focus on higher-value work.

- Personalization is a huge theme in GenAI, and we can expect all organizations to unearth new opportunities to provide personalized solutions for customers. GenAI can assist with this by understanding the customer's history and preferences, and generating thoughtful suggestions and recommendations.

- Personalization also enables a new level of proactive responsiveness for organizations. From identifying potential issues and malfunctions before they occur, to delivering proactive advice that helps customers achieve their goals, GenAI can help businesses better anticipate their customers' needs.

- And finally, we can expect to see GenAI built into all sorts of everyday devices and appliances, such as cars, ovens, and washing machines. AI has been creeping into devices for years, but GenAI will accelerate this trend and allow for more intuitive, natural language conversations with everyday items.

Customer engagement is a topic that applies to any organization across any industry. Next, we'll drill into a specific sector to explore GenAI opportunities. Turn the page to read about GenAI uses in retail.

Notes

1. AI doing the work of over 200 people at Octopus, chief executive says; *CityAM*; https://www.cityam.com/ai-doing-the-work-of-over-200-people-at-octopus-chief-executive-says/
2. From cost center to value creator; *IBM Institute for Business Value*; https://www.ibm.com/thought-leadership/institute-business-value/en-us/report/ceo-generative-ai/customer-service
3. How Generative AI Is Already Transforming Customer Service; *BCG*; https://www.bcg.com/publications/2023/how-generative-ai-transforms-customer-service
4. ChatGPT will be used by Air India as part of system modernization; *Analytics Insight*; https://www.analyticsinsight.net/chatgpt-will-be-used-by-air-india-as-part-of-system-modernization/
5. Strategic Progress report; *BT*; https://www.bt.com/about/annual-reports/2022summary/assets/documents/Strategic_progress_2.pdf
6. Say hello to Freddy AI; *Freshworks*; https://www.freshworks.com/freddy-ai/
7. PGA Tour teams up with AWS to improve fan engagement during tournaments; *Computer Weekly*; https://www.computerweekly.com/news/252497159/PGA-Tour-teams-up-with-AWS-to-improve-fan-engagement-during-tournaments
8. Exploring the Transformative Potential of Generative AI in Fintech and Banking; *Medium*; https://medium.com/@seyhunak/exploring-the-transformative-potential-of-generative-ai-in-fintech-and-banking-c01977c33a64
9. Generative AI for Banking and Financial Services; *Medium*; https://medium.com/@jeevan_6696/generative-ai-for-banking-financial-services-the-next-frontier-c98d5c42ba30#
10. Visa Invests $100M in Generative AI to Transform the Way We Shop and Pay; *Medium*; https://medium.com/@jhakon/visa-invests-100m-in-generative-ai-to-transform-the-way-we-shop-and-pay-4f18dfd9e268
11. Samsung may be adding AI to its home appliances; *TechRadar*; https://www.techradar.com/computing/artificial-intelligence/samsung-may-be-adding-ai-to-its-home-appliances-im-so-ready-to-chat-to-my-oven
12. Artificial intelligence for best taste as well as for self-help error prevention in case of appliance malfunctions; *Miele*; https://www.miele.de/en/m/artificial-intelligence-for-best-taste-as-well-as-for-self-help-and-error-prevention-in-case-of-appliance-malfunctions-6669.htm

13. How LG Is Using AI to Change How Consumers User Appliances, Improve Sustainability and Do Our Laundry Better; *Forbes*; https://www.forbes.com/sites/amandalauren/2020/01/20/how-lgs-artificial-intelligence-is-changing-how-consumers-use-appliances-improving-sustainability-and-doing-our-laundry-better/#

14. Google Cloud and Continental to equip generative AI in cars; *Techwire Asia*; https://techwireasia.com/2023/09/how-is-generative-ai-in-cars-making-talking-cars-real/

15. Mercedes-Benz takes in-car voice control to a new level with ChatGPT; *Mercedes-Benz Group*; https://group.mercedes-benz.com/innovation/digitalisation/connectivity/car-voice-control-with-chatgpt.html

9

RETAIL REIMAGINED: THE RISE OF VIRTUAL TRY-ONS, AI SHOPPING ASSISTANTS, AND MORE

Incredible GenAI tools like ChatGPT will clearly have an effect on every industry, and the retail sector is no different. In this chapter, we'll explore some of the main ways GenAI can be used in retail – and how it might transform the shopping experience for both customers and retailers. Fashion will crop up a lot in this chapter but make no mistake, GenAI will impact all kinds of retailers. We're talking immersive virtual stores and websites optimized for GenAI technologies. We're talking interactive displays in physical stores. We're talking hyper-personalization on a mass scale. And we're talking optimized behind-the-scenes processes. Are you ready to reimagine retail? Let's get into it.

Improved Digital Shopping Experiences

From optimized websites to virtual stores in the metaverse, GenAI could shape the way we shop online.

Virtual storefronts: immersive shopping in the metaverse

With augmented and virtual reality becoming more mainstream, GenAI can help to create immersive virtual shopping experiences. This ties in with the concept of the metaverse – immersive virtual worlds where we can shop, game, work, and more. Forward-thinking retailers are already building a presence in the metaverse, creating immersive, interactive and personalized virtual stores, and brand experiences. Nike is a real leader in the metaverse space with its part-game, part-showroom Nikeland experience on the Roblox metaverse platform. Nikeland features buildings, arenas, and games, as well as a virtual showroom complete with digital products.[1] Another brand to pitch up in Roblox is Forever 21, which has created a virtual brand experience that allows users to "run" their own virtual Forever 21 store.[2]

GenAI can help to make these virtual experiences more responsive. For example, as a user navigates these digital realms, AI can generate personalized store layouts, product placements, and even virtual sales assistants tailored to the user's shopping history and preferences.

Delivering a better website (and app) experience

Outside of the metaverse, GenAI will also enable better, more intuitive experiences on regular websites and apps. Take Expedia Group as an example. Users can now plan their travel arrangements by having an open-ended "chat" with the app, from discussing accommodation to pinpointing the best sights to see. It's as close as you can get to the old-school travel agent experience in app form. Expedia says the feature will also let users know when there are exclusive rewards and discounts, which they can take advantage of directly via the ChatGPT interface.[3]

As this chapter shows, we'll see more and more ecommerce sites incorporate ChatGPT-style features into their websites and apps. The technology can be used to create personalized shopping assistants (more on that coming up), deliver enhanced customer support, and even be used as a market research tool, gathering data from customer interactions.

Another way GenAI can prove useful is in summarizing customer reviews. Ever wanted to check out a product only to find hundreds of reviews offering a multitude of (sometimes conflicting) opinions? GenAI can provide helpful summaries that save you wading through all that mess. Online electronics retailer Newegg has done just that, adding a ChatGPT-powered feature that summarizes reviews into either brief snippets or a longer paragraph that highlights what customers frequently say about a product.[4] Amazon is also beginning to use GenAI to summarize customer reviews into one digestible paragraph.[5]

The key takeaway here is that GenAI can enhance the shopping journey by adding new, more intuitive, and more personalized features that increase customer satisfaction and help find exactly the right product for them.

The rise of virtual try-on features

The online shopping experience can often fall short because you can't try something before you buy it. Determining what an item of clothing will look like on *you* (instead of the model), or visualizing what an item of furniture would look like in *your* house can be a total guessing game. And those issues apply just as much to glasses, beauty items, and other products.

Until now, virtual try-on features have been fairly rudimentary – for example, picking from a small list of body shapes to see what a particular dress might look like on your body. But thanks to augmented reality (AR) technology, virtual try-ons are getting better. Typically, this is done using a phone camera, but it can also be done using "smart mirrors" (more on these coming up). The AR technology then layers digital elements (say, glasses, or an item of clothing) over the real-world image in the camera.

GenAI will bring a new level of realism to such features. Imagine creating a realistic avatar of yourself, based on a photo and your exact measurements, and then being able to generate an image of yourself wearing a particular outfit (even combining different items to see how well they go together), *and* seeing yourself wearing those items in a range of different settings, all to help you fully visualize whether the product's right for you. GenAI makes all that possible. Having an item arrive only to discover it's not right could be a thing of the past. For retailers, this means lower return rates and higher customer satisfaction.

Some of the brands experimenting with virtual try-on features include Sephora (digitally superimposing makeup shades onto the user's face), Ray-Ban (for eyewear), and Baume & Mercier (for luxury watches).[6]

In fashion, start-up Body Labs (owned by Amazon) has created mixed reality technology that enables shoppers to "see" themselves wearing virtual clothing in a virtual setting, such as a formal event or the beach.[7] Google has also introduced virtual try-on technology that uses GenAI to show clothes "on a wide selection of real models."[8] Google says the GenAI model can take just one picture of an item of clothing and accurately show how it would cling, drape, etc. on a diverse range of real models from sizes XXS to 4XL, and representing different skin tones and ethnicities. The feature is available for brands such as Anthropologie and H&M.

Even furniture and home décor can benefit from virtual try-before-you-buy features powered by GenAI. Wayfair, for example, has introduced a new GenAI feature called "Decorify," which creates photorealistic images that help customers see their homes in new styles (choosing from themes such Bohemian and Farmhouse).[9] Users can then shop the Wayfair catalog directly from their reimagined room.

By the way, virtual try-on features can also apply to the physical, in-store shopping experience. Which brings us to. . .

Augmenting Physical Stores

The in-store experience could also be enhanced with GenAI technology, particularly when it comes to creating interactive store displays and smart mirrors for virtual try-on experiences in stores.

GenAI can be used to create responsive store displays that change based on real-time data. Say, for example, a cold front is moving into an area, a clothing store's digital window display might adapt to showcase winter gear and generate a live snowfall backdrop to attract people in. Combined with personalized customer data, in the future, store displays could even adapt to each customer, showing them products they might be interested in locating in the store.

As for smart mirrors (or smart fitting rooms), GenAI combined with AR technology could ensure that a digital representation of clothing on a customer is accurate, giving a photorealistic visualization of the fit and look. Why would we want to virtually try on clothes when we've traveled to a physical store? Well, the store in question may not have all styles, colors, and sizes available in the store to try on. Before they order your particular item, wouldn't it be nice to see how it might realistically look on you?

I mentioned earlier that beauty brand Sephora is using virtual try-on technology; the company has also installed kiosks in stores that offer the same try-on experience for customers visiting physical stores. Handbag and accessory brand Coach has also experimented with smart mirror technology. To celebrate the launch of its Tabby Bag campaign, the brand installed a smart mirror in its Soho New York store.[10] Customers using the mirror could see themselves with different digital variations of the bag (and other digital effects, like butterfly wings). They could also download their image to share online. So, as an added bonus, Coach benefited from free social marketing thanks to users sharing their images on social media.

Even when trying on a physical, real item of clothing, AI-powered mirrors could still add value for customers. They could, for example, provide real-time feedback, suggesting sizes, colors, or alternative styles based on the clothes being tried on. The mirror might even generate virtual previews of how different accessories or shoes would complement the chosen outfit.

Bottom line, while GenAI is set to enhance the digital shopping experience, it could also give us a more engaging real-world shopping experience.

Personalizing the Customer Journey

Once again, personalization crops up as a major use case for GenAI. This applies to all aspects of retail, but let's explore a few specific ways retailers can provide a more personalized shopping experience.

Personalized, unique product designs

No longer confined to a one-size-fits-all approach, retailers can employ GenAI to craft custom product designs based on individual consumer behaviors and preferences. For instance, a fashion brand could generate unique clothing patterns or accessories that align closely with evolving trends and individual tastes. Fashion tech specialists Space Runners have created a GenAI tool that allows people to design their own unique clothing, just using simple text prompts.[11] Called "Ablo," the AI design tool allows individuals to effectively become their own fashion brand – and for brands, Ablo allows amazing co-creation opportunities with their customers.

Combine this trend with the growing trend of 3D printing, and we have more opportunities than ever for individuals and brands to create one-offs that can be printed without having to worry about economies of scale.

Personalized shopping journeys

Online platforms can use GenAI to redesign the shopping journey dynamically, amending what the user sees on-the-fly. For example, as a user browses, the AI might rearrange product placements based on the customer's interests, showcase user-generated content to encourage longer engagement, or even change the website's color scheme to resonate with the shopper's preference.

According to research by McKinsey, 7 out of 10 consumers expect brands to personalize the content they see, such as ads and recommendations, and 76% get frustrated when they don't feel their experience is personalized.[12]

Amazon and Netflix's recommendation engines are well-known examples of personalizing the customer journey. But with GenAI, we can expect this personalization to become more intelligent. Instead of simply grouping customers into personas based on interests or past habits (e.g., "people who bought X"), AI-based personalization can deliver information and recommendations based on the individual, not a generic persona.

We're talking about true, one-on-one personalization, in other words. Remember Newegg from earlier in the chapter? As a way to personalize the customer journey, the online retailer has integrated ChatGPT into its "PC Builder" online shopping tool, which allows customers to build a customer desktop PC system. The new, improved functionality allows customers to type their desired attributes, and then ChatGPT will make recommendations.[13] We'll see more and more retailers introduce features like this, where the shopper can describe what they're looking for, and a chat AI will be able to make relevant recommendations. And that brings us to the notion of personal shopping assistants. . .

Virtual AI shopping assistants

Product recommendations with personality – that's what GenAI brings to the customer journey. Expedia's use of ChatGPT to help travelers plan the perfect journey is a great example of using GenAI to create what's effectively a virtual, personal shopping assistant. We're talking, then, about conversational bots that help customers through the shopping journey, giving thoughtful responses to their queries and recommending products.

French retailer Carrefour has done this, integrating an advice robot called "Hopla" (based on ChatGPT) into its website.[14] Customers can ask the bot natural language questions that help them complete their shopping – for example, which products are best for their budget, food constraints, or menu ideas, and how to reuse ingredients to save wasting food.

eBay has introduced ShopBot, an AI personal shopping assistant available (at the time of writing) in Facebook Messenger. ShopBot is designed to help customers navigate through eBay's one billion product listings and find the best deals for them – by typing or saying what they're looking for, or snapping a picture. The bot then asks questions to better understand the customer's needs, and it makes personalized recommendations. eBay says its goal is to "make shopping with eBay as easy as talking to a friend, whether you are looking for something specific or just browsing for inspiration."[15]

Meanwhile, Walmart's forthcoming GenAI shopping assistant (forthcoming at the time of writing) will be able to help shoppers plan the perfect event. Say you want to throw a unicorn-themed party for a six-year-old, the tool will recommend relevant products, such as unicorn-themed balloons and banners – without you having to do multiple individual searches.[16]

Second-hand marketplace Mercari has unveiled its own AI shopping assistant called "Merchat AI," powered by (you guessed it) ChatGPT.[17] Instead of having to search and scroll through multiple options, shoppers can simply tell the AI what they're looking for and it'll point them in the right direction.

I believe AI shopping assistants is a major use case for GenAI in retail, and I expect traditional "search and scroll" experiences will be increasingly replaced with conversational search and recommendations. As someone who's frequently frustrated by the online shopping experience, that sounds pretty good to me.

What's more, AI shopping assistants won't just help with shopping – they'll be able to provide more contexts and, in turn, deliver greater value for customers. Take, for example, the "Ask Instacart" AI search tool unveiled by Instacart. It doesn't just help customers with shopping questions and personalized recommendations – it can also provide extra info about food preparation, dietary considerations, and more.[18] So you can ask it which side dishes go well with your protein of choice, or what kinds of sauce would work well, or ideas for "free-from" foods.

Tailored promotions, discounts, and loyalty programs

We talked about this already in terms of hyper-personalized advertising and marketing (see Chapter 7), but let me briefly reiterate that GenAI can create custom promotions and offers for each shopper – by analyzing their individual buying habits and preferences. For example, if a customer often purchases sustainable products, the AI might generate special discounts or bundle offers related to eco-friendly items during their next visit. This can be done automatically, and at scale.

GenAI can also be used to develop highly personalized loyalty programs that evolve based on each member's interactions with the brand. So, instead of a generic point system, members might be offered personalized challenges, rewards tailored to their preferences, or unique experiences curated just for them.

Other Potential Uses in Retail

As well as augmenting the online and real-world shopping experience, and enabling a personalized customer journey, GenAI could support retailers in other innovative ways. It can be used to provide marketing and sales support through automated and personalized marketing messages (again, see Chapter 7). It can upsell customers by telling them about similar or complementary products. It can be used to manage inventory levels in a more intelligent way, by analyzing sales data and forecasting demand – thereby helping retailers ensure they stock the right products in the right quantities. Or it can help customers handle returns and exchanges, answering questions about the returns process and guiding customers through the process step-by-step.

Let's explore a couple of use cases in a little more detail.

Generating product descriptions

One area in which GenAI excels is in writing descriptions, including bespoke descriptions that tell a story about a product. For example, a coffee brand might create a dynamic story for each coffee blend, detailing its journey from a specific farm, its unique roasting process, and flavor notes. For companies that emphasize storytelling as part of their brand identity, GenAI can add huge value.

The same goes for generic product descriptions. A retailer or online seller might not want to craft a compelling story for each individual product, but simply want to streamline the process of creating informative, search-friendly descriptions.

eBay is helping sellers do just that with a new GenAI "magical listing" tool that writes product listings from photos.[19] So, a seller can simply take or upload a photo in the app and then let the AI complete the product details for them. Shopify has a similar tool that it calls Shopify Magic – which automates the content creation process for descriptions, email subject lines, and headers for an online store.[20] Likewise, Amazon has debuted a GenAI tool that helps sellers create product descriptions.[21]

Diesel has also turned to AI to enhance its product data, using automated product tagging to enhance product discovery online. By switching from manually tagging products according to various attributes and categories to automated tagging, the company was able to save 30 hours of time per week per person. [22]

Automating supplier negotiations

As well as creating a personal AI shopping assistant, we know that Walmart has been experimenting with GenAI across internal operations (see Chapter 3). One particularly interesting use case is in supplier negotiations. In an experiment, the retailer used a chatbot to close deals with 89 suppliers of items like shopping carts and other store equipment. Of those suppliers, the chatbot closed deals with 64%, gaining an average of 1.5% in cost savings, and an extra 35 days in extended payment terms. An impressive 83% of suppliers actually liked the chatbot negotiation.[23]

Deploying GenAI across the organization

Spanish fashion retailer, Mango, has introduced its own conversational GenAI platform called "Lisa," which is designed to help employees across the business make improvements – and this can span anything from enhancing the after-sales service to developing new clothing collections. The tool has been described as a "co-pilot for our employees."[24] Mango has also previously developed a GenAI image platform called "Inspire," aimed at helping the design team find inspiration and come up with new concepts for prints, fabrics, and garments. But we'll talk more about GenAI in the design process in Chapter 14.

Key Takeaways

Make no mistake, retail will be utterly transformed by GenAI tools. To recap some of the main use cases from retail:

- GenAI enables more immersive digital experiences – for example, through a dynamic, responsive customer journey in metaverse shops. But it will also enable a better shopping experience on regular websites and apps, with realistic virtual-on features and handy summaries of customer reviews.

- GenAI will augment the physical in-store experience, too, thanks to dynamic displays and smart mirrors.

- Once again, personalization is a huge theme. GenAI enables hyper-personalization for retailers in a number of ways, including one-off products, personalized shopping journeys, AI shopping assistants, and tailored promotions.

- Other uses in retail include automatically generating product descriptions, automating aspects of the supply chain, and even automating supplier negotiations.

Now let's go back to school and see how GenAI will transform how people learn, *what* people learn, and how educators teach.

Notes

1. What Will Fashion Retail Look Like in the Future?; *Forbes*; https://www.forbes.com/sites/bernardmarr/2023/07/13/what-will-fashion-retail-look-like-in-the-future/
2. What Will Fashion Retail Look Like in the Future?; *Forbes*; https://www.forbes.com/sites/bernardmarr/2023/07/13/what-will-fashion-retail-look-like-in-the-future/
3. The Amazing Ways Expedia Is Using ChatGPT to Simplify Travel Arrangements; *Bernard Marr*; https://bernardmarr.com/the-amazing-ways-expedia-is-using-chatgpt-to-simplify-travel-arrangements/
4. Newegg adds ChatGPT-powered feature to save you from review analysis paralysis; *ZDNet*; https://www.zdnet.com/article/neweggs-ai-review-summary-tool-could-make-shopping-for-electronics-a-little-easier/
5. Amazon now using generative AI to summarize customer reviews; *ZDNet*; https://www.zdnet.com/article/amazon-now-using-generative-ai-to-summarize-customer-reviews/
6. 7 Brands Using Virtual Try-on Tech to Boost Sales; *ThreeKit*; https://www.threekit.com/blog/7-brands-using-virtual-try-on-boost-sales
7. Virtual Try-on for Clothing: The Future of Fashion?; *3D Look*; https://3dlook.ai/content-hub/virtual-clothing-try-on/
8. Virtually try on clothes with a new AI shopping feature; *Google*; https://blog.google/products/shopping/ai-virtual-try-on-google-shopping/
9. Shop Virtually with Wayfair's Generative AI Decorify; *RetailWire*; https://retailwire.com/discussion/shop-virtually-with-wayfairs-generative-ai-decorify/

10. Why the New Generation of AR Smart Mirrors Are Catnip for Fashion and Beauty Retail; *Forbes*; https://www.forbes.com/sites/stephaniehirschmiller/2023/05/19/how-ar-mirrors-offer-visual-marketing-meets-user-generated-content-for-fashion-and-beauty-retail/

11. Collaborative Fashion Innovation: Unlocking Creativity with AI; *Medium*; https://medium.com/@spacerunners/collaborative-fashion-innovation-unlocking-creativity-with-ai-91b424d9e5ba

12. The value of getting personalization right – or wrong – is multiplying; *McKinsey*; https://www.mckinsey.com/capabilities/growth-marketing-and-sales/our-insights/the-value-of-getting-personalization-right-or-wrong-is-multiplying

13. Newegg Uses ChatGPT to Improve Online Shopping Experience; *Business Wire*; https://www.businesswire.com/news/home/20230327005151/en/Newegg-Uses-ChatGPT-to-Improve-Online-Shopping-Experience

14. Carrefour integrates OpenAI technologies and launches a generative AI-powered shopping experience; *Carrefour*; https://www.carrefour.com/en/news/2023/carrefour-integrates-openai-technologies-and-launches-generative-ai-powered-shopping

15. Say 'Hello' to eBay ShopBot Beta; *eBay*; https://www.ebayinc.com/stories/news/say-hello-to-ebay-shopbot-beta/

16. Walmart experiments with generative AI tools that can help you plan a party or decorate; *TechCrunch*; https://techcrunch.com/2023/10/04/walmart-experiments-with-new-generative-ai-tools-that-can-help-you-plan-a-party-or-decorate-a-space/

17. ChatGPT can help you shop now via Mercari's AI-powered assistant; *ZDNet*; https://www.zdnet.com/article/chatgpt-can-now-help-you-shop-via-mercaris-new-ai-powered-shopping-assistant/

18. Instacart launches new in-app AI search tool powered by ChatGPT; *TechCrunch*; https://techcrunch.com/2023/05/31/instacart-in-app-ai-search-tool-powered-by-chatgpt/

19. eBay's new AI tool generates product listings from photos; *Retail Dive*; https://www.retaildive.com/news/ebay-ai-magical-listing-product-descriptions-listings/693185/

20. Shopify Magic; *Shopify*; https://help.shopify.com/en/manual/shopify-admin/productivity-tools/shopify-magic

21. Amazon debuts generative AI tool that helps sellers write product descriptions; *TechCrunch*; https://techcrunch.com/2023/09/13/amazon-debuts-generative-ai-tools-that-helps-sellers-write-product-descriptions/

22. Product tagging for Diesel; *Vue AI*; https://vue.ai/resources/case-studies/product-tagging-for-diesel/

23. The Supply Side: Generative AI or ChatGPT next holy grail for retailers, suppliers; *Talk Business & Politics*; https://talkbusiness.net/2023/06/the-supply-side-generative-ai-or-chatgpt-next-holy-grail-for-retailers-suppliers/

24. Mango launches conversational generative AI platform; *Fashion United*; https://fashionunited.uk/news/business/mango-launches-conversational-generative-ai-platform/2023100571951

10
PERSONALIZED LEARNING: THE FUTURE OF EDUCATION

AI has been making inroads into education for the last few years, and as with many sectors, GenAI will massively accelerate this trend. Indeed, it could be a game-changer, having a profound effect on how teachers teach and how students learn – not to mention *what* students learn. But GenAI comes with risks and challenges for educators. How can we make sure students don't cheat on assessments and homework? How should educators prepare for this new era of on-demand, personalized AI tools?

It's still early days for GenAI in education, but let's paint a picture of where the sector is headed.

Rethinking How Learners Learn, and How Teachers Teach

In any education setting, from schools and colleges to self-directed lifelong learning, GenAI has the capacity to provide super-personalized learning, make teachers' jobs easier, and help students understand topics more easily. As such, we may see vast changes in how students learn and how teachers teach. We'll talk more about what this means for education policy later in the chapter, but for now let's explore the practical uses of GenAI in education.

How GenAI can add value for educators and students

Arguably the biggest advantage of GenAI is the ability to provide a more personalized learning experience. One of the many challenges teachers face is identifying where each student needs additional support, and then providing that support in a busy classroom setting (or, indeed, in a remote learning environment). GenAI can assist with this by creating assessments and questions in real time – giving educators more feedback to help them identify how students are progressing and pinpoint which students might be struggling with a concept. And, of course, GenAI can help to provide the extra support when needed. For instance, when a student struggles with a math problem, a GenAI tutor can explain the concept step-by-step, adapting its explanations to the student's level of understanding. GenAI can also be used to generate personalized follow-up questions to help cement understanding. Plus, GenAI can create individual homework plans for each student. We're talking about adaptive learning, basically – learning that is tailored to each student's needs, and to their pace.

Another significant application is in content creation. GenAI can generate educational materials such as quizzes, interactive games, flashcards, lesson plans, and even entire textbooks or video courses, making it easier for educators to create engaging and relevant learning resources for use in class. And again, these materials can be easily personalized if desired.

Moreover, language models like GPT-4 have enabled AI-powered chatbots that can answer students' questions in real time, enhancing accessibility and support for students (especially for remote and online learners). As the following examples will show, GenAI can be used to create dedicated virtual tutors that are available 24/7, allowing students to learn entirely at their own pace. And even outside of formal classroom settings or online learning platforms, GenAI is already making its way into education. With developments like ChatGPT being integrated into Snapchat, children are already beginning to access GenAI, ask it questions, and use it as part of their learning, even in informal ways.

Overall, then, GenAI will revolutionize education by enhancing personalization, accessibility, and efficiency in the learning process. No wonder the UK government has said GenAI has the potential to "reduce workload across the education sector" and "free up teachers' time, allowing them to focus on delivering excellent teaching."[1] The UK Department for Education says it is working with the education sector to "identify opportunities to improve education and reduce workload using generative AI." More on this coming up.

Helping teachers teach

Now let's explore some of the many GenAI tools designed specifically for education. MagicSchool is just one example of a GenAI tool designed for teachers. Based on OpenAI technology, the tool can be used to create word problems, worksheets, tests, and lesson plans. It can also adjust the reading level of materials based on individual students' needs, advise teachers on how to deal with behavioral problems in class, and more. Promising to save teachers time, reduce stress, and avoid burnout, tools like this will become increasingly popular among teachers. Indeed, MagicSchool amassed an impressive 150 000 users in its first four months.[2]

Kortext is another interesting example. The education platform is designed to help universities and colleges provide AI-enhanced teaching and personalized learning experiences. Kortext tools can instantly summarize content, generate study notes, and create interactive Q&As to cement learning. It can also deliver valuable data to course leaders on student engagement, study patterns, and content usage. And, importantly, unlike many other GenAI tools, Kortext uses only trusted content (textbooks, etc.) that has been prescribed as part of the institution's own curriculum. Among the thousands of universities using Kortext is Middlesex University, University of Manchester, and University of Oxford.[3]

GenAI can also be used internally to help staff and students with daily admin tasks. In one example, Purdue University says it has used GenAI to give technical advice – for example, explaining how to set up a networked printer – and has plans to use the technology for other advice, such as how to find buildings on campus.[4]

Helping learners learn

Meanwhile, students can benefit from GenAI-powered learning tools such as Chegg, which is designed to facilitate 24/7 study and help learners access instant, step-by-step explanations on any subject or question. According to Chegg, 94% of its users say they get better grades when they use Chegg to understand their coursework.[5]

There's also Khan Academy, a nonprofit organization on a mission to provide free education for anyone, anywhere. Khan Academy has partnered with OpenAI and is using the GPT-4 language model to create Khanmigo, a virtual tutor for students that can, among other things, ask each student individualized questions to prompt deeper learning.[6] (Khan Academy is also exploring using GPT-4 as a classroom assistant for teachers – e.g., creating instructional materials and classroom prompts.)

Udacity is another online course provider using GPT-4 to create a virtual, on-demand, AI tutor – a tutor that can provide detailed explanations tailored to each individual learner, summarize concepts, and even translate learning materials into other languages. Udacity says the chatbot tutor is a "real-time complement to our human mentors," not a replacement for human mentors.[7] And importantly, the AI tutor can handle thousands of interactions at once.

There's also Quizlet's GenAI study aid, which provides personalized AI tutoring, automatic flashcards, quick summaries of concepts, and questions that help students understand topics (instead of just telling them the answer). Over a million students have used Quizlet's Q-Chat chatbot, and Quizlet research shows that more than two-thirds of students believe the AI helps them better understand materials and learn faster.[8]

And for lifelong learners whose school days are long behind them, GenAI can make learning any topic easier. Take learning a second language as an example. Duolingo is the poster child for using AI in language learning, and has collaborated with OpenAI to integrate GPT-4 into its offering.[9] The result is a much more personalized language-learning experience. In particular, the partnership has introduced two new features to Duolingo: the first feature, called "Explain My Answer," provides users with detailed explanations of their responses, mimicking the feedback you might get from a human language tutor; and the second "Role Playing" feature allows users to engage with AI personas for immersive language practice in diverse scenarios. For example, say you're planning a trip to Paris and have specific dietary requirements;

you can tailor your role-playing lessons to have conversations with an AI barista. The AI personas are designed to be fully fleshed-out characters with their own personality and backstory that learners can uncover through conversations. With these new additions, Duolingo is able to cater to each of its 500-million-plus students as individuals, which is an impressive feat.

Transforming *What* We Teach

As well as transforming how subjects are taught, the rise of GenAI may change *what* subjects are taught. We talked about this a little in Chapter 5 – about how the important skills for success will be different in a world where machines can do more and more jobs. This is the subject of my book, *Future Skills: The 20 skills and competencies everyone needs to succeed in a digital world*, and I recommend you seek it out if you'd like a more in-depth look at skills. But from a formal learning perspective, we may see institutions incorporate subjects and skills that are complementary to machines in our increasingly AI-driven world. Skills like creative thinking, empathy, and teamwork.

We will also need to teach young people how to critically assess the information they access, especially given the huge potential for AI-generated misinformation. For example, students will need to learn to search for clues in text to determine the authenticity and accuracy of the text. They will need guidance on how to gather evidence – and what constitutes good evidence – in a world where you can just ask a chatbot for information and immediately be given an answer.

And of course, students will need to learn how to be digitally literate. I'm not talking about teaching every young person how to code; rather, I'm talking about teaching every young person about AI and its impact on our world. That includes understanding the potential for misinformation, understanding the potential for data bias, understanding how AIs are trained (and how that impacts the information they serve up), and understanding how AI dictates so much of the content we see online (leading to information bubbles). I would love to see young people learning how to thrive in a digital world, and how humanity can get the best out of AI without losing what makes us human.

Given its transformational potential, we may see GenAI integrated into core curricula around the world. I certainly hope so. As more and more jobs will be augmented by GenAI, it makes sense that students should learn how to harness GenAI to solve problems, enhance their productivity, and boost innovation. The California Department of Education is one authority "encouraging" districts to explore the potential benefits of AI as part of the curriculum.[10] But we need more formal frameworks than that – not just in terms of including AI in the curriculum, but also how to harness GenAI properly in education settings. Which brings us to. . .

The Need for Formal Policy and Guidance in Schools

It should be clear by now that I'm broadly in favor of schools, colleges, and individual students embracing GenAI. But GenAI isn't without its challenges. For one thing, we need teachers (and students) to be aware of potential bias and misinformation in educational content generated by AI. We need institutions to ensure GenAI is inclusive. We need to use GenAI as a *complement* to human teachers, not a replacement. And we may even need to rethink how students are assessed – cheating being a big concern among some educators. Say, for example, a student is wearing a smart watch in an exam, what's to stop them having ChatGPT dictate answers to them via unseen wireless earbuds? At the very least, there's the danger of students relying on ChatGPT to write their homework for them. So how can educators prepare for this – and prepare their students to use GenAI responsibly?

Of course, institutions faced similar conversations when calculators and, later, computers were introduced, but the question remains: How can we encourage students to use these GenAI tools effectively but not *rely* on them?

Despite teachers and students already beginning to experiment with GenAI tools, the education sector remains largely unprepared for the rise of GenAI. A UNESCO study of over 450 schools and universities around the world found that less than 10% had institutional policies or formal guidance in place outlining the use of GenAI applications – largely due to lack of government frameworks.[11] This has led UNESCO to call for governments to provide formal regulation and teacher training on the use of GenAI in education settings. UNESCO says the lack of scrutiny, checks or regulations on the use of GenAI is worrying, especially given the scrutiny applied to other aspects of education, such as which books are taught in the classroom.

Some authorities are beginning to grapple with AI policy. New York City Public Schools, for instance, has collaborated with AI experts to launch an AI Policy Lab to guide the school district's approach to AI. The Policy Lab will focus on "human-centered AI implementation, equity, safety, ethics, effectiveness, and transparency."[12] That's an encouraging and pragmatic turnaround, considering the district initially banned the use of ChatGPT on school networks.

The use of GenAI in college applications is another hot topic. Common App, the college application tool used by more than 1000 institutions, has included a restriction on the use of "substantive content or output of an artificial intelligence platform" in college applications.[13] (Although, my question is, how on earth do they police this? How do they intend to identify when a "substantive" amount of content has been written by GenAI?)

Here in the UK, I've already mentioned that the UK Department for Education (DfE) is keen to explore the use of GenAI in schools. At the time of writing, the DfE had launched a "call for evidence" to gather views from education professionals on the ethical considerations, risks and possibilities of AI, and invited teachers to participate in a "hackathon" event designed to explore AI's potential across different scenarios. Results were due to be published at the end of 2023.[14]

Also in the UK, the Russell Group, comprising 24 universities, has drawn up "guiding principles" for the use of GenAI in its universities – designed to help universities capitalize on the technology while maintaining academic rigor. The new policies "make it clear to students and staff where the use of generative AI is inappropriate, and are intended to support them in making informed decisions and to empower them to use these tools appropriately and acknowledge their use where necessary."[15]

We'll no doubt see more education institutions around the world begin to account for GenAI in their policies and guidance, but this cannot happen soon enough. At present, the use of GenAI in education is reminiscent of the old Wild West. For now, anything goes. . .

Key Takeaways

In this chapter, we've learned:

- GenAI is revolutionizing education by enhancing personalization, accessibility, and efficiency in the learning process. Adaptive, on-demand tutoring is a particularly hot area. The use of GenAI in education promises not only to help students learn, but also to help teachers teach – freeing up teachers' time to focus on students rather than, say, writing lesson plans and devising tests.

- The rise of GenAI may also influence *what* is taught in institutions. From school to university level, students will need to be equipped with the skills and knowledge to thrive in an AI-driven world.

- At present, few institutions have formal policies on how GenAI should be used by teachers and students, prompting concerns about cheating and the potential for misinformation and bias in educational content. This is something education providers need to think about, and fast!

I like talking about education because it's a subject that's close to many of our hearts – we've all been learners at one time or another and many of us have children in education. Now let's turn to another sector with universal interest: healthcare. How will GenAI transform the healthcare sector and, hopefully, improve healthcare outcomes for us all? That's the subject of our next chapter.

Notes

1. Generative artificial intelligence (AI) in education; *Department for Education*; https://www.gov.uk/government/publications/generative-artificial-intelligence-in-education/generative-artificial-intelligence-ai-in-education#:~:text=Generative%20AI%20refers%20to%20technology,large%20language%20models%20(%20LLMs%20)

2. Teachers Are Going All In on Generative AI; *Wired*; https://www.wired.com/story/teachers-are-going-all-in-on-generative-ai/

3. Kortext; *Kortext*; https://www.kortext.com/

4. AI Buzz Dominates Annual Ed-Tech Conference; *Inside Higher Ed*; https://www.insidehighered.com/news/tech-innovation/artificial-intelligence/2023/10/12/ai-buzz-dominates-annual-ed-tech-conference

5. Chegg; *Chegg*; https://www.chegg.com/

6. Khan Academy; *OpenAI*; https://openai.com/customer-stories/khan-academy

7. Announcing our new AI chatbot; *Udacity*; https://www.udacity.com/blog/2023/03/announcing-our-new-ai-chatbot-on-demand-learning-guidance-made-easy.html

8. Quizlet is using AI to make studying easier – with personalized tutoring, automatic flashcards, and even songs; *Fortune*; https://fortune.com/education/articles/quizlet-ai-powered-tools-q-chat-magic-notes-quick-summary-gpt/

9. The Amazing Ways Duolingo Is Using AI and GPT-4; *Forbes*; https://www.forbes.com/sites/bernardmarr/2023/04/28/the-amazing-ways-duolingo-is-using-ai-and-gpt-4/

10. 'We Can't Pretend It Away': Schools Grapple with Guidelines for Using Generative AI on College Applications; *KQED*; https://www.kqed.org/news/11964259/we-cant-pretend-it-away-schools-grapple-with-guidelines-for-using-generative-ai-on-college-applications#:~:text=The%20California%20Department%20of%20Education,broader%20lessons%20in%20media%20literacy.

11. UNESCO: Governments must quickly regulate generative AI in schools; *UNESCO*; https://www.unesco.org/en/articles/unesco-governments-must-quickly-regulate-generative-ai-schools

12. NYC Schools Working with AI Experts to Launch AI Policy Lab; *Government Technology*; https://www.govtech.com/education/k-12/nyc-schools-working-with-experts-to-launch-ai-policy-lab

13. Application Fraud; *Common App*; https://www.commonapp.org/files/Common-App-Fraud-Policy.pdf

14. Teachers to join DfE's AI workload reduction trial; *TES Magazine*; https://www.tes.com/magazine/news/general/artificial-intelligence-reduce-teacher-workload-government-trial

15. UK universities draw up guiding principles on generative AI; *The Guardian*; https://www.theguardian.com/technology/2023/jul/04/uk-universities-draw-up-guiding-principles-on-generative-ai

11

HEALTHCARE TRANSFORMATION: FROM PERSONALIZED ADVICE TO OPERATIONAL IMPROVEMENTS

GenAI is ushering in a transformative era in healthcare, with far-reaching implications for patient care, diagnostics, and more. There's a lot happening in this field, so this chapter touches on key developments only, with a particular focus on:

- Personalized advice for patients

- Detection of diseases

- Personalized treatment

- And operational improvements

We'll return to healthcare in Chapter 19, where we'll look at the use of GenAI in drug discovery and development. But for now, let's get into the amazing ways GenAI can improve healthcare and deliver better outcomes for patients (not to mention a better working experience for healthcare professionals).

Giving Patients Personalized Health Advice

This goes beyond basic chatbots that can help patients book appointments, refill prescriptions, or answer routine enquiries (although such chatbots do have a valuable place in healthcare, as we'll see later in the chapter). Sophisticated large language models like GPT-4, combined with human doctor expertise, has led to a new wave of virtual health assistants – developed to give actual medical advice that's personalized to each patient's specific health concerns. With millions of people around the world unable to access medical care (either because of their geographical location, for economic reasons, or simply because their local services are too stretched), we can expect to see AI increasingly pick up the slack. These AI systems not only improve patient engagement but also relieve the burden on healthcare professionals by handling routine healthcare concerns and directing patients accordingly.

As an example, Ada is a doctor-developed, AI-driven app designed to assess symptoms and offer patients medical guidance, in multiple languages (including English, German, French, Spanish, Portuguese, and Swahili). So far, the app has amassed 13 million users and has completed more than 30 million symptom assessments.[1] It works by asking you questions about your symptoms (you can also create separate symptom profiles for loved ones), then pointing you to possible conditions and medical guidance. The app also tracks your symptoms as they progress.

Image Analysis and the Early Detection of Diseases

AI has been making a mark in this area for a little while, but GenAI will significantly enhance the analysis of medical images. As such, we'll increasingly see GenAI tools being used to help radiologists identify and diagnose diseases from X-rays, MRIs, and CT scans with greater accuracy and speed.

But can an AI really be as effective as a human doctor when it comes to detecting and diagnosing issues from images? Absolutely. Numerous studies have shown that AI tools deliver comparable accuracy to human doctors – if not higher accuracy. (After all, machines don't get tired at the end of a long shift.) But let's explore one particular example. . .

Detecting issues in chest radiographs

One study explored the use of AI to interpret chest radiographs and generate radiograph reports in the emergency department. Since many emergency departments don't have 24/7 access to dedicated radiology services, images are often interpreted by a remote radiologist (known as "teleradiology") or even by ER doctors. The study found that the AI tool generated rapid radiograph interpretations and reports with comparable levels of quality and accuracy as radiologist reports – and to a *higher quality* than teleradiology reports.[2] In one of the cases, the AI performed even better than a human radiologist, detecting an issue that the radiologist failed to report. And in another case, the human radiologist reported that opacities in a patient's lungs appeared consistent, while the AI detected that the opacities had worsened – a finding that could be significant in that patient's case.

The authors of the study suggest that the short processing time and high accuracy of AI diagnostics could help to streamline the processing of patients in emergency departments. This shows that not only can AI help radiologists perform their work more quickly and effectively – it can also help clinicians in other departments interpret medical images and accelerate the processing of patients.

Helping patients self-examine

GenAI is rapidly emerging as a viable tool in medical diagnostics. But it can also help patients identify issues and seek early medical intervention. That's the idea behind SkinVision, the AI-powered app for early detection of skin cancer. SkinVision is a regulated medical service that teaches people how to self-examine their skin and determine when they need to take action. And while SkinVision is quick to say its service is *not* a medical diagnosis, the idea is to help people quickly detect signs of the most common kinds of skin cancer, so that they can seek a formal diagnosis where needed. Research has shown that the app can detect skin cancer with 95% accuracy.[3]

Providing Personalized and Improved Treatment for Patients

GenAI can help doctors enhance patient treatment – by analyzing vast patient datasets to recommend personalized treatment plans, optimizing medication dosages, and predicting potential adverse reactions, all based on the individual. Plus, it can assist in the creation of tailored rehabilitation exercises and therapy programs, enabling more precise and effective care for individual patients.

GenAI can also help to enhance preventive medicine. For example, clinics and hospitals could employ GenAI to create personalized health plans based on a patient's unique genetic makeup, health history, and lifestyle. This sort of AI-driven approach could not only help people lead healthier lives and, in turn, prevent illness – it would also help patients feel more understood and cared for as an individual.

Supplementing patient–doctor conversations

Imagine a scenario where a patient consults with a doctor, and a GenAI system operates in the background, listening, taking notes, and formulating potential questions for the doctor to ask – based on the patient's history and symptoms. Like a cross between a medical chatbot and a diagnostic tool, but designed to be used in sessions with patients to inform conversations and help the doctor uncover symptoms and diagnoses. (Indeed, later in the chapter we'll see how GenAI is already being used to listen to and summarize patient consultations.)

This sort of AI-augmented approach could help doctors get the most out of patient appointments (which can be as brief as 10 minutes), while tailoring their care to the individual in front of them. Plus, it could prove particularly valuable in the diagnosis of rare or difficult-to-diagnose conditions, such as endometriosis, which affects 1 in 10 women but has symptoms which are often dismissed or misdiagnosed.

Helping busy doctors provide precision care

A good example comes from GenAI experts RhythmX AI, who have created a precision care platform that helps doctors deliver hyper-personalized care.

In essence, the system uses GenAI and predictive AI algorithms to provide patient-specific prescriptive actions and recommendations. Doctors can then drill into the recommendations via the natural language interface – an AI co-pilot for doctors, if you will. As Dr Gregg Meyer, part of the clinical advisory board at RhythmX put it, "Physicians are now considering clinical experience, social determinants, lifestyle factors, and mental health factors to deliver hyper-personalized interventions . . . There is a critical need in the industry for a platform that can aid physicians to solve these issues."[4]

Healthcare Research and the Development of New Drugs

We'll talk more about this in Chapter 19, which is all about the use of GenAI to design the products and solutions of the future. But I just want to flag here that the implications of GenAI for healthcare research and drug discovery are huge. GenAI can help researchers understand disease markers more easily, and find optimal combinations of chemicals (and even invent entirely new combinations) to create new pharmaceutical treatments. As such, GenAI will revolutionize drug discovery and development by generating novel molecular structures, swiftly screening compounds, predicting drug interactions, repurposing existing drugs for new applications, optimizing clinical trials, and enhancing drug formulations. Not only will this help clinicians treat diseases better in future, it will also make treatment more personalized – because drugs can, in theory, be tailored based on individual patient data.

Delivering Administrative and Operational Improvements

GenAI can help to reduce the administrative burden in healthcare by automating tasks such as medical coding, billing, routine enquiries, and notetaking. If we think about the tasks that GenAI is capable of – writing, listening, and interpreting human speech and text – it's clear that GenAI can add a lot of value behind the scenes in clinical settings. Even just a few minutes saved on each patient encounter with automated notetaking could add up to considerable operational improvements – freeing up healthcare professionals to spend more time with patients and less time on admin tasks.

Conversational AI for answering routine calls and messages

Hyro is a HIPAA-compliant "conversational AI" designed to help clinics automate common interactions, overcome staffing shortages, and enhance patient engagement. Using natural language text and speech, Hyro helps healthcare teams automate straightforward tasks and requests from patients, including appointment scheduling and prescription refills – meanwhile, more complex cases are routed to the appropriate department. Hyro says its AI assistants can resolve around 85% of calls.[5]

Using GenAI for notetaking and clinical documentation

Another good example comes from NextGen Healthcare and its Ambient Assist notetaking tool, which listens to conversations between patients and clinicians, then provides summary notes. Notes are available for the clinician to review within just 30 seconds of completing the patient encounter, with the tool documenting appointments with over 90% accuracy.[6]

A 2017 study found that primary care doctors spend nearly half their working day on electronic health record and admin tasks, and just 27% of their time with patients – with admin burden being cited as a leading cause of clinician burnout.[7] Tools like NextGen help clinicians cut down on admin tasks without compromising clinical records.

In another example, Baptist Health, a South Florida health system comprising 11 hospitals, is also using GenAI to reduce the time spent on clinical documentation. It is implementing a GenAI-powered documentation app that blends medical transcription technology with AI language models – meaning the system can transcribe patient conversations and quickly generate clinical notes from the conversations. The automation is expected to reduce documentation time down to around two minutes post-visit, giving clinicians more time to attend to patients.[8]

Helping clinicians search information more easily

GenAI isn't just about generating content for clinicians; it can also help clinicians access and digest information more easily. That's the idea behind Google Cloud's Vertex AI Search platform, which has now been tailored specifically for healthcare and life-sciences organizations. Using the tool, clinicians can search for information across data sources – not just electronic health records, but potentially the organization's entire data ecosystem, including raw unstructured data. Among the companies integrating Google Cloud's GenAI search capabilities is care.ai. The AI company says its 'Smart Care Facility Platform' will use Google's GenAI technology to enable new ways to analyze data, generate insights, and enhance care delivery.[9]

Predicting outbreaks to optimize resources

Another way that AI may streamline healthcare provision is in forecasting disease outbreaks, or predicting how viruses may change. An exciting example comes from an AI tool called "EVEscape," developed by researchers at Harvard Medical School and the University of Oxford. EVEscape uses generative models to predict how a virus could evolve to escape the immune system, thereby predicting new mutations of viruses. (The tool successfully predicted the most concerning new variants of COVID-19.[10]) Not only could this help global health systems prepare for and manage pandemics, it could also inform the development of vaccines and therapies for rapidly changing viruses.

Could Generative AI Help to Solve the Healthcare Crisis?

Around the world, healthcare systems are coming under enormous strain. In many regions, there is a critical shortage of doctors and healthcare professionals. The World Health Organization (WHO) estimates a projected shortfall of 10 million healthcare professionals by 2030, primarily affecting low- and lower-middle-income countries.[11] Even in a rich country like the US, the Association of American Medical Colleges is predicting a shortage of up to 139 000 physicians by 2033.[12]

What's more, healthcare systems are plagued by rising waiting times. At the time of writing, the waiting list for planned treatment in England's National Health Service hit another record high of 7.75 million patients, with thousands waiting more than 18 months to start treatment.[13] And that's the situation in a country with universal healthcare – something that many people aren't fortunate enough to enjoy. Shockingly, WHO figures from 2021 indicate that around 4.5 billion people around the world are not fully covered by essential health services.[14]

The promise of GenAI

There's no substitute for receiving amazing care from human doctors and other healthcare professionals. But it's clear that GenAI offers solutions that can help to bridge the gap between growing healthcare needs and apparently dwindling healthcare resources. We needn't be afraid of this. GenAI tools have demonstrated remarkable medical knowledge – to the extent that some are competent enough to pass medical certification exams.[15] And as we've seen in this chapter, they can even outperform human doctors when it comes to diagnosing issues. So a future where clinicians and GenAIs work together – where human intuition and expertise combines with machine precision – is enticing. As healthcare systems become more stretched, combining human and machine expertise will likely be the best way to diagnose patients and provide appropriate treatment.

What's more, GenAI tools can empower individuals to take charge of their own healthcare, by engaging in discussions with healthcare chatbots about potential diagnoses and treatment options, and seeking medical help when needed. Think of it as the new version of Googling your symptoms, only much more advanced and precise! And when a patient does interact with a doctor, GenAI can add value in the background, generating medical notes and helping doctors search information.

But there are challenges

When a GenAI tool generates inaccurate or "hallucinated" content in a sector like marketing, it's probably rather embarrassing for the company using that content. But if a healthcare GenAI generates inaccurate or incoherent responses, that's a whole other story. So while large language models and other GenAI models hold great promise for solving problems in healthcare, providers obviously need to ensure the accuracy and reliability of responses.

Are there challenges to deploying GenAI in healthcare? Absolutely. But given the current state of healthcare provision and access around the world, I believe GenAI promises more solutions than obstacles.

Key Takeaways

To summarize the key applications of GenAI in healthcare:

- Through more intelligent, responsive chatbots, GenAI can be used to deliver personalized advice to patients, allowing them to discuss concerns, get potential diagnoses, and understand when they may need treatment. New tools are already emerging to meet this demand for more immediate access to healthcare advice.

- When it comes to the early detection of diseases, AI has already proven itself to be as capable and reliable as human doctors at interpreting medical images and generating reports based on those images. Not only can this help radiologists in their work, it can also help doctors in other departments (such as the ER) to quickly diagnose issues and accelerate patient treatment.

- Personalized treatment is a particularly hot area in medicine, but one that's challenging to deliver given each patient has a different medical history, different needs, and a different lifestyle. GenAI can help clinicians overcome this challenge by acting as a medical "co-pilot" – suggesting potential treatments and next steps.

- Behind the scenes, GenAI can also deliver huge operational improvements – particularly when it comes to streamlining medical notetaking, dealing with routine calls and enquiries at clinics, and more. This could improve the patient experience and help to reduce clinician burnout.

- Healthcare systems around the world are struggling and waiting times can be frustratingly long. GenAI can help to solve some of the biggest challenges facing global healthcare systems and make healthcare much more accessible and efficient.

Now let's turn to something completely different: the world of gaming. In the next chapter, we'll explore how video game design is being transformed by GenAI, and how the games of the future will be more responsive, personalized, and immersive than ever before. Ready Player One? Then turn the page.

Notes

1. About Ada; *Ada*; https://ada.com/about/
2. Is generative AI the future of rapid and accurate chest radiograph interpretation in the ER?; *News Medical Life Sciences*; https://www.news-medical.net/news/20231008/Is-generative-AI-the-future-of-rapid-and-accurate-chest-radiograph-interpretation-in-the-ER.aspx
3. Accuracy of a smartphone application for triage of skin lesions based on machine learning algorithms; *Journal of the European Academy of Dermatology & Venereology*; https://onlinelibrary.wiley.com/doi/10.1111/jdv.15935
4. New Generative AI-Native Health Company RhythmX AI Announces Precision Care Platform For Doctors to Deliver Hyper-Personalized Care to the Right Patient at the Right Time; *PR Newswire*; https://www.prnewswire.com/news-releases/new-generative-ai-native-health-company-rhythmx-ai-announces-precision-care-platform-for-doctors-to-deliver-hyper-personalized-care-to-the-right-patient-at-the-right-time-301947898.html
5. Conversational AI for healthcare; *Hyro*; https://www.hyro.ai/healthcare/
6. NextGen Healthcare reveals AI notetaking product; *Healthcare Dive*; https://www.healthcaredive.com/news/nextgen-healthcare-generative-ai-clinical-documentation-ambient-assist/696029/
7. Yet another study highlights EHR burden on physicians; *Healthcare Dive*; https://www.healthcaredive.com/news/another-study-highlights-ehr-burden-on-physicians/504805/
8. In pilot, generative AI expected to reduce clinical documentation time at Baptist Health; *Healthcare IT news*; https://www.healthcareitnews.com/news/generative-ai-reduces-clinical-documentation-time-baptist-health
9. Google Cloud Launches New Generative AI Capabilities for Healthcare; *Forbes*; https://www.forbes.com/sites/saibala/2023/10/09/google-cloud-launches-new-healthcare-generative-ai-features/?sh=3de773ac7e5b
10. An AI Tool That Can Help Forecast Viral Outbreaks; *Harvard Medical School*; https://hms.harvard.edu/news/ai-tool-can-help-forecast-viral-outbreaks
11. Health Workforce; *World Health Organization*; https://www.who.int/health-topics/health-workforce#tab=tab_1

12. New AAMC Report Reinforces Mounting Physician Shortage; *AAMC*; https://www.aamc.org/news/press-releases/new-aamc-report-confirms-growing-physician-shortage#:~:text=According%20to%20new%20data%20published,and%20specialty%20care%2C%20by%202033

13. NHS waiting list in England rises to record 7.75 million; *BBC News*; https://www.bbc.com/news/health-67087906

14. Universal health coverage; *World Health Organization*; https://www.who.int/news-room/fact-sheets/detail/universal-health-coverage-(uhc)

15. Generative AI in Medicine and Healthcare; Promises, Opportunities, and Challenges *Future Internet*; https://www.mdpi.com/1999-5903/15/9/286

12

VIDEO GAME DESIGN AND TESTING: THE GENERATIVE AI APPROACH

I wanted to include a chapter on video games because it's something that is a little different and also since there are some really interesting advances happening in this area. Plus, I'm sure a lot of my readers are keen gamers and would be interested to know how games will evolve in the GenAI era. (Hint: we can look forward to more personalized experiences and NPCs [non-player characters] that are capable of proper conversations.)

GenAI will play such a key role in the video game industry that one survey of video game execs found that GenAI is expected to contribute to more than half of video game development within the next 5–10 years – freeing up game designers from the more mundane development work and helping to reduce costs and development time.[1]

In addition to helping develop new, better video games, GenAI also has a role to play in quality control and testing of video games. Let's explore both factors, along with some emerging examples from the video game industry. (Alongside, you can read about the impact of GenAI on coding in Chapter 16.)

Generative AI in Video Game Development and Testing

In this age of GenAI, creating video game environments and characters no longer needs to be done painstakingly by hand. GenAI can automate many development tasks, freeing up developers to focus their time on the most impactful aspects of game design.

Plus, as GenAI tools become more sophisticated, it will be possible to build the technology into real-time games that offer personalized environments and NPCs that adapt and evolve based on a player's style and strategy – as opposed to the pre-built worlds and pre-programmed NPCs of today's video games. This could potentially transform the gaming industry, ensuring each gamer's experience is different.

GenAI uses in game development

For developers, GenAI offers exciting new ways to create engaging content, realistic visuals, and immersive gameplay experiences. As an example, let's say part of a video game takes place in a forest. Pay attention and you may start to notice that there's only a small number of individual tree models that repeat over and over again. Once you've noticed it, you can't help but keep seeing the same trees, which is jarring and takes you out of the game experience. But if that forest was created with GenAI, it could potentially be populated by thousands of completely unique trees and critters – which is not only more visually appealing and immersive, it keeps you focused on the gameplay experience, without being distracted by technical limitations.

Let's break down some of the main elements of game development and see how GenAI can facilitate the process:

- **Procedural generation:** By leveraging algorithms to create vast, intricate, and unpredictable environments, games can potentially deliver a unique, dynamic experience in each gameplay session.

- **Terrain generation:** GenAI can assist in the generation of realistic terrains, enhancing the visual appeal of game worlds.

- **Automated modeling:** GenAI can streamline the creation of 3D models for characters and other elements, thereby reducing the time and expertise required.

- **Voice synthesis:** Developers can utilize AI to create diverse and realistic voiceovers for characters.

- **Voice modification:** GenAI provides the means to modify voice recordings easily, thus creating a diverse range of voices for characters, with limited resources.

- **Generative music:** Thanks to GenAI, it's possible to automatically create music scores for games – and even create dynamic scores that change based on in-game events, thereby enhancing the emotional impact of games.

- **Sound effects:** GenAI can also be used to generate realistic sound effects – again, potentially on-the-fly, to support the immersion and realism of game worlds.

- **Ambient soundscapes:** Immersive ambient soundscapes that enhance the game's atmosphere can be generated with GenAI.

- **Dialogue generation:** GenAI can also write realistic dialogue for characters, again, potentially on-the-fly.

- **Personality generation:** GenAI is capable of crafting unique and consistent character personalities that enrich storytelling.

- **Dynamic storytelling:** Non-linear storylines that adapt based on player choices are another possibility thanks to GenAI. This helps to create a more personalized gaming experience.

- **Automated quest generation:** GenAI can also be used to automatically create quests and missions that align with the game's overarching narrative.

Bottom line, GenAI can autonomously create hugely immersive and engaging gaming elements – thereby speeding up game development and reducing the costs associated with bringing new games to market. And in the future, GenAI will be increasingly used to create dynamic elements, characters, and worlds that can evolve and adapt to each player. Make no mistake, GenAI marks a huge leap forward in video game development.

GenAI in video game testing

Another way GenAI can add value to video games is in game testing and quality assurance. GenAI can be used to automatically detect bugs and defects in games, and rank them according to priority and their impact on the game. Plus, the predictive capabilities of AI mean it can be used to analyze data to predict potential issues within a game, allowing developers to take proactive action. GenAI can also be used to create multiple simulated players (i.e., bots) to test the game, all playing in different ways according to their AI-generated play styles. This allows game developers to quickly work out where players get stuck, where players are most likely to spend money (on in-game accessories), and which factors lead to less satisfying gaming experiences.

All of this will help to speed up the quality assurance process, while simultaneously increasing the accuracy and overall experience of video games.

Examples of GenAI in games

Let's turn to some real-world examples that show how developers are already using GenAI in their work.

Video game company, Ninja Theory, has reportedly tapped into GenAI to generate vocal performance – using the Altered AI voice library.[2] Meanwhile, Ubisoft, creator of Assassin's Creed, has developed its own in-house GenAI tool called "Ghostwriter" to create "barks," those brief phrases spoken by NPCs when triggered by certain events.[3] The idea is to automatically create first drafts of character dialogues (e.g., enemy dialogue during a battle scene), which scriptwriters can then select from and, if necessary, polish up. By automating these little lines of dialogue – of which there could be hundreds within a game – scriptwriters can instead focus their time on core plot dialogue.

It's no wonder the developer of Ubisoft's Assassin Creed game, Jade Raymond, says AI in the development of big-budget games is "unavoidable" due to its ability to cut expenses and speed up game development.[4]

Hexworks, creators of the game Lords of the Fallen, also used GenAI during development – not to create artwork, dialogue, or characters, but to optimize the game.[5] Today's stunning graphics-heavy games present problems in terms of memory usage and computational oomph (technical term). Hexworks says GenAI can help with this by automatically detecting inefficiencies and suggesting solutions, such as reducing texture sizes. Interestingly, AI-generated voices were also used in an early build of the game, with voice actors being brought in for the final version. For me, this shows that GenAI can help to speed up prototyping and get new game projects up and running faster, without replacing human creativity.

It's even possible to create entire games with GenAI. That's the case with the Angry Pumpkins game, inspired by the popular Angry Birds game and created entirely using GenAI – with ChatGPT being used to write the code, and AI imaging tools like Midjourney and Dall-E creating the images. Its creator, Javi Lopez, says the game is more of a "proof of concept" rather than a direct competitor for Angry Birds. Basically, he wanted to show what was possible with GenAI tools.[6] And the end result is pretty impressive, especially considering its developer didn't have to write a single piece of code. It just goes to show how easy it is to create games with GenAI.

GenAI is also helping to breathe new life into classic computer games. Revolution Software, the UK game developer that scored a big hit with the Broken Sword series of adventure games in the 1990s, has been using GenAI to help update the early games in the series so they can be played on the latest generation of consoles and PCs. The first games in the series had hand-drawn graphics that were scaled to fit the far lower resolution displays that were used in the 1990s. Recreating all that hand-drawn artwork at a higher resolution would have been prohibitively expensive. So the team worked with GenAI researchers at the University of York, who were able to take a few sample pieces of art designed for a modern-day update and use them to train a GenAI model – the result being a model capable of creating a piece of in-game artwork (such as an object or character) in as little as five minutes.[7] Human artists were then used to retouch some of the AI-generated art (e.g., making faces more realistic). So basically, instead of having to redraw everything, the team could focus human efforts where it was most beneficial, and let GenAI take care of the rest. And this made the whole endeavor economically feasible for Revolution Games.

New GenAI tools for developers

Meanwhile, new tools are emerging to help developers harness GenAI. As an example, leading game software company Unity has announced an AI marketplace where developers can gain access to GenAI solutions that help to accelerate game development – including solutions for asset creation, NPC platforms and voice generators.[8] Unity has also created the Muse and Sentis generative platforms, which further help developers harness AI technology in their workflows.

There's also a new animation tool called "Animate Anything," created by Anything World, which can be used to easily animate 3D models. This means users can upload a static 3D model and have the tool create an animated 3D version in minutes.[9]

Or there's the SyncDreamer GenAI tool, which creates multiple 2D perspectives of an object based on a single 2D image (whether a drawn image or a photorealistic image). This allows game developers to streamline the process of creating 3D representations from 2D images – something that has proven stubbornly difficult and laborious until now.[10]

Similarly, there's the Auctoria platform, which uses GenAI to create video game assets and game levels from scratch. Users can convert images into 3D equivalents, or create assets using simple text prompts.[11]

Microsoft is also embracing GenAI, partnering with Inworld AI to create Xbox tools that enable game developers to create GenAI characters, storylines, and quests. Additionally, the "AI design co-pilot" can create detailed scripts and dialogue trees.[12] Microsoft's partner, Inworld, has also been working on using GenAI to create NPCs that react to questions from a player.

Elsewhere, Google Cloud has formed strategic partnerships with the leading game developers in Vietnam, enabling the use of Google Cloud GenAI solutions for games. Plans include building advanced chatbots for more realistic conversations with characters, and enabling games that respond dynamically to players.[13]

In another example, software company NVIDIA has unveiled its Avatar Cloud Engine (ACE) for Games, a custom GenAI model that "aims to transform games by bringing intelligence to NPCs through AI-powered natural language interactions."[14] As NVIDIA points out, even in today's most sophisticated games, interactions with NPCs still tend to be transactional, scripted, and brief, with dialogue options being quickly exhausted. But with ACE for Games, developers can improve the conversational skills of NPCs, making them more intelligent with consistent personalities that evolve over time. Importantly, this enables dynamic responses that are unique to the player. So instead of brief, scripted conversations, gamers could, in the future, have endless interesting conversations with NPCs.

Generative AI Will Shape the Future of Video Games

GenAI will be so impactful in game development that Xbox CFO, Tim Stuart, has described its power as "magical." Speaking at the MIT Sloan Gaming Conference in 2023, Stuart said GenAI will help even more people create games, describing "a world where we go from 2 million or 3 million core game developers to 200 million game developers that can now use AI as a tool."[15] He also noted that gaming business models are shifting – moving away from the model where companies sell a console and games, to a model where gamers have more flexible ways to access games. Which means key performance indicators revolve less around sales of consoles and games, and more around factors like the number of hours played and revenue per hour (e.g., from players buying accessories within the game). Which means it's more important than ever to keep players immersed in games for longer periods – something that GenAI can support.

As we've seen in this chapter, GenAI is likely to bring huge changes to the video game industry by automating some of the menial development and testing tasks, and enabling the creation of truly dynamic games. Think about it – developers will no longer have to painstakingly code every single line of dialogue or every little movement by an NPC; a GenAI tool can do it for them, even reacting on-the-fly to individual player interactions. If you're a gamer who likes to feel fully immersed in a world and its characters, this is no doubt a tantalizing concept.

In other words, while GenAI can help to unlock huge efficiencies in game development workflows, perhaps the biggest win of all is for the game-playing experience. That's why new game studio Jam & Tea Studios is putting GenAI at the heart of its vision – because of its ability to "empower previously impossible levels of player agency . . . While we're confident there will be improvements to workflows, we are far more focused on using AI to unlock game experiences folks have never seen before."[16]

Looking further ahead, we may even see tools emerge that allow players to create their own games, without any development knowledge. Pahdo Labs, the studio behind the Halcyon Zero anime game, is planning to launch its own GenAI tools for game creation, after raising US$15 million in funding.[17] The plan is to open up creator tools to players, allowing them to build their own anime games with GenAI.

Does all this mean we'll no longer need game developers? No. There will always be a vital place for human creativity in game development. But as with other industries, the work of developers will evolve as they increasingly work alongside AIs to create games.

Key Takeaways

In this chapter, we've learned that the video game industry is set to be transformed by GenAI. Key points to note are:

- GenAI marks a huge leap forward in video game development. The technology can be used to create immersive environments, game assets, levels, objects, music, dialogues, and NPCs that make for a more realistic, immersive, and engaging gaming experience.

- In the future, GenAI will enable games to evolve dynamically based on the individual player, with characters and the storyline reacting to the player's style and strategy.

- GenAI can also help to streamline game testing and quality assurance, for example, by creating bot testers that play the game using multiple different styles to spot flaws.

From the world of gaming to something completely different: the legal sphere. Let's find out how GenAI can assist in the work of lawyers – and potentially make legal advice more affordable and accessible to anyone.

Notes

1. Generative AI will contribute to more than half of video game development within next 5 to 10 years, finds Bain & Company; *Bain & Company*; https://www.bain.com/about/media-center/press-releases/2023/generative-ai-will-contribute-to-more-than-half-of-video-game-development-within-next-5-to-10-years-finds-bain--company/
2. How generative AI is revolutionizing the gaming landscape; *Techwire Asia*; https://techwireasia.com/2023/06/gaming-ai-revolutionizing-generative-landscape-for-developers-and-gamers/
3. Ghostwriter AI tool; *Ubisoft*; https://news.ubisoft.com/en-us/article/7Cm07zbBGy4Xml6WgYi25d/the-convergence-of-ai-and-creativity-introducing-ghostwriter
4. Assassin's Creed Developer Says AI Is Unavoidable in Future AAA Titles; *Fandom Wire*; https://fandomwire.com/assassins-creed-developer-ai-unavoidable-aaa-titles/
5. Lords of the Fallen dev experimented with generative AI during development; *Creative Bloq*; https://www.creativebloq.com/features/lords-of-the-fallen-created-using-gen-AI
6. This Video Game Was Made Entirely Using ChatGPT 4 and AI Imaging Tools; *Augustman*; https://www.augustman.com/my/gear/gaming/chatgpt-game-like-angry-birds-made-using-ai-tools/
7. Generative AI Is Breathing New Life into Classic Computer Games; *Forbes*; https://www.forbes.com/sites/bernardmarr/2023/09/22/generative-ai-is-breathing-new-life-into-classic-computer-games/
8. Generative AI Will Change Game Dev Forever; *Analytics India*; https://analyticsindiamag.com/generative-ai-will-change-game-dev-forever/
9. New AI tool could be a game-changer for 3D animation; *Creative Bloq*; https://www.creativebloq.com/news/anything-world-animate-anything-ai
10. This generative AI model can transform the gaming industry; *Cryptopolitan*; https://www.cryptopolitan.com/generative-ai-can-transform-gaming-industry/
11. Auctoria uses generative AI to create video game models; *TechCrunch*; https://techcrunch.com/2023/09/20/auctoria-uses-generative-ai-to-create-video-game-models/
12. Microsoft is bringing AI characters to Xbox; *The Verge*; https://www.theverge.com/2023/11/6/23948454/microsoft-xbox-generative-ai-developer-tools-inworld-partnership

13. Google Cloud forms strategic partnerships with Vietnam's top game devs; *Data Center News*; https://datacenternews.asia/story/google-cloud-forms-strategic-partnerships-with-vietnam-s-top-game-devs

14. Generative AI Sparks Life into Virtual Characters with NVIDIA ACE for Games; *NVIDIA*; https://developer.nvidia.com/blog/generative-ai-sparks-life-into-virtual-characters-with-ace-for-games/

15. Xbox CFO on gaming content, business models, and generative AI; *MIT*; https://mitsloan.mit.edu/ideas-made-to-matter/xbox-cfo-gaming-content-business-models-and-generative-ai

16. Industry vets form Jam & Tea Studios to build multiplayer RPG using generative AI; *Game Developer*; https://www.gamedeveloper.com/business/industry-vets-form-jam-tea-studios-to-build-multiplayer-rpg-using-generative-ai

17. Pahdo Labs Raises $15M to Let Players Make Anime Games with AI Tools; *Decrypt*; https://decrypt.co/155895/pahdo-labs-raises-15-million-players-make-anime-games-ai-tools

13

THE LEGAL SPHERE: AI-ASSISTED DOCUMENT CREATION AND REVIEW

You may raise an eyebrow at AI being used in the legal sector. But now, thanks to the latest large language models, GenAI is much better at understanding the context and nuance of complex legal texts. As such, it is proving a useful tool in the work that lawyers do, particularly when it comes to reviewing legal documents and drafting text.

GenAI has so much promise in the legal sphere that two-thirds of large law firms in the United Kingdom say they are exploring the potential of GenAI (along with approximately a third of smaller law firms).[1] Meanwhile, in the United States, 67% of in-house counsels expect their outside law firms to use GenAI tools in their work.[2] Another report asked 379 lawyers and other legal professionals about ChatGPT – with more than 90% saying they'd used it.[3] We can therefore expect the workload of lawyers and other legal professionals to change as they increasingly find themselves working alongside AIs.

But that's not all. As we'll see in this chapter, GenAI can also help everyday people tackle legal questions and issues.

The Use of Generative AI in Law Firms

GenAI holds transformative potential for the legal profession. As GenAI systems become more sophisticated, they will facilitate the work of lawyers in several ways.

Potential GenAI uses

We'll get to specific examples later in the chapter. But for now, let's explore overarching use cases. GenAI can support legal professionals with the following:

- **Document drafting:** GenAI can assist in automating the creation of standard legal documents such as contracts, wills, and leases – tailoring them to the client's needs, according to specific parameters. GenAI can also be used to draft communications to clients.

- **Legal research:** Researching existing case law and legal precedents can be enormously time consuming. By providing a set of criteria or keywords, lawyers can use GenAI to generate summaries or briefs on relevant case law, statutes, and regulations.

- **Discovery and data review:** GenAI can assist in the discovery process by generating queries to identify relevant documents or data. It can also help in summarizing vast amounts of data.

- **Contract analysis:** AI can generate summaries, highlight key terms, and identify potential issues in lengthy contracts.

- **Predictive analysis:** AI may even be used to predict the outcomes of legal cases based on historical data, which can be useful for advising clients or strategizing for litigation.

- **Legal advice chatbots:** For firms looking to expand their service offering, GenAI can be used to create legal advice chatbots, which generate responses to common legal queries on websites or through messaging apps.

Such uses promise to enhance the efficiency of law firms, enabling lawyers to tackle more cases in a shorter amount of time, while also reducing the margin for human error. Furthermore, AI can help democratize legal services by making basic legal assistance more accessible and affordable to the general public through automated platforms – but we'll talk more about that later in the chapter.

Here comes the caveat. . .

With these exciting advancements come challenges. Lawyers will need to adapt their roles, acquiring new skills to effectively utilize and supervise these technologies – for example, making sure the GenAI is delivering accurate outputs. There are also ethical considerations, particularly when it comes to the potential for over-reliance on GenAI, which could lead to a lack of nuanced human judgment that is so crucial in legal situations. There may also be issues around data bias that could skew GenAI responses. (A major concern for any law firm, but especially in the case of, say, a legal chatbot delivering biased advice and answers.) And there's the risk that information given to a GenAI tool by a law firm could be used for AI training purposes and potentially disclosed to other users.

In essence, while generative AI presents an array of opportunities for the legal world, its integration must be approached thoughtfully to ensure that the essence and integrity of the legal profession remain intact. We'll talk more about GenAI implementation in Chapter 18.

Examples from the legal profession

Now let's look at some examples of how law firms and other legal organizations are beginning to harness GenAI.

You may have heard of the California Innocence Project (CIP), which was established by the California Western School of Law to assist in cases where there is compelling evidence that someone has been wrongly convicted. This is complex, labor-intensive work requiring many hours of reviewing case law and poring over evidence for each case. So CIP has turned to GenAI to help speed up the painstaking work of its lawyers – and hopefully, reduce the amount of time innocent people spend behind bars. CIP lawyers have deployed a GenAI platform called "CoCounsel," which was developed by AI company, Casetext, in partnership with OpenAI. CoCounsel, which has been specifically trained on legal documents, case law, and court proceedings, is capable of reviewing and summarizing legal documents, drafting documents, analyzing contracts, and preparing depositions. According to CIP lawyers, using the tool for essential but mundane tasks saves precious time – for example, reducing the time spent drafting a letter to a client from 15 minutes down to one minute – thereby allowing the team to spend their time on more impactful tasks that require human interaction.[4] Importantly, in order to reduce the potential for bias and "hallucinations" (i.e., fabricated responses), CoCounsel was beta-tested by 400 lawyers from boutique and multinational firms – and Casetext says the sensitive information entered into the system isn't stored or fed back into the platform for training.[5]

Dentons, one of the world's largest global law firms, is launching its own proprietary ChatGPT-style tool called "fleetAI," based on the GPT-4 large language model. Dentons says the tool will enable its lawyers to "conduct legal research, generate legal content, and identify relevant legal arguments."[6] Again, Dentons says all data uploaded won't be used to train the model, can't be accessed by anyone outside of the firm, and is deleted after 30 days. Plus, any Dentons lawyers using the tool are required to independently verify and validate all outputs, and disclose to clients that they have interacted with the AI tool as part of their work.

As you might expect, there is a plethora of GenAI-powered tools and services springing up to serve legal firms. As an example, legal research and software company LexisNexis is embracing GenAI, building the technology into its Lexis+ AI platform – which is designed to help lawyers conduct case research, and draft summaries, legal documents, and communications.[7] With a simple interface that acts rather like ChatGPT (indeed, the platform is built on OpenAI's GPT language model, among other models), the GenAI responds to prompts in seconds. It also provides citations for its responses. And as with Casetext's CoCounsel platform, Lexis+ AI is focused on private interactions, to ensure that sensitive information won't be shared with other users.

Another GenAI service designed for the legal profession comes from AI start-up Harvey, which builds custom large language models for law firms. Among the firms partnering with Harvey are major London law firm Macfarlanes and multinational firm Allen & Overy.[8] Lawyers can use Harvey for conducting research, analyzing documents, summarizing texts, and creating draft communications (for human lawyers to review).

Information specialist Thomson Reuters is also building GenAI into its legal offerings, including the Westlaw legal research platform and Practical Law, which provides how-to guides, templates, and checklists.[9] GenAI means lawyers and legal researchers can engage with these platforms in a more intuitive, conversational way and get natural language answers to their questions. Thomson Reuters also offers GenAI-powered contract review software called "Document Intelligence," which it says can cut the amount of time spent searching for information in contracts by 50%.[10]

Helping Everyday People Digest Legal Documents and More

Clearly GenAI can help cut the workload of lawyers, which in itself may help to make legal advice more affordable and accessible for people. But, we will also see new tools become available that allow lay people to directly interact with GenAI legal tools. This can prove useful in several ways, such as digesting lengthy contracts and legal letters, drafting contracts, and even accessing basic legal advice. It's early days in this field, but some interesting tools are beginning to emerge that promise to democratize legal advice.

One example is called "Legal Robot," which is designed to automatically translate "legalese" into everyday language that anyone can understand. So a lay person faced with a complex contract or other legal document can get a plain-English translation and properly understand what they're reading or signing. (Legal Robot also says its tool can be used by lawyers to ensure their documents are easy for anyone to understand, but whether lawyers actually *want* their documents to be easily understood is another matter!)

Another example comes from AI Lawyer, which offers 24/7 expert legal help and information – so, you can, in theory, ask any legal question and get a response. You can also use the tool to draft contracts without having to hire a lawyer. Plus, it can be used to simplify or summarize legal text.

It's really exciting seeing tools emerge to help people access legal support without the huge bills that can come with engaging a law firm. Who knows, maybe developments like this will further encourage legal firms to embrace GenAI in order to provide a more streamlined, affordable service to the public.

Key Takeaways

In this chapter, we've learned that GenAI is impacting the legal sector in two main ways:

- Legal firms are embracing GenAI to help lawyers work in a more efficient way. In particular, GenAI can be used to review legal documents and cases, analyze contracts, draft documents, prepare depositions, and write communications. Several GenAI platforms and tools are emerging to serve the legal profession.

- GenAI can also help to make legal advice more accessible to everyday people, thanks to new tools that offer simple legal advice, and help with translating complex legal jargon into everyday language. Such tools can even help people draw up contracts without having to hire a lawyer.

Now let's turn to a topic that spans many sectors and industries: design and innovation. In the next chapter, we'll see how GenAI is helping to enhance the research and design process in everything from fashion and jewelry to potentially life-saving drugs.

Notes

1. Two-thirds of large law firms researching generative AI; *Legal Futures*; https://www.legalfutures.co.uk/latest-news/two-thirds-of-large-law-firms-researching-generative-ai
2. 60% of in-house counsel expect law firms to use generative AI; *Legal Dive*; https://www.legaldive.com/news/law-firms-generative-ai-use-cases-lexisnexis-ai-survey/691913/
3. Generative AI: a legal revolution is coming – eventually; *FT*; https://www.ft.com/content/0f36eb4e-b90f-4ffe-befc-daf01829c182

4. How Generative AI Is Used to Fight Miscarriages of Justice at the California Innocence Project; *Forbes*; https://www.forbes.com/sites/bernardmarr/2023/10/06/how-generative-ai-is-used-to-fight-miscarriages-of-justice-at-the-california-innocence-project/
5. Casetext Unveils CoCounsel, the Groundbreaking AI Legal Assistant Powered by OpenAI Technology; *PR Newswire*; https://www.prnewswire.com/news-releases/casetext-unveils-cocounsel-the-groundbreaking-ai-legal-assistant-powered-by-openai-technology-301759255.html
6. Dentons to launch client secure version of ChatGPT; *Dentons*; https://www.dentons.com/en/about-dentons/news-events-and-awards/news/2023/august/dentons-to-launch-client-secure-version-of-chatgpt
7. LexisNexis announces new generative artificial intelligence platform; *ABA Journal*; https://www.abajournal.com/web/article/lexisnexis-announces-new-generative-ai-platform-lexis-ai
8. UK law firm is latest to partner with legal AI startup Harvey; *Reuters*; https://www.reuters.com/legal/transactional/uk-law-firm-is-latest-partner-with-legal-ai-startup-harvey-2023-09-21/
9. AI @ Thomson Reuters; *Thomson Reuters*; https://www.thomsonreuters.com/en/artificial-intelligence.html
10. Document Intelligence; *Thomson Reuters*; https://legal.thomsonreuters.com/en/products/document-intelligence

14

CRAFTING TOMORROW: AI IN DESIGN AND DEVELOPMENT

GenAI is poised to revolutionize the design, research, and product development processes by injecting advanced computational power and creativity into these traditionally human-centric domains. Drug development is a super-interesting and leading-edge application of GenAI, so this chapter will kick off with a look at how GenAI will shape the drug therapies of the future. We'll then explore the concept of generative design, and see how GenAI can help design all manner of products. And we'll finish up with a brief look at digital twins and academic research. There's a lot to cover in this chapter, so let's get started.

Generative AI in Drug Discovery

For me, drug discovery is an area that perfectly demonstrates the transformative power of GenAI. The process of bringing a new drug to market is long and eye-wateringly expensive. It can take up to 15 years from starting the discovery process to the point at which a drug is approved for sale – and 9 out of 10 drugs that enter clinical trials never make it to the approval stage. No wonder the cost of bringing a new drug to market can reach US$2.5 billion, once you account for the cost of both successful and failed programs.[1] GenAI may help to speed up the drug discovery phase, thereby helping to get drugs to the clinical trial phase more quickly (and with less money spent).

How GenAI is accelerating the search for new drugs

To get an overview of GenAI's role in drug discovery, I spoke with Kimberly Powell, VP and general manager of healthcare at NVIDIA.[2] Powell's team works with industry leaders, academics, pharma companies, and tech bio companies to apply AI to the drug discovery process. Essentially, they exist to make AI technology accessible across the ecosystem. So if anyone knows how GenAI could potentially transform the search for new drug therapies, it's Powell.

As Powell explained it to me, GenAI excels at bringing the world's knowledge together in one place. If we think of ChatGPT, for instance, it was trained on everything available on the internet, including books and articles. This natural language prowess can be applied to the R&D phase of drug discovery by trawling through research papers and electronic health record data to discover, for example, how existing drugs are affecting people.

But what gets the team at NVIDIA really excited is the potential to apply GenAI to other languages related to drug development: the languages of biology and chemistry. Think of human DNA as a sequence of four letters (A, T, C, and G) strung together into a 3-billion-letter-long sentence. That's a language of its own. We also have proteins, which form the building blocks of biology. Proteins have their own alphabet – 20 letters for amino acids, strung together in lengths of tens of thousands, or even hundreds of thousands. Chemicals, too, have a language known as "SMILES" (Simplified Molecular Input Line Entry System) – characters that, together, define the structures of chemistry.

As Powell puts it, "We can now take these languages . . . and we can apply the method of generative AI and GPT-type methods . . . Once we do that, the language models can really help us understand a lot more about biology that maybe we haven't been able to observe in the real world." This means, not only can we discover new drugs with GenAI, we can also do it with less time and less cost. And in the process, Powell's hope is we can improve that 90% failure rate I mentioned earlier.

But how exactly does GenAI apply to the drug discovery process? Powell described the drug discovery process as having three phases:

The first phase is about establishing the target (disease or condition) that they want to go after with a new drug. In this phase, GenAI can be used to study genomics, understand the gene that's causing the disease, or understand whatever is happening in the body. Basically, the aim is to understand the target better. In Chapter 11 we saw how one GenAI model was able to predict variants of the COVID-19 virus. Another example comes from the GenSLMs model, developed by researchers from NVIDIA, Argonne National Laboratory, the University of Chicago, and more. The model was trained on COVID-19 genome data from the first year of the pandemic, and from that it successfully generated sequences that closely matched the Eris and Pirola variants from 2023.[3] In other words, it was able to accurately predict how the virus would later mutate. This sort of modeling could potentially inform drug discovery in future, and would also help governments track and manage infectious diseases.

The second phase of drug discovery is about coming up with leads, i.e., chemicals or proteins that could be used to target that disease. And this is where the scale of the problem becomes truly mind-boggling. Because there are more than 10^{60} chemicals and 10^{160} proteins that could potentially be made to target a disease. No wonder drug discovery is often described as searching for a needle in a haystack! GenAI can sift through these potential chemicals and proteins and start generating ideas – potentially even inventing new chemicals and proteins with the desired structure and function to target the disease in question. This creates a tremendous number of new leads to explore, which is really exciting.

And the third phase is about optimization. Say the GenAI model has generated one billion compounds that could potentially be effective; the drug company then needs to test those against the target. GenAI can assist with this screening process at a scale and speed that's never been seen before. In one example, NVIDIA worked on a project with Recursion Pharmaceuticals to screen more than 2.8 quadrillion small-molecule-target pairs (using Recursion's matchmaker GenAI algorithm running on NVIDIAs supercomputing technology). Within a week, they were able to complete screening that would have taken 100 000 years with traditional methods.[4]

In short, then, GenAI can help pharma companies explore potential new drugs with unprecedented scale, speed, and accuracy – which, in turn, allows them to proceed to clinical trials more quickly. As an example of this, Insilico Medicine used GenAI in the drug discovery process to develop a drug to treat idiopathic pulmonary fibrosis. Using traditional methods, the process would have cost more than US$400 million and taken up to six years. But with GenAI, NVIDIA says Insilico accomplished the task in one-tenth of the cost and one-third of the time, proceeding to clinical trials in just two and a half years.[5] (Incidentally, Insilico has also made the news for developing a new AI-generated COVID drug that has entered clinical trials, and is reported to be effective against all variants.)[6]

Imagine that sort of acceleration across the entire pharma industry and you can see how GenAI can absolutely transform this aspect of healthcare.

Enabling truly personalized medicine

Looking further ahead, Powell says GenAI will also help to realize truly personalized medicine. GenAI can be used to analyze patient genetic and health data to suggest personalized drug treatments based on the individual's unique profile. This approach might be particularly beneficial in cancer therapy, where the genetic makeup of tumors can vary widely.

As Powell predicts, "This true opportunity of personalized medicine will *only* be realized through these generative methods. Because you have to associate so much information: my history, my DNA, what you've discovered about whatever disease state I have . . . it's completely unique to me. And only through these methods and being able to synthesize that level of information will we get there. And once you understand my issue, then you can have a very fast-track discovery process so that you can treat me, not in the five years it takes to discover a drug, but maybe in five weeks."

Other examples from the world of medicine

Of course, NVIDIA isn't the only provider working to aid drug discovery. Pharma company Merck has developed a GenAI-powered drug discovery platform called "Addison," which is designed to help drug designers explore that vast chemical landscape I mentioned and come up with drug candidates much more quickly.

As Merck explains, there are an estimated 166 billion molecules in the chemical universe database GDB-17, yet even libraries that vast "barely scratch the surface of all possible structures."[7] Which is where a platform like Addison can add tremendous value – by helping researchers "explore unbounded chemical space and generate ideas for entirely new compounds."

In another example, GenAI was used by British biotech company Etcembly to design a cutting-edge immunotherapy drug for cancer. Called "ETC-101," the new drug is a type of T-cell engager (T-cells being a type of white blood cell). These types of drugs basically harness the power of T-cell receptors (TCRs), which recognize foreign antigens in the body, to identify and destroy cancer cells. The trouble is, they can also recognize targets in healthy cells. Etcembly's solution to this is to engineer TCRs that are more sensitive and selective – so they can effectively target cancer cells, with minimal side effects.

To do this, Etcembly deployed GenAI to decode the "language" of TCRs and "rewrite" the genetic code of the TCR to make it more potent. The resulting drug, ETC-101, has been designed to target PRAME, a protein associated with many cancers known for their low survival rates. The drug reportedly binds to PRAME with a millionfold greater affinity than natural TCRs (again, without targeting health cells), and was developed in 11 months, as opposed to the two-year timeframe typical for TCR discovery.[8] The drug may enter clinical trials as early as 2025.

Elsewhere, Dell has teamed up with the University of Limerick to create an AI platform for cancer diagnostics and predictive research. The goal is to use AI to speed up cancer biomarker testing and enhance the treatment of patients with B-cell lymphoma.[9]

GenAI may also play a role in artificial DNA synthesis (gene synthesis), which allows virtually any DNA sequence to be generated in a laboratory setting. Again, if we think of DNA as a language, it makes sense that GenAI can help researchers "decode" and "rewrite" this language. Given that the majority of cancers are caused by sporadic mutations of genes, as opposed to genes that we're born with, it's clear that gene synthesis can help us understand more about, and better treat, cancer. The human genome is enormously complex and the array of genetic factors that contribute to health and disease is vast. This poses a problem for researchers looking to understand disease. But technology – specifically GenAI – can help.

Google DeepMind is another tech company looking to support health and drug research. It has created a new AI tool that classifies the effects of 71 million "missense" mutations – genetic mutations that result in changes in a DNA sequence. These mutations can be benign or they can be pathogenic, and the average person carries more than 9000 missense variants. Understanding these millions of variants – particularly whether they are benign or disease-causing – is a complicated, resource-heavy task. According to DeepMind, only 0.1% of all 71 million possible variants have been classified as pathogenic or benign.[10] DeepMind's AlphaMissense platform has been developed to help accelerate classification.

All of this is super-exciting to me. But could it also pose a threat to humanity? After all, if you can use AI to design new drugs, the other end of the spectrum is using GenAI to design the most poisonous drugs or identify new toxins that are dangerous to humans. (Case in point: AI was able to come up with 40 000 potential new chemical weapons in just six hours!)[11] In the wrong hands, this technology is terrifying. But the rewards of being able to better understand and target diseases, and increase health spans of people around the world, are worth striving for.

Designing Anything with Generative AI and Generative Design

The field of *generative design* uses AI to conceptualize myriad design possibilities that adhere to specific constraints and performance parameters, offering a breadth of optimized solutions that would be nearly impossible for humans to create manually. So, designers enter parameters such as what materials should be used, the size and weight of the desired product, what manufacturing methods will be used, and how much it should cost, and then the generative design algorithms cough up designs. This transformative approach not only accelerates the ideation phase but also enhances innovation, allowing designers and engineers to explore a wider range of design options, and then pick and choose the best ones. And that applies to designing anything – products, buildings, potential solutions for climate change, anything at all.

Generative design software has been around for a few years, but now, we're beginning to see generative design being combined with GenAI to make the process of designing with AI more intelligent and more intuitive. Indeed, the rise of GenAI means you won't necessarily need to be a professional designer or an expert in design software to design amazing products in future. You'll be able to tell a GenAI interface what you want to achieve and it will come up with various designs for you.

How GenAI will enhance generative design

To learn how GenAI is transforming the design process, I spoke with Mike Haley, head of research at Autodesk. Autodesk has a huge focus on cutting-edge technologies – so much so that they were talking about generative design as early as 2009.

Haley says that across all sorts of industries, Autodesk clients are trying to design more complex things, with more complex requirements and constraints, while at the same time wanting to design more efficiently and cheaply. There's a lot of pressure on the design process, basically, which is why generative design is so valuable – it helps designers come up with complex designs in a more efficient, cost-effective way.

So how can GenAI make generative design even better? It turns out, generative design tools can actually be quite difficult to use because, to get the best out of generative design software, you have to be able to specify what you want in a very exacting way. Trouble is, most designers don't necessarily know all the constraints right at the beginning of a design project. Often, constraints and requirements will emerge during the design process. Plus, generative design solutions can be expensive because there's a lot of computational power involved.

GenAI can help to solve these issues. GenAI is fast, and it's super-easy and intuitive to use because you can just talk to the system or type in what you want. So, combining GenAI with generative design gives professional designers (and even non-professional designers) the best of both worlds. With a generative design system, you get incredible precision, and with GenAI you get a system that's much easier to use. This is what Autodesk is particularly excited about – combining the two technologies to make generative design more accessible to more people, and to enhance the creativity of Autodesk customers.

Haley's Autodesk research lab works with forward-thinking customers to come up with new design solutions. He gave an example of working with one client, a large construction company, who had concerns about how long it took to do the early conceptual designs for skyscrapers. The customer found this early explorative process took months, and they wanted to accelerate the process for future buildings. By applying GenAI to this initial conceptual design process, they were able to shrink the process from multiple months down to a week. Clearly, GenAI's ability to quickly synthesize and iterate on design concepts helps designers explore a larger landscape of potential solutions in a much shorter time period – leading to more innovative and creative outcomes. Imagine such technology being applied across the design process for pretty much everything – houses, products, cars, etc. – and you can see how GenAI can add serious value to the design process.

(As an aside, Autodesk's 60 000-square-foot Toronto offices, named "Autodesk Technology Centre," was one of the first AI-designed offices of its scale. The designers consulted with Autodesk employees about their preferences for factors like daylight, views, and proximity to other desks, and those parameters were fed into the AI design tool.[12])

What's more, the combination of GenAI, generative design *and* 3D printing may prove to be particularly impactful. Generative design and GenAI can be used to better understand what can be done with 3D printing, since the range and complexity of shapes that can be created with 3D printing is so vast. Increasingly, this winning combination will be used to create new components and products that are cheaper, lighter, and sturdier, thereby improving the overall quality of many products, from cars and aircraft to prefabricated houses and structures.

When I asked Haley about the future of GenAI and design, he was passionate about the idea of design software (indeed, all software) becoming much easier to use, because GenAI allows us to express ourselves however we want – by speaking, typing, sketching, whatever. "The nature of user interfaces of all software, whether it's a word processor or a complex building design product, are going to fundamentally change in the next five years . . . all of a sudden, computers have this ability to interpret us."

He also predicts that design software is going to become more proactive, interjecting with helpful suggestions based on what it knows the user wants to design, and what the system has learned from past data. "We're going to see, emerging in the design process, these tools that are not just overwhelming you with the volume of data but are coming to say, 'Hey, I notice you're designing this. Here's something you may want to know that I've noticed in all the data that may be relevant to what you're designing now.' So it helps you focus your attention."

The business argument for GenAI-powered design (and manufacturing)

While many designers are already accustomed to designing with AI, it's clear that GenAI is going to further aid and improve the design process. It will give designers the ability to generate designs more quickly, and work with AI in a more intuitive way. It can be used to model how materials or products will perform, without always having to build physical prototypes. It can even be used to incorporate customer feedback data or user data from existing products (or buildings) into future designs. So, the whole design phase becomes less of a trial-and-error process, basically; which clearly reduces the time and resources involved. Plus, it can help to create better products. As an example, with Autodesk's help, General Motors was able to design a new car component that was 40% lighter and 20% stronger than its predecessor.[13]

All this will bring significant advantages to organizations, not least the ability to quickly innovate, explore a wide range of creative options in a shorter time period, accelerate the process of iterating and refining prototypes, and bring new (better) products to market, faster. Plus, GenAI opens up a whole new world of product personalization, especially when combined with 3D printing.

GenAI can also be used as part of intellectual property processes. For example, it can analyze whether patents are necessary in order to comply with a particular product standard. It can analyze existing patent text, research papers, and market trends to help companies target their R&D efforts. And it can analyze vast amounts of data online to monitor for potential trademark infringements.

We can also expect GenAI to become integrated into the manufacturing process, which is why Microsoft and Siemens have partnered on a new GenAI assistant designed specifically for manufacturing.[14] The companies say the Siemens Industrial Copilot tool will improve human-machine collaboration, thereby increasing productivity and speeding up manufacturing tasks. As an example, the companies say tasks such as debugging automation codes and running simulations can be done in mere minutes using the GenAI assistant. Microsoft and Siemens have plans to develop GenAI co-pilot tools for a wide range of industries beyond manufacturing, including transportation and healthcare.

Examples from jewelry and fashion

Jewelry designers are already harnessing AI for their designs, enabling them to push the boundaries of new designs, accelerate prototyping, and streamline the design process. Jewelry companies that have used AI as a co-creator include high-end Parisian jeweler Boucheron, and Vancouver-based private jeweler Volund Jewelry.[15] Combined with 3D printing, AI-aided design allows jewelers to quickly create prototypes and see how their designs look in the real world (since printing even an elaborate prototype can be done in hours, versus the weeks it might take to hand-craft a wax mold). Tiffany & Company is one major jewelry designer that has used both AI-enhanced design and 3D printing to create prototypes.[16]

In the future, GenAI could even enable customers to design their own bespoke jewelry. Using GenAI tools, customers could create their own unique designs according to their preferred materials, design preferences, and cost, and then generate images to see how the design would look on themselves before they order. And with 3D printing – which can be used to print all sorts of materials, including plastic, metals, concrete, and even chocolate – one-of-a-kind products could be manufactured without having to worry about economies of scale.

Big-name fashion and sports brands are also routinely using AI to augment their design process, including Nike.[17] It makes sense that fashion designers can benefit hugely from AI-enhanced design, since it enables them to originate multiple new designs more quickly.

In one example, fashion technology company, Fashable, has partnered with Microsoft to bring GenAI to the clothing design process. Fashion is one industry with particularly high expectations of quick turnarounds and endless new styles – driven especially by "fast fashion." But instead of adding to the problem of the "throwaway culture," Fashable believes GenAI can help designers meet demand while reducing waste. How? In part by allowing designers to innovate multiple new designs without wasting fabric, but also by using AI to remove much of the guesswork that goes into creating new clothing. After all, trends are unpredictable and it's not obvious whether inventory will sell. So Fashable uses AI to analyze data from multiple sources, including social media and retail sites, to better understand trends. Designs can be augmented in real time to take account of trends, and the resulting images can be shared to social media for A/B testing with consumers. So designers can better understand demand before going into production. According to Fashable, instead of taking months to get a new collection from design to store, it can now be done in minutes – by designing quickly and marketing directly to customers, without wasting fabric.[18]

Examples from the automotive industry

The automotive industry has been using AI to help design cars and components for years. But GenAI can help to further streamline and improve the design process in several ways. For example, GenAI can be used to generate new design concepts and virtual prototypes. The process of moving from early concept ideas and sketches, through to the development of full-sized clay prototypes, can take many months – but GenAI can help to speed up the early parts of this process by instantly translating 2D sketches into lifelike 3D virtual models, enabling designers to explore a wide range of options in less time. Designers can also use text prompts such as "rugged" or "sleek" to generate design ideas. Plus, for interiors, GenAI can be used to generate realistic visuals of textures based on simple descriptions.

Toyota's Research Institute has been experimenting with using GenAI to speed up vehicle design. It has developed a new technique that allows designers to integrate initial design sketches and engineering constraints (around performance, safety, and usability) into GenAI tools early in the creative process. According to Toyota, this approach could "reduce the number of iterations needed to reconcile design and engineering considerations."[19] In other words, this helps designers come up with designs according to their creative vision (e.g., for a rugged, SUV-type vehicle), while optimizing for the many complex engineering and safety considerations that are essential.

Speaking of safety, GenAI can also be used to detect and prevent defects in vehicles, and generate realistic simulations of accidents, which can be used to train autonomous vehicles and identify potential safety hazards in existing vehicles.

GenAI is even being used to help battery development for electric vehicles (EVs). This is the focus of start-up Aionics, which is using GenAI to speed up EV battery research. It's like the drug discovery process I talked about earlier in the chapter – there are billions of procurable molecules that could be combined to make electrolyte materials in batteries, and hence lots of potential combinations to explore! Find the optimal combination, and you have an EV battery that can charge faster and be more efficient; but *finding* that optimal combination can take years (and may involve a lot of trial and error). Aionics is using GenAI to accelerate discovery and even create new molecules designed for certain applications.[20]

The Impact of Generative AI on Digital Twins

A digital twin is a digital copy of a real-world physical asset (such as a product, process, or system) that can be used to run virtual simulations. The idea behind a digital twin is to let us see what might happen if we were to make certain adjustments in real life. The adjustments can be trialed on the digital twin without having to test potentially expensive changes on the real-world counterpart.

Digital twins have been a trending technology for a few years now, used in industries as diverse as manufacturing (e.g., to optimize machine performance) and Formula 1 (to test different car setups). Creating and using digital twins has, until now, been a pretty technical process. But with GenAI, in theory, you can ask a GenAI tool to create the digital twin for you, making it so much easier for organizations to harness digital twin technology and create simulations of real-world products, objects, and systems. So, for example, you'll be able to create a digital twin of your product to see how it performs under many different circumstances without having to conduct expensive and time-consuming tests on the physical product.

Importantly, you will be able to interact with simulations and digital twins using natural language technology. For example, you could ask it, "now test the product in temperatures below zero," or whatever you like. And in the case of a digital twin of an entire factory floor – with the digital twin reflecting real-world performance – a supervisor could simply ask the system, "Hey, what's happening on the floor today?" or "What are the top three predictive maintenance issues that need our attention today?" The supervisor could oversee their operations via a real-time 3D computer representation. (The same idea applies to all sorts of premises or operations – factories, retail premises, sports stadiums, energy grids, you name it.) It's yet another example of how GenAI promises to make technology more accessible.

Aiding Academic Research

Before we close out this chapter, I wanted to briefly mention academic research as another area where GenAI can add enormous value. In fact, new tools based on large language models are already emerging to aid academic research – for example, by scanning through thousands of research articles for information and providing summaries.

One example comes from a tool called "Consensus," which provides answers to yes/no questions based on the consensus of the academic community. So you can ask a question like, "Is immigration good for the economy?" and it will reply with the academic consensus (in this case, studies show that immigration is generally an economic benefit). It will also provide a citation list and summaries of the academic articles used in its analysis. So far, Consensus focuses on six topics: economics, sleep, social policy, medicine, mental health, and health supplements.

Another tool, called "Elicit," can find relevant academic papers for you based on a specific question you have. It will then summarize the key information from those papers. It's described as an "AI research assistant." Scite does a similar thing, unearthing relevant academic papers.

It's easy to see how GenAI could transform academic study and research in future, and even allow non-academics to access academic information in a more user-friendly way.

Key Takeaways

In this chapter, we've learned:

- GenAI will shape the drug therapies of the future by accelerating the drug discovery process and helping to bring drugs to clinical trials much faster – potentially years faster.

- In design, generative design (which uses AI to optimize the design process) has been around for a few years, but the addition of GenAI interfaces promises to improve AI-aided design even further. GenAI can, among other things, help designers work with complex generative design tools more easily, generate endless potential designs according to parameters and criteria, simulate products, and accelerate the product development lifecycle. This can apply to all sorts of fields, from jewelry to automotive design, to building design.

- Related to this, GenAI will also enable companies to create digital twins more easily for simulations of real-world products, objects, and systems – using natural language prompts.

- And finally, GenAI is also making academic research more accessible. New tools are emerging to help answer questions based on the consensus of the academic community, and provide easy-to-digest summaries of research papers.

Clearly GenAI is going to positively disrupt the fields of design, development, and manufacturing. But now let's turn to another sector that's set to be transformed by GenAI –banking and finance.

Notes

1. AI's potential to accelerate drug discovery needs a reality check; *Nature*; https://www.nature.com/articles/d41586-023-03172-6
2. How Generative AI Is Revolutionizing Healthcare & Drug Discovery; *Bernard Marr*, YouTube; https://www.youtube.com/watch?v=dIOBS-T0Z-g
3. Gen AI for the Genome: LLM Predicts Characteristics of COVID Variants; *NVIDIA*; https://blogs.nvidia.com/blog/generative-ai-covid-genome-sequences/
4. Recursion Bridges the Protein and Chemical Space with Massive Protein-Ligand Interaction Predictions Spanning 36 Billion Compounds; *Recursion*; https://ir.recursion.com/news-releases/news-release-details/recursion-bridges-protein-and-chemical-space-massive-protein
5. Quicker Cures: How Insilico Medicine Uses Generative AI to Accelerate Drug Discovery; *NVIDIA*; https://blogs.nvidia.com/blog/insilico-medicine-uses-generative-ai-to-accelerate-drug-discovery/
6. New AI-generated COVID drug enters Phase I clinical trials: 'Effective against all variants'; *Fox News*; https://www.foxnews.com/health/new-ai-generated-covid-drug-enters-phase-i-clinical-trials-effective-variants
7. Aiddison: Harnessing generative ai to revolutionize drug discoveries; *Merck*; https://www.merckgroup.com/en/research/science-space/envisioning-tomorrow/future-of-scientific-work/aiddison.html
8. Gen AI may power the next generation of immunotherapies; *Omnia Health*; https://insights.omnia-health.com/technology/gen-ai-may-power-next-generation-immunotherapies
9. Dell partners with the University of Limerick to develop an AI platform for cancer research; *Windows Central*; https://www.windowscentral.com/hardware/dell/dell-university-of-limerick-ai-for-cancer-research

10. Google DeepMind Introduces a New AI Tool that Classifies the Effects of 71 Million 'Missense" Mutations; *Market Tech Post*; https://www.marktechpost .com/2023/09/23/google-deepmind-introduces-a-new-ai-tool-that-classifies-the-effects-of-71-million-missense-mutations/

11. AI suggested 40,000 new possible chemical weapons in just six hours; *The Verge*; https://www.theverge.com/2022/3/17/22983197/ai-new-possible-chemical-weapons-generative-models-vx

12. 4 examples of generative design in action; *Archistar*; https://www.archistar.ai/ blog/4-examples-of-generative-design-in-action/

13. Autodesk's Generative Design: Optimizing Design Through AI; *Direct Industry*; https://emag.directindustry.com/2023/03/15/autodesks-generative-design-optimizing-design-through-ai/

14. Microsoft and Siemens Team Up to Introduce a GenAI Assistant for Manufacturing; *Investopedia*; https://www.investopedia.com/microsoft-and-siemens-team-up-to-introduce-a-genai-assistant-for-manufacturing-8384823

15. Technology Could Turn You into a Tiffany; *NY Times*; https://www.nytimes .com/2021/04/23/fashion/jewelry-technology-augmented-reality.html

16. Technology Could Turn You into a Tiffany; *NY Times*; https://www.nytimes .com/2021/04/23/fashion/jewelry-technology-augmented-reality.html

17. How Nike used algorithms to help design its latest running shoe; *Wired*; https:// www.wired.co.uk/article/nike-epic-react-flyknit-price-new-shoe

18. Fashable reimagines the future of fashion design with Azure Machine Learning and Pytorch; *Microsoft*; https://customers.microsoft.com/en-us/ story/1558909662014453187-fashable-retail-azure

19. Toyota's Research Institute develops new AI technique with potential to help speed up vehicle design; *Toyota*; https://media.toyota.co.uk/toyota-research-institute-develops-new-ai-technique-with-potential-to-help-speed-up-vehicle-design/

20. How generative AI is creeping into EV battery development; *TechCrunch*; https:// techcrunch.com/2023/10/14/how-generative-ai-is-creeping-into-ev-battery-development

15
BANKING AND FINANCIAL SERVICES: AI AS A DISRUPTIVE FORCE

AI has always been a game-changer in finance, but GenAI will take this to a whole new level. GenAI's ability to create content, analyze data, simulate scenarios, and optimize processes will enable financial institutions to make more informed decisions, innovate in product design, improve the services delivered to customers, enhance risk management practices, and maintain compliance more efficiently. As such, GenAI will profoundly change the landscape of banking operations.

As we'll see in this chapter, banks and other financial institutions are already starting to implement GenAI. It's not something they're shying away from. In fact, I think GenAI will end up bringing one of the biggest shakeups the financial world has seen – for example, by democratizing financial advice for everyone. According to McKinsey, GenAI could add between US$200 and US$340 billion in value for banks *per year* (9–15% of operating profits).[1] Safe to say, any bank that doesn't embrace GenAI, risks being left behind.

Generative AI Uses in Banking and Financial Services

So how exactly can banks and financial services companies use GenAI? Let's explore the main use cases from this industry.

General use cases and possibilities

We'll get to real-world examples later in the chapter, but for now let's explore some overarching uses for GenAI.

One of the obvious uses is in **customer services** – such as banking chatbots that can answer questions and respond to complaints 24/7. GenAI can also help to onboard new customers in a more efficient way, for example, by using a tool like ChatGPT to help customers fill out forms correctly and answer their questions about switching banks. We talked about customer service a lot in Chapter 8, so do circle back there if you want a refresh, but the key takeaway in relation to banking is this: GenAI will give rise to a new era of *conversational banking* that simulates human conversations. More like the way we used to do banking.

Just as with other sectors, **personalization** is a major use case in banking, such as personalized tools and advice, designed to help customers use their money more wisely. GenAI can deliver in-depth insights into customer behavior and preferences, and this will help banks create new products and services that are more thoughtful and customized. By simulating how different product and service features meet the needs of individual customers or market segments, GenAI can help banks create highly tailored products and additional services that better serve their customers. A good example comes from Square financial services company, which we'll look at later in the chapter (Hint: they're using GenAI to help business customers generate content for their business).

Another major use case is **automating** many of the behind-the-scenes processes and operations in financial institutions, such as conducting financial analysis and writing reports. This may include:

- **Credit decisioning:** GenAI can produce more nuanced credit models that consider a plethora of variables, including unconventional data sources that might be predictive of creditworthiness. By generating complex behavioral profiles, these models could potentially reveal insights that lead to safer (and more equitable) lending.

- **Denial explanations:** As well as aiding the credit decision process, GenAI can be used to generate user-friendly explanations of why a certain decision was made. Not only does this help customers with future applications; it builds trust in AI decision-making.

- **Fraud detection frameworks:** GenAI can be employed to simulate patterns of fraudulent behavior, which can train fraud detection systems to recognize and block sophisticated scams and security breaches before they happen. And later in the chapter, we'll see how GenAI is helping banks and payment providers search communications for potential scams.

- **Payment processing systems:** As well as helping to detect fraud, GenAI can optimize payment processing systems in other ways, for example, optimizing cross-border payments.

- **Financial modeling and scenario analysis:** GenAI can create sophisticated financial models that simulate various economic and market conditions to predict their effects on investment portfolios, asset values, or institutional risk exposure. Banks can use these models to prepare for a range of future scenarios, making their operations more resilient to shocks and stresses.

- **Quantitative trading:** GenAI algorithms can create numerous strategies and test them against historical and simulated future market data. They can generate predictive models that improve over time, potentially offering higher returns or lower risk on investment strategies.

- **Asset and portfolio management:** GenAI could significantly enhance asset management by simulating the performance of different asset combinations under a range of market scenarios, thus generating optimized portfolios based on predicted future performance.

- **Regulatory compliance:** GenAI can be instrumental in developing compliance systems that continuously learn and adapt. It can generate and test thousands of compliance scenarios to ensure that new financial products or services meet stringent regulatory standards across different jurisdictions.

- **Know Your Customer (KYC) and Anti-Money Laundering (AML):** These processes are critical for banks to mitigate financial crime and maintain regulatory compliance. GenAI can assist in automating these processes by analyzing large amounts of customer data, including personal data and transaction history, and identifying potential compliance issues.

- **Operational risk management:** By simulating various operational failure scenarios, GenAI can help in forecasting and mitigating potential operational risks, leading to more robust risk management practices.

- **Legacy software maintenance:** Did you know that many banks still rely on extremely outdated software written in legacy programming languages like COBOL (which is a 60-year-old programming language)? Not many developers are fluent in these old languages, which can make maintenance an issue. But GenAI can easily be trained to understand these legacy programming languages and maintain older software.

Supporting accountants and internal accounting functions

GenAI can also play a vital role in aiding accountancy firms and internal accounting functions within organizations. While this won't be the main focus of this chapter, I wanted to highlight that GenAI can help accounting teams augment accounting and finance processes, such as:

- Creating and summarizing reports

- Forecasting financials

- Analyzing data

- Mitigating risks

- Delivering user-friendly recommendations for business leaders

- Generating simulations of various scenarios to aid decision-making

- Automating everyday processes, such as generating invoices

As with other sectors, we can expect to see more AI tools emerge to support accounting professionals in their work – for example, by helping them create more forward-looking insights that drive business performance.

The Risks of Generative AI

GenAI will bring major changes to the financial sector. It will also bring new risks. A report by the International Monetary Fund cites four main areas of risk for the financial services industry:[2]

- **Inherent technology risk:** This includes factors like data privacy (e.g., leakage of personal data through training data), and the risk of embedded bias in data perpetuating discrimination.

- **Performance risk:** This includes the risk of GenAI systems "hallucinating" incorrect (but convincing) information, and the problem of "explainability" (which is particularly important because financial institutions must be able to explain the reasoning behind their actions and decisions).

- **Cybersecurity threats:** This spans both the possibility of a GenAI system being attacked, and the use of GenAI by hackers to target financial systems.

- **Financial stability risk:** The IMF suggests that GenAI could pose a systemic risk, especially if advisors over-rely on the technology. One example given is GenAI systems potentially encouraging financial institutions to follow the same decision-making process ("herd behavior"), thereby impacting market liquidity.

Despite these threats, it's worth noting that the IMF still believes GenAI shows great promise for the financial sector, helping to drive efficiency, increase compliance, and enhance the customer experience. However, GenAI tools must be deployed with caution and careful (human) oversight to realize their full potential.

Examples from the Financial Sector

Now let's explore some real-world examples of how banks and financial service providers are harnessing GenAI:

Helping banks (and insurance companies) provide a better service

Let's kick off with British bank, NatWest, which has collaborated with IBM to deliver enhancements to the bank's virtual assistant, Cora.[3] Thanks to GenAI, Cora+ will be able to provide NatWest customers with a wider range of information, all through personalized, conversational interactions. The idea is to provide a more human experience for customers looking for information or looking to compare products and services across NatWest's offering.

Private Iranian bank, Saman Bank, is also using GenAI to provide personalized financial solutions. It has developed Saman Bot, a virtual AI assistant that can answer customer queries and deliver financial advice 24/7.[4] These are early examples of banks deploying GenAI in customer-facing solutions, but they certainly won't be the last.

Square, the financial services platform owned by Block Inc., is embracing GenAI in a really interesting way – using the technology to provide new tools for customer content creation, onboarding, and setup.[5] Among the new features is a Menu Generator tool, which allows restaurants to create a menu in minutes for their website. There's also a GenAI-powered email feature, which helps businesses create personalized messages for customers. There's even a website copy generator, which can write headlines, copy, and blog posts for business websites. This gives us a taste of how banks could use GenAI to create time-saving new tools and products for their business customers in future.

Another example comes from insurance and financial services company, Nationwide, which has been using GenAI to improve pet insurance provision by helping pet owners take better care of their pets' health. The company turned to GenAI to create easy-to-understand summaries for 71 different health conditions – information that was used by Nationwide's Pet Health Zone platform, which uses pet claims data to provide personalized information about pet health risks. Thanks to GenAI, the team accelerated the creation of 35 000 words of medical content, saving more than 300 hours.[6]

Streamlining banking operations with GenAI

Meanwhile, several banks in China are reportedly embracing GenAI for behind-the-scenes functions. For example, Industrial and Commercial Bank of China is exploring GenAI language models as a wealth management tool. Fintech giant, Ant Group, is doing something similar; developing its own language model for wealth management and insurance that can assist finance professionals.[7]

In the US, KeyBank is taking a similar approach – using GenAI to streamline internal operations before deploying it across customer-facing channels. The bank is reportedly using GenAI to support its documentation teams to minimize their manual workload.[8]

Global bank, HSBC, isn't shying away from GenAI, either; the bank has reportedly unearthed a "few hundred" use cases for GenAI that could potentially be deployed.[9]

Asset management company, Schroders, has built its own internal version of ChatGPT, trained on its own proprietary data and that is proving useful in a number of ways. One of those is in translating content into other languages. The company says translations that previously took two days can now be done in two minutes, and the translations have, over time, become "near perfect."[10] Schroders is also exploring how GenAI can be used to analyze data and identify future needs that may inform product design.

GenAI tools as a "co-pilot" for financial professionals

Morgan Stanley has been experimenting with OpenAI's GPT-4 model, using the language model as a sort of encyclopedia for financial advisors. The company trained GPT-4 on content from over 100 000 documents, to help financial advisors answers questions on investment recommendations, general business performance, and internal processes (such as how to complete certain applications).[11] Several times throughout this book we've seen how

GenAI can serve as a "co-pilot" for professionals, helping them do their job in a more efficient way – and the financial industry is no exception.

Meanwhile, Moody's, the company best known for risk assessment and credit ratings, is partnering with Google Cloud to help financial service professionals leverage large language models to accelerate financial analysis. In essence, the idea is to use GenAI to help professionals gain new financial insights and summarize financial data in a quicker, easier way.[12] As an example, users will be able to easily analyze and extract "decision-ready insight" directly from financial disclosures and other financial reports.

Enhancing the payments industry

Examples are also emerging of using GenAI to facilitate payments. Mastercard, for instance, already uses AI to secure billions of transactions annually, and helps banks predict or spot fraudulent activity. But the payments provider is now actively looking to use GenAI to improve the customer experience, aid product testing, and generally help customers solve business challenges (such as reducing bias in credit decisions).[13]

Elsewhere, Stripe was an early collaborator with OpenAI on its GPT-4 large language model. Stripe employees were encouraged to come up with exciting ways to use the model to identify new products and improve workflows, and one of the uses they came up with is monitoring for fraud. Stripe has now started using GPT-4 to analyze posts in Stripe forums on platforms like Discord. (These forums can be used by bad actors posing as legitimate community members to try and defraud people or get them to give up personal information.) Using GenAI-powered syntax analysis, Stripe can now monitor these communications for potentially dodgy interactions – with GPT-4 flagging posts that require investigation so they can be passed on to Stripe's fraud team.[14]

Stripe is also building new user tools based on the GPT model.[15] One of these is Stripe Docs, a GPT-powered tool that allows developers to pose natural language queries to the language model, rather than having to wade through documentation. Stripe says this allows developers to spend less time reading and more time building solutions.

GenAI in accounting

I've also mentioned that GenAI can assist accountants and internal finance functions in their work. As such, accounting software companies are keen to integrate GenAI into their products. One example comes from Intuit, the software giant behind QuickBooks online accounting software, which has introduced an AI helper called "Intuit Assist."[16] The tool can deliver personalized insights and recommendations to help users solve problems (routing the customer to a human expert for issues that need in-depth guidance). For example, for individuals using Intuit software to manage their personal taxes, Intuit Assist can create a personalized tax checklist to help them file their tax return and access refunds more easily. And for small businesses using QuickBooks accounting software, Intuit Assist can examine customer behavior and business performance to pinpoint potential cash flow issues, highlight the most successful products, and more. And this can all be done via natural language queries, such as, "Which invoices are overdue?"

Oracle subsidiary, NetSuite, is a provider of cloud-based enterprise resource planning (ERP) applications. Now, NetSuite has added a GenAI feature called "NetSuite Text Enhance" to help finance teams (and HR, supply chain and sales team) generate contextual and personalized content.[17] The tool can generate draft text for team members to review, based on just a few starter words. It's one of several AI-powered features being rolled out by NetSuite, including a new feature that helps businesses automate data analysis for preparing budgets.

Key Takeaways

In this chapter, we've learned that the financial sector is set for a major shakeup thanks to GenAI:

- AI has been a game-changer within the financial sector for many years, but GenAI will take this to new heights. GenAI can help banks deliver a better, more thoughtful service to customers through AI assistants. It can also be used to develop customized products and services, and deliver personalized advice to clients. And it can be used to automate and augment internal processes – such as credit decisioning, detecting fraud, asset management, and compliance.

- GenAI can also be used by accountants and internal finance teams to augment their work. For example, GenAI can be used to forecast financials, generate or summarize reports, and provide more forward-looking recommendations.

- However, GenAI does bring new risks to the financial sector. Specifically, there are risks around data privacy, data bias, the risk of AI systems hallucinating incorrect financial information, cybersecurity threats, and risks to financial stability. Therefore, GenAI tools must be deployed with careful human oversight.

- GenAI is already being used by banks and financial services providers in a number of different ways – from customer-facing chatbots that give advice 24/7, to behind-the-scene operations, to AI "co-pilot" tools for financial advisors. It is also being deployed by payment providers such as Mastercard, and being built into accounting solutions for individuals and businesses.

- Bottom line, any bank or financial services operator that ignores GenAI risks being left in the dust.

Now let's turn to coding and computer programming and see how GenAI can support the work of developers (and lay people) in interesting new ways.

Notes

1. The economic potential of generative AI: The next productivity frontier; *McKinsey & Company*; https://www.mckinsey.com/capabilities/mckinsey-digital/our-insights/the-economic-potential-of-generative-ai-the-next-productivity-frontier
2. Generative Artificial Intelligence in Finance: Risk Considerations; *IMF*; https://www.imf.org/en/Publications/fintech-notes/Issues/2023/08/18/Generative-Artificial-Intelligence-in-Finance-Risk-Considerations-537570
3. NatWest and IBM collaborate on generative AI initiative to enhance customer experience; *PR Newswire*; https://www.prnewswire.com/news-releases/natwest-and-ibm-collaborate-on-generative-ai-initiative-to-enhance-customer-experience-301977636.html
4. Revolutionising banking: The role of AI in shaping the future; *Zawya*; https://www.zawya.com/en/opinion/business-insights/revolutionising-banking-the-role-of-ai-in-shaping-the-future-x5p6syun

5. Square's new AI features include a website and restaurant menu generator; *TechCrunch*; https://techcrunch.com/2023/10/18/squares-new-ai-features-include-a-website-and-restaurant-menu-generator/

6. Nationwide's innovation with generative AI across business lines; *Columbus Business First Journal*; https://www.bizjournals.com/columbus/news/2023/10/30/nationwide-s-innovation-with-generative-ai.html

7. Chinese banks jump on AI bandwagon to cut costs; *Asia Nikkei*; https://asia.nikkei.com/Spotlight/Caixin/Chinese-banks-jump-on-AI-bandwagon-to-cut-costs

8. KeyBank implements gen AI internally; *Bank Automation News*; https://bankautomationnews.com/allposts/ai/keybank-implements-gen-ai-internally/

9. Now HSBC has a 'few hundred' potential use cases for generative AI: HK CEO; *CNBC*; https://www.cnbc.com/video/2023/11/03/hsbc-has-a-few-hundred-potential-use-cases-for-generative-ai-hk-ceo.html

10. Asset Managers Benefit from Generative AI; *Markets Media*; https://www.marketsmedia.com/asset-managers-benefit-from-adopting-generative-ai/

11. How Morgan Stanley Is Training GPT to Help Financial Advisors; *Forbes*; https://www.forbes.com/sites/tomdavenport/2023/03/20/how-morgan-stanley-is-training-gpt-to-help-financial-advisors/

12. Moody's and Google Cloud Partner on Generative AI Applications Tailored for Financial Services Professionals; *PR Newswire*; https://www.prnewswire.com/news-releases/moodys-and-google-cloud-partner-on-generative-ai-applications-tailored-for-financial-services-professionals-301964682.html

13. 9 new AI moves in the payments industry; *American Banker*; https://www.americanbanker.com/payments/list/9-new-ai-moves-in-the-payments-industry

14. How Stripe is using GPT-4 to fight fraud; *Free Think*; https://www.freethink.com/robots-ai/stripe-gpt4

15. Stripe and OpenAI collaborate to monetize OpenAI's flagship products and enhance Stripe with GPT-4; *Stripe*; https://stripe.com/en-bg/newsroom/news/stripe-and-openai

16. Intuit Assist Brings Generative AI to Small Business and Consumer Portfolio; *Forbes*; https://www.forbes.com/sites/patrickmoorhead/2023/09/11/intuit-assist-brings-generative-ai-to-small-business-and-consumer-portfolio/?sh=7f6a414d29dd

17. NetSuite adds generative AI to its entire ERP suite; *CIO*; https://www.cio.com/article/655912/netsuite-adds-generative-ai-to-its-entire-erp-suite.html

16
CODING AND PROGRAMMING: THE AI REVOLUTION

This new wave of advanced GenAI large language models isn't just capable of writing text – they can write computer code. Which makes sense when you think that computer code is just another type of language. This means GenAI can aid the work of coders, programmers, and developers, and speed up the software development process.

(If you're new to this topic and wondering what the difference is between coders, programmers, and developers, coders use programming languages to tell a computer or software what to do, whereas programmers or developers are generally more experienced coders who can work across multiple programming languages and oversee projects, including developing the logic and mapping the project from start to finish. People often use the terms interchangeably, which is what I'll do in this chapter, although technically speaking, coding is a part of the overall programming process.)

But how good is GenAI at creating computer code? Well, when the Alphabet-owned DeepMind lab pitted its AlphaCode AI model in competition against human coders, AlphaCode's performance roughly corresponded to "a novice programmer with a few months to a year of training."[1] Not bad at all for an AI. And given that GenAI's capabilities are progressing so fast, we can expect the technology to catch up to more experienced coders in the not-so-distant future.

Another interesting aspect of this is GenAI can also help people like me – someone who has relatively little knowledge of programming languages – write computer code for various applications. Let's explore the role of GenAI in coding.

The Impact of Generative AI on Programming

We'll kick off this section by exploring exactly what GenAI is capable of and then see how this may impact the work of programmers (and every-day people).

What can GenAI do?

Developing new software is like building a house – it always seems to take longer and cost more than you expect! GenAI can help to accelerate the process in several ways:

- **Gathering requirements:** All software development starts by identifying requirements (such as "User wants to do X, Y, and Z"). GenAI can aid this process by generating a list of requirements. It can also be used to review requirements and check nothing has been missed (e.g., security requirements).

- **Generating code:** GenAI can turn natural language instructions into functioning code. Which essentially turns English (or whatever your native tongue is) into a computer programming language. . .

- **Completing code:** As coders type, the GenAI can suggest code completions – which saves coders time, especially when working on repetitive or mundane tasks. Code completion can also help to reduce human error.

GenAI can also be a useful tool when it comes to reviewing and testing software, by:

- **Reviewing code:** GenAI can check through existing code and suggest improvements or create alternatives that are more efficient. It can also analyze code according to coding style guidelines, to ensure code is consistent.

- **Fixing bugs:** GenAI can be used to identify and fix bugs in code, to create a better end product.

- **Testing software:** GenAI can carry out many of the testing phases, such as generating test cases, generating test code, and analyzing test results.

Looking ahead, GenAI may also be able to predict how systems and software might fail *before* the code goes into production – and, of course, tell developers how to fix it. That's the goal of software company Dynatrace, which has been building "predictive AI" to predict how systems will fail for years. In an interview with ZDNET, co-founder and chief technology officer of Dynatrace Bernd Greifeneder says, the next stage is building GenAI into that process – so the GenAI can tell coders how their code may cause faults and how to fix it.[2] "The typical request from a CIO is, please fix my system before it actually fails," he said. In other words, the holy grail of programming is to prevent coding that causes faults, as opposed to having to fix faults further down the line. It's still early days for using GenAI in this way, but Dynatrace is certainly working toward that holy grail.

Of course, there are issues with using GenAI in programming – particularly when it comes to hallucinations, data security, and IP. (For example, you don't want your precious code hoovered up for training purposes, potentially to be shared with other users outside of the company.) As in any industry, human oversight and clear guardrails are needed.

So does this mean we won't need software developers in the future?

No. But it does mean they will increasingly work alongside AI, just as other professionals like journalists and doctors will. While it's true that GenAI can be used to automate coding (thereby putting the work of junior coders potentially at risk), I see an even bigger application being the use of GenAI as a co-pilot or co-coder for even the most experienced programmers. Especially when you consider that GenAI can be used to gather requirements and debug codes, or make sure that code adheres to certain requirements, as well as write the code itself.

And let's not forget that, for someone like a higher-level developer or programmer, writing code isn't the main thing they do all day. In fact, writing code may take up as little as 20% of their time,[3] with the rest of their time spent on gathering requirements, testing, meetings, collaborating with users, overseeing projects, etc.

What's more, even when using GenAI tools to automate or help with programming work, we'll still need experienced developers to write detailed prompts that get the best out of the AI. (You could argue writing detailed prompts that tell the AI *exactly* what you want it to do is just another form of programming. . .)

So rather than replacing programmers, GenAI will support the work of programmers by automating repetitive tasks, accelerating software development, and enhancing productivity. GenAI could thereby prove to be a game-changing tool for programmers. In one example, GenAI was shown to increase developer productivity by 10%; in another, it cut the menial work that developers are expected to do (such as internal communication and documentation) by a huge 70–80%.[4] Perhaps it's no wonder that many developers are on board with the idea of using GenAI. According to a survey by GitHub, 92% of US-based developers are already using AI coding tools, and 70% believe AI coding tools will give them an advantage at work – with better code quality and faster completion time among the anticipated benefits.[5]

GenAI will change how programming is done, in other words – and hopefully make the work better for programmers.

This has advantages for everyday people, too

Clearly, GenAI is going to be a revolutionary tool for programmers. But it may also prove a useful tool for everyday folks who want to, say, build an app or create a piece of software, but don't know any programming languages.

With a GenAI tool, you can tell the GenAI what you want to achieve and voila! It will deliver (in theory, at least, since we know that GenAIs can sometimes confidently give incorrect but plausible-looking answers).

This means anyone can potentially become a coder, regardless of expertise. Even me.

For my YouTube Short videos, I have to complete these annoying templates that are super-restrictive (e.g., requiring a specific number of characters for the title, description, and so on). Doing this for each video (I create a lot of content) and sticking to the character restriction was proving really tricky and time consuming. So I asked ChatGPT to write me a little program to help me create HTML templates for my YouTube videos. And it works. And it saves me precious time. And I haven't got any real programming experience. . .

Adoption and New Coding Tools: Real-World Examples

Now that we know what GenAI is capable of, let's see how companies are putting this into practice – starting with companies who have deployed GenAI for their software development, and then looking at some of the new tools that promise to help people (professionals and non-professionals) create code.

Examples of companies using GenAI internally

Coders at software company, Freshworks, have been using ChatGPT to write code – and, in the process, cut the development time from around 10 weeks down to less than a week.[6] ChatGPT can write code in a number of programming languages, including JavaScript, Python, and C++. It can also act like a coding tutor, explaining how code works, and debug code.

Collaboration software company, Augmend, is using Microsoft's GitHub Copilot tool and ChatGPT for development, debugging, and learning – helping the small start-up accelerate the software development cycle and be more competitive. As CEO and co-founder, Diamond Bishop, puts it, "Going back to coding without this augmentation feels a lot like working without the internet at your fingertips."[7] He also noted that GenAI tools have nearly doubled the team's productivity – which is impressive for a team of just five developers.

Meanwhile, at cloud technology company, Oracle, CTO and founder, Larry Ellison, has said Oracle will develop future applications using GenAI, based on developer prompts. "We're not writing it anymore. We're generating that code. It fundamentally changes how we build applications, how we run applications. It just changes everything."[8] He also noted that GenAI enables faster development with smaller development teams, and reduced security flaws.

GenAI is also proving useful for non-technology businesses (if there's any such thing as a non-technology business these days). Dubai Electricity and Water Authority (DEWA) has adopted the GitHub Copilot tool, using it to help its software developers write code and develop applications.[9] As the name suggests, Copilot acts like a co-pilot, giving suggestions and guidance to programmers writing code to help speed up the process.

Seattle-based real estate company, Redfin, has used large language models (LLMs) including ChatGPT to help with programming tasks. As Redfin CTO, Bridget Frey, says, GenAI has proven useful for "migrating from one programming language to another, helping developers understand legacy code written by other colleagues, or writing functions for converting data formats. These are good examples of tasks that our engineers can do without the assistance of LLMs, but with these models, they can move much faster. Something that used to take an engineer 30 minutes to do can now be done by AI in one minute."[10]

Meanwhile, at General Motors, Chief Data and Analytics Officer, Jon Francis, has said AI is a huge area of investment for the auto giant, noting that it will be used "in the back office with HR chatbots, on the factory floor with predictive maintenance, and in IT operations by scaling and productionizing software development."[11]

New coding tools are emerging

Now let's take a quick look at some of the many tools that are emerging to help coders code. Obviously ChatGPT is one that you've already heard of, but let's explore a wider list (in alphabetical order, not order of preference):

- **Auto-GPT:** This open-source tool harnesses OpenAI's GPT-4 model to perform tasks – including, for example, creating a simple app. Ask it to create an app and not only will it break the project down into specific tasks, it will autonomously complete the tasks.

- **Bard:** Google's ChatGPT, basically. Bard can function as a coding assistant, generating code from prompts, and explaining code pasted in. It's not explicitly designed for this (see Google Codey below), but it can do it.

- **ChatGPT:** OpenAI's ChatGPT wasn't designed to generate code, but it can write code in various languages when prompted. Like Bard, it's perhaps not the best tool out there for programming, but the easy-to-use interface makes it a decent starting point for those experimenting with AI-generated code.

- **Codacy:** An AI code quality/code analysis tool that helps to automate code analysis. It's designed to help developers create better software, faster.

- **Code Llama:** Meta (Facebook) fine-tuned its Llama 2 LLM to create this tool for coding in various programming languages.

- **CodeWhisperer:** This is Amazon's code generation tool, developed using open-source code and Amazon's own data. The tool takes natural language prompts and creates code based on the programmer's objectives, in their style. It can also be used for code completion.

- **CodeWP:** WordPress's code generation tool is designed for developers who build sites on WordPress's hugely popular content management system.

- **Codey:** Google's AI coding assistant is designed to streamline workflows and increase productivity – as such, it can do the things you'd expect, including code generation and code completion. Its "code chat" function lets developers chat with a bot to get help with learning new concepts, answering questions about code, and debugging.

- **GitHub Copilot:** Microsoft's GenAI for writing code is a code-suggestion and generation tool, designed to enhance the work of developers. One of the ways it can do this is by suggesting code snippets as developers' type. It was created in collaboration with OpenAI.

- **SAP Build Code:** SAP's tool for application development is optimized for Java and JavaScript, and can be used for coding, testing, integrations, and application lifecycle management.

- **Salesforce Anypoint Code Builder:** This code builder tool is designed to help developers reduce costs and speed up software development. So far, so standard. But Salesforce also offers industry-specific integration via packaged tools for sectors like healthcare and financial services.

- **Tabnine:** A coding assistant built on OpenAI's Codex model, Tabnine, can generate code suggestions, autocomplete lines of code, and match in-house conventions.

- **Tynker Copilot:** Designed for coders aged 6–12, Tynker Copilot applies GenAI to coding education. This game-based coding platform, which was created by fine-tuning Meta's Llama 2 LLM, helps young coders turn their imaginative ideas into visual block code for apps and games.

- **Uizard:** This tool uses GenAI to help people design mobile apps, websites, and landing pages in minutes. With its intuitive interface, it simplifies the design process enabling quick and easy prototyping.

- **Watsonx Code Assistant:** IBM's GenAI tool is designed to speed up code generation and increase developer productivity.

- **What The Diff:** A GenAI-powered code review assistant, What The Diff reviews the "diff" of pull requests. A pull request is a way for developers to notify colleagues that they have completed something (such as a bug fix) and are ready to begin merging new code changes into a project. This tool explains the differences between the new and old code in plain English, so everyone in the team (including non-techies) can understand what's been done.

This is by no means an exhaustive list of the many coding assistant tools coming onto the market. I just wanted to give you a flavor of what's available, from huge tech corporations and lesser-known companies alike. As GenAI tools like these become more commonplace, developers will increasingly incorporate them into their everyday work – hopefully making the work of developers easier and better.

Key Takeaways

In this chapter, we've learned that GenAI can serve as a useful tool in software development:

- GenAI can automate or assist in the writing, reviewing, and testing of computer code.

- Rather than making developers extinct, GenAI will support the work of developers by automating repetitive tasks, accelerating software development, and enhancing productivity. Examples have shown how GenAI can accelerate the development process from weeks down to days.

- Tech and non-tech companies are beginning to use GenAI for their software development tasks, and new GenAI coding assistant tools are rapidly emerging to help developers create better code, faster.

Now let's turn to another somewhat unexpected skill of GenAI – analyzing data. Turn to the next chapter to see how GenAI can help us solve some of the biggest problems around working with (and understanding) data.

Notes

1. Can coding academies survive the AI era?; *Fast Company*; https://www.fast company.com/90931184/can-coding-academies-survive-the-ai-era
2. AI aims to predict and fix developer coding errors before disaster strikes; *ZDNet*; https://www.zdnet.com/article/ai-aims-to-predict-and-fix-developer-coding-errors-before-disaster-strikes/
3. AI Won't Eliminate Programming, But Can Make It Better; *Inside Big Data*; https://insidebigdata.com/2023/11/13/ai-wont-eliminate-programming-but-can-make-it-better/

4. How Generative AI Can Increase Developer Productivity Now; *The New Stack*; https://thenewstack.io/how-generative-ai-can-increase-developer-productivity-now/

5. Survey reveals AI's impact on the developer experience; *GitHub*; https://github.blog/2023-06-13-survey-reveals-ais-impact-on-the-developer-experience/

6. Software company CEO says using ChatGPT cuts the time it takes to complete coding tasks from around 9 weeks to just a few days; *Business Insider*; https://www.businessinsider.com/chatgpt-coding-openai-ceo-save-time-ai-jobs-software-2023-5?r=US&IR=T

7. AI and coding: How these tech companies are using generative AI for programming; *Geek Wire*; https://www.geekwire.com/2023/ai-and-coding-how-seattle-tech-companies-are-using-generative-ai-for-programming/

8. Larry Ellison outlines Oracle's generative AI strategy; *Oracle*; https://www.oracle.com/artificial-intelligence/larry-ellison-cloudworld-genai-strategy/

9. DEWA adopts new Microsoft generative AI tool to drive digital transformation; *Zawya*; https://www.zawya.com/en/business/technology-and-telecom/dewa-adopts-new-microsoft-generative-ai-tool-to-drive-digital-transformation-yh60rr4j

10. AI and coding: How these tech companies are using generative AI for programming; *Geek Wire*; https://www.geekwire.com/2023/ai-and-coding-how-seattle-tech-companies-are-using-generative-ai-for-programming/

11. Every enterprise plans to increase AI spending next year; *ZDNet*; https://www.zdnet.com/article/every-enterprise-plans-to-increase-ai-spending-next-year/

17

DATA INSIGHTS: HARNESSING THE POWER OF GENERATIVE AI

Data is a vital asset for today's businesses. It is the fuel that powers better decision-making in organizations. As such, it's crucial that people across the organization are able to extract insights from data. However, that is more easily said than done. Rather than being empowered by data, many people find themselves intimidated (or even paralyzed) by it.

In this chapter, we'll explore the problem of being rich in data but poor in insights, and discover how GenAI can help businesses get more out of data.

What Is the Data Problem and How Does Generative AI Help?

We live in a world that's full of data – indeed, everything we do generates data, and the average business is absolutely swimming in the stuff. But what is the problem with having such a vast sea of data? You can end up drowning in it.

The thorny issue of data overwhelm

Useful as data is, the sheer volume of data can simply overwhelm people. This phenomenon is described by software leader Oracle as the "Decision Dilemma." You could also call it "decision paralysis" or "data anxiety."

Whatever you call it, the basic gist is that more data causes anxiety and lack of action, instead of better decisions.

For its 2023 Decision Dilemma report, Oracle surveyed more than 14 000 employees and business leaders across 17 countries, and the results were eye-opening:[1]

- 83% agreed that access to data is essential for helping businesses make decisions, BUT. . .

- 86% said that data makes them feel less confident, and

- 72% said that data has stopped them being able to make a decision.

When I spoke to Oracle's James Richardson, VP for Product Strategy, Analytics, he told me, "It's the anxiety that comes from having the wealth of data we have at our fingertips, but perhaps a limited amount of time to use it . . . one of the interesting findings was a significant number of people said that at the point of making a decision, they were so overwhelmed by the data that they didn't make the decision. So the question is, how do we deal with that?"

I've certainly noticed this myself in my own consultancy work – organizations are rich in data but that doesn't necessarily mean they have the *insights* they need to make decisions and take action. It's perhaps no wonder that 70% of business leaders would sometimes prefer to simply leave these decisions in the hands of a robot or AI.[2] Richardson doesn't believe this means that people are looking to abdicate all responsibility for decision-making; we're just desperate for assistance. "What they are really saying is 'help me'", he says.

So what do we do about this? As we'll see in this chapter, part of the solution may lie in GenAI's ability to make sense of data and extract useful information that helps us make better decisions.

The importance of data literacy

To truly harness GenAI, we need businesses to embrace a new era of "self-service" analytics, where anyone has the power to find the answers they need.

(As opposed to the traditional approach where insights would be handed down from business analysts within the organization.) To successfully make this transition, organizations must put resources into supporting workforces through these changes – for example, by setting up data and analytics hubs where those who have professional data skills can assist those who don't.

Because, if we're honest about the situation, there's a startling lack of data literacy out there. (By data literacy, I don't mean being a data analyst; I mean the ability to confidently work with data to get the information you need.) Partly, this lack of data literacy is down to anxiety around working with data, and the overwhelm that can come with having so much data at your fingertips, but it's also down to a lack of training in data literacy. According to one telling survey, 82% of leaders expect all employees to have basic data literacy, and 79% say their departments are equipping workers with critical data skills – *yet* only 40% of employees say they're being provided with the data skills their employers expect.[3]

We urgently need people to become more confident and competent at working with data. Which is why all organizations must invest in a data literacy program that not only provides data training, but also instills a data-driven culture from top to bottom. Importantly, GenAI can also play a role in increasing data literacy. How? By giving anyone the ability to analyze vast amounts of data in an intuitive way, using natural language questions.

GenAI and its ability to understand data

GenAIs are able to create outputs (such as text or images) by learning from vast amounts of data and recognizing patterns in that data. Which is a massive simplification, of course, but the truth is even the best AI experts aren't able to explain exactly *how* GenAIs do what they do. The point is, GenAI systems are adept at analyzing huge amounts of data, and organizations can use this to their advantage.

GenAI has the potential to democratize data analytics by making advanced data interpretation and insight generation accessible to companies of all sizes. GenAI streamlines the analysis and interpretation of data by automating complex processes such as pattern recognition and trend analysis, allowing for real-time insights that turn vast datasets into easy-to-understand narratives and visualizations. (Because with multi-model systems that are able to produce, say, graphs as well as text, you could have your data presented in the exact way you want.) Plus, GenAI can in theory work with all sorts of messy, unstructured data, including photos and video data, or social media posts – meaning, it isn't just limited to neatly structured data in databases.

All this makes data much more actionable for decision makers across the organization – regardless of their data expertise. Decision paralysis, begone! Which is good news, considering that three-quarters of business leaders say the daily volume of decisions they need to make has increased tenfold over the past three years.[4]

As well as alleviating the problem of decision paralysis, this democratization of data through GenAI can also help to level the playing field between large corporations and smaller enterprises. With GenAI, you don't need an army of data scientists to gain competitive advantage; you just need to ask GenAI the right questions. As such, analytics software vendors such as Microsoft, Qlik, and Tableau are increasingly embedding GenAI in their analysis tools. But we'll talk more about tools later in the chapter.

Use cases for GenAI

So how exactly can GenAI be used to work with data? Potential use cases include:

- **Driving faster and better decision-making through better insights:** Through real-time tracking of data, decision makers can gain a better grasp of what's happening across the business and be presented with actionable insights suggested by the GenAI. And this can be achieved through natural language prompts, such as "What are our top three customer behavior trends for the previous month?"

- **Acting as a decision-making co-pilot:** Thanks to GenAI's conversational abilities, these tools can function as virtual advisors – a sounding board to help discuss and generate ideas.

- **Generating summaries of data:** GenAI can sift through vast quantities of data and create executive summaries that pull out the key points, along with best-practice recommendations. GenAI can even be used to suggest what information to include in reports for different audiences (execs, department heads, managers, and so on), so that everyone gets the information they need to make better decisions.

- **Visualizing data:** GenAI can generate analytics reports in an easy-to-digest format –presenting insights from the data not just as text narratives but also in visual format (graphs, charts, etc.).

- **Automating data analytics:** GenAI can potentially automate the data analysis process and provide automatic notifications for, well, anything you want. Spikes in sales, trending website activity, a drop in factory machine performance, increased sick leave, you name it. . .

- **Harnessing predictive capabilities:** Throughout this book we've seen how GenAI can help people take action before an issue becomes a real problem. So as well as understanding what's going on in the business right now, GenAI can help decision makers pre-empt what might be coming down the line.

- **Using synthetic data to test ideas and scenarios:** By creating large amounts of synthetic data that mimic real-world data, leaders can model scenarios that may be difficult to model with real-world data (e.g., because an event is a rare, but impactful, occurrence, or because gathering that much data would be difficult and expensive). Remember that synthetic data can often be generated with just a small amount of real-world data as a starting point – which makes large-scale data analysis possible for even smaller businesses.

- **Preparing data:** GenAI can also be used to take care of data preparation tasks such as tagging, classification, segmentation, and anonymization.

- **Helping to clean up data for better analysis results:** Because GenAI is so good at spotting patterns, it can be used to detect anomalies and inconsistencies in your data – things that could potentially skew results.

Again, later in the chapter we'll look at some of the analytics tools that are building such GenAI capabilities into their products.

Will GenAI put data analysts out of work?

If a business leader can simply ask a GenAI analysis tool, "What do I need to do to improve customer satisfaction?" will we really need analytics professionals in future?

I believe the answer is yes. If anything, as GenAI becomes more accessible and mainstream, data teams may even become more critical to organizations than they already are. After all, today's GenAI tools still lack vital abilities like critical thinking, strategic planning, and complex problem-solving. We will still need people who are experts in data and who can help organizations apply their data in the most strategic way.

Having said that, as with many jobs, the work of data analysts, business analysts, and data scientists will undoubtedly change. Routine and repetitive analytics tasks will likely be automated, leaving analysts to focus on more strategic tasks and collaborating with teams within the business. Plus, knowledge of how to work with tools like ChatGPT will become increasingly important for analysts.

What about the limitations of GenAI?

If this all sounds great so far, hold your horses, because, as always, there are limitations and challenges around deploying GenAI for data analysis.

Once again, data security and privacy is a major concern here. You don't really want your precious organizational data to be used for training large language models – potentially exposing information to users outside of the company. And you'll certainly need to take care when it comes to using GenAI for personal data, of either customers or employees. There's also the perennial issue of biased data, potentially skewing your results. Plus, there's the old "black box" issue (where we don't really understand how these systems work and how they arrive at answers), not to mention the risk of "hallucinations."

That's not to put you off using GenAI to help boost data literacy and democratize data in your organization. I absolutely think businesses should be exploring GenAI in this context. But it's important to balance the technology with human judgment and oversight. It's also important to remember that we're not looking to abdicate all responsibility to machines. Which means we still need leaders and decision makers to cultivate skills like judgment, complex decision-making, and strategic thinking. Read more about successful implementation in Chapter 18.

Real-World Examples and New Analytics Tools

Now let's see how organizations have already begun to use GenAI to get more out of their data. After that, we'll explore some of the many analytics tools that are now incorporating GenAI features.

Organizations using GenAI for data analysis

It's early days for organizations adopting GenAI in their internal analytics, but there are a couple of interesting examples we can learn from. JetBlue is on a mission to be the "most data-driven airline in the world,"[5] with data informing every part of the business, including operations, commercial, and support functions. To help JetBlue staff leverage data and enhance decision-making, the airline created an internal system called "BlueSky" that functions as an AI-driven operating system. JetBlue has also created an LLM called "BlueBot," which is integrated with BlueSky, that can be used by all teams at JetBlue to access data and insights.

Elsewhere, communications company, TELUS, partnered with AI specialists, HEAVY.AI, to improve performance analytics and the customer experience. TELUS used interactive GenAI visualization features to extract key insights from customer information that pinpointed upsell opportunities. As a result, TELUS was able to focus its wireless services in the most profitable locations – just by querying and visualizing the data in a more intelligent way.[6]

We'll certainly see more companies publicizing their own GenAI success stories in the near future.

GenAI-powered analytics tools

Providers of analytics software and platforms have been building AI into their products for years to enable more intelligent data analytics. But now they're increasingly adding GenAI capabilities that allow for natural language querying and easy summaries of data. Let's look at a few examples.

One example comes from Microsoft Power BI, which now incorporates Microsoft Copilot's large language model technology. Basically, Copilot brings GenAI capabilities to Power BI users. This means a user can ask a question or describe the insights or visualization they're looking for – all in conversational language – then Copilot analyzes the data and pulls the relevant information into a report with actionable insights.[7] Users can tailor reports to their liking, including the tone, scope, and style of narratives.

Another example comes from Terradata, which has recently launched a new GenAI natural language interface for its VantageCloud Lake enterprise analytics solution.[8] The new capability, called "ask.ai," allows anyone with approved access to ask questions of their company's data and get instant answers. Because no complex coding or querying is needed, this expands the use to non-technical roles.

Qlik also offers GenAI capabilities, including fully interactive search, chat, and multi-language support. To expand on this, the analytics software company has launched a new suite of OpenAI connecters that essentially give users the ChatGPT experience in the Qlik Cloud platform.[9] Qlik says this new functionality will drive broader insights and help engage more users in data analysis.

Meanwhile, data visualization company, Tableau, is also getting on board with GenAI, aiming to "reimagine the data experience" and bring a more "personalized, contextual, and smart" experience to users.[10] Tableau AI, which is powered by Salesforce's Einstein AI technology, is designed to make analyzing data as simple as asking a question – with insights delivered in plain language. Tableau AI can even proactively suggest the questions you might want to ask next. There's also a new feature called "Tableau Pulse," which will help organizations make data accessible to everyone in the business, regardless of their level of expertise. Pulse delivers personalized insights through "data digests" delivered inside workflow tools that people are already using, as well as a personalized metrics homepage that functions rather like a curated newsfeed. Tableau says the homepage will become even more personalized over time as it learns what information the user is most interested in.

Oracle has unveiled new GenAI features that allow companies to integrate large language interfaces in their apps, enabling users to generate text from data, summarize data, and more.[11]

Big data company, Alteryx, is also leveraging GenAI to help non-skilled workers better visualize and understand the trends within their data.[12] With its AI Studio, Alteryx customers can also use those insights to build new applications that streamline business operations, enhance processes, and improve productivity – through a conversational interface.

Then there's analytics and BI company, MicroStrategy, which has launched MicroStrategy AI – a GenAI product that is designed to make interacting with data faster, simpler, and more accessible for everyone.[13] It includes a feature called "Auto Answers," which allows users to engage in natural language chats with their data, asking questions and getting instant replies. There's also the Auto Dashboard feature, an AI collaborator that suggests questions and can autocomplete queries.

Kinetica, specialists in harnessing machine and sensor data, have unveiled a feature called "SQL-GPT," which effectively allows users to ask anything of their data in natural language. Type an answer, get an answer. Kinetica says its tool outperforms other tools when it comes to accuracy and dealing with complex questions, such as, "Show me all the aircraft over Missouri."[14]

Cloud-based data company, Snowflake, has also brought GenAI to its data cloud platform. Snowflake Cortex allows users to chat with their data, detect sentiment in data, extract answers, summarize information, and translate text to a selected language.[15]

Elsewhere, Akkio is on a mission to bring GenAI-powered analytics to small and mid-sized businesses. The company's Generative Reports tool makes business intelligence accessible to SMBs by letting them quickly understand their data, get insights, and share live reports with the team. The tool is designed to go beyond standard dashboard tools and understand the user's specific problems, project requirements and use cases. In other words, it understands the problem the user wants to solve and serves up a report to answer questions. As Akkio describes it, "it's like speaking with an analyst."[16]

As you can tell, providers of data analytics tools are extremely keen to build GenAI capabilities into their products. As these tools become more commonplace, users of all skill levels will be able to interrogate organizational data in a more intuitive, easy way – and get the answers they need to do their jobs better. Which is good news, because companies that use data to drive their decisions will outperform those who base their decisions on instinct and gut feeling alone.

Key Takeaways

In this chapter, we've learned that GenAI will help organizations solve some of their biggest data challenges:

- By making it easier for people to interact with and query data (e.g., through natural language questions), GenAI promises to democratize data, boost data literacy, and solve the problem of data anxiety.

- GenAI can automate or assist with a wide range of data analysis tasks, including preparing data, reviewing data, analyzing data, delivering automated notifications, creating summaries of data, surfacing important insights, generating reports, and creating engaging visuals that highlight insights.

- With GenAI's help, people across the organization will be able to use data to make better decisions and improve performance – regardless of their technical abilities.

- However, human oversight and human skills like judgment, complex decision-making, and strategic thinking will still be important. The goal is not to abdicate all decision-making responsibility to machines!

- Providers of analytics platforms are rapidly building GenAI features into their products – features that allow users to ask questions of their data, generate insights more easily, and share insights with others in the business.

Throughout this book, we've touched on some of the challenges that come with GenAI. So how can you best avoid these pitfalls and implement GenAI in the most thoughtful way? In the next chapter, we'll look at tips for successful implementation.

Notes

1. The Decision Dilemma: How More Data Causes Anxiety and Decision Paralysis; *Bernard Marr*; https://bernardmarr.com/the-decision-dilemma-how-more-data-causes-anxiety-and-decision-paralysis/
2. The Decision Dilemma: How More Data Causes Anxiety and Decision Paralysis; *Bernard Marr*; https://bernardmarr.com/the-decision-dilemma-how-more-data-causes-anxiety-and-decision-paralysis/
3. Data literacy; *Tableau*; https://www.tableau.com/why-tableau/data-literacy
4. How AI Can Help Leaders Make Better Decisions Under Pressure; *Harvard Business Review*; https://hbr.org/2023/10/how-ai-can-help-leaders-make-better-decisions-under-pressure
5. How JetBlue is leveraging AI, LLMs to be 'most data-driven airline in the world'; *Constellation Research*; https://www.constellationr.com/blog-news/insights/how-jetblue-leveraging-ai-llms-be-most-data-driven-airline-world
6. 5 main uses of generative AI in business intelligence and data analytics; *Hackernoon*; https://hackernoon.com/5-main-uses-of-generative-ai-in-business-intelligence-and-data-analytics
7. Introducing Microsoft Fabric and Copilot in Microsoft Power BI; *Microsoft*; https://powerbi.microsoft.com/en-us/blog/introducing-microsoft-fabric-and-copilot-in-microsoft-power-bi/
8. Terradata Launches ask.ai, Brings Generative AI Capabilities to Vantage-Cloud Lake; *Business Wire*; https://www.businesswire.com/news/home/20230911090555/en/Teradata-Launches-ask.ai-Brings-Generative-AI-Capabilities-to-VantageCloud-Lake
9. Experience Generative AI with Qlik; *Qlik*; https://www.qlik.com/blog/experience-generative-ai-with-qlik
10. How Tableau Pulse powered by Tableau AI are reimagining the data experience; *Tableau*; https://www.tableau.com/blog/tableau-pulse-and-tableau-ai

11. Oracle Doubles Down on Generative AI Trend at CloudWorld 2023; *Forbes*; https://www.forbes.com/sites/danielnewman/2023/10/03/oracle-doubles-down-on-generative-ai-trend-at-cloudworld-2023/?sh=5ccf33364acf

12. Alteryx launches no-code AI Studio to simplify the development of generative AI applications; *Silicon Angle*; https://siliconangle.com/2023/10/05/alteryx-launches-no-code-ai-studio-simplify-development-generative-ai-applications/

13. Introducing MicroStrategy AI: Generative AI on Trusted Data; *Business Wire*; https://www.businesswire.com/news/home/20231003746515/en/Introducing-MicroStrategy-AI-Generative-AI-on-Trusted-Data

14. Ask Anything of Your Data; *Kinetica*; https://www.kinetica.com/blog/sqlgpt-ask-anything-of-your-data/

15. Snowflake's Cortex to bring generative AI to its Data Cloud platform; *InfoWorld*; https://www.infoworld.com/article/3709518/snowflake-s-cortex-to-bring-generative-ai-to-its-data-cloud-platform.html

16. Akkio Launches Generative Reports to Turn Data into Decisions Instantly; *Akkio*; https://www.akkio.com/press-release/akkio-launches-generative-reports

Part 3
MOVING FORWARD WITH GENERATIVE AI

Now that we've seen how organizations across multiple sectors are using GenAI, it's time for you to think about deploying the technology in your business – using it to enhance your products and services, boost your processes, and more. But where do you start?

In Part 3, we'll look at tips for implementing GenAI successfully in your business. And in the final chapter, we'll explore where GenAI might be headed in the future.

18

IMPLEMENTING GENERATIVE AI: KEYS FOR SUCCESS

Okay, you've seen how other companies are using GenAI to great effect. You understand that the technology will be utterly transformative, and you're inspired to get started.

So now you're ready to dive straight into the technology and start using tools like ChatGPT for everything, right? Not quite. Because if there's one thing I've learned from my long career consulting with organizations on transformative technologies it's that transformation never starts with the technology itself. If anything, technology is the last piece of the puzzle.

With GenAI, it's not just a case of "have a play around and see how it might be useful." You can't just tell everyone in your business to start using ChatGPT right away, because there are very real challenges and limitations, especially around privacy. You can't have your sales team uploading customer data to a tool like ChatGPT, for example, because that could potentially expose people's personal data. Yes, you want people to be using these sorts of tools as quickly as possible, but *thoughtfully*. Thoughtfully, carefully, and with all the support and guidance they need to get the best out of new technology.

If you're going to successfully effect change – and bring people in the organization along with that change – you need the right building blocks in place to support that change. And the very first, arguably most important, building block centers around culture and mindset.

Fostering the Right Culture and Mindset for Success

Adopting such a transformative technology requires a shift in culture and mindset. It requires an organizational culture where people in the business continually challenge the status quo, are comfortable with change (and failure), are not afraid to experiment, and are open to learning new things.

I'm talking about a culture where people constantly ask questions like, "How can we better serve our customers?" "How can we create more value for customers?" "How can we create more value for the world?" and "How can we use technology to do that?"

The GenAI mindset

I firmly believe that as this new era of GenAI unfolds, a separation will emerge among businesses (and individuals): those who leverage the technology to enhance innovation and productivity, and those who lag behind. The decisive factor here is mindset.

The starting point for managing any change is usually working out how we need to change ourselves. For most of us, that means adopting a "GenAI mindset" (or "growth mindset" if you prefer). This goes beyond skills (which are undoubtedly important, and we'll talk about later in the chapter). It's about embracing certain beliefs and cultivating certain attributes. In particular:

- Understanding that GenAI is *a tool*: It won't do our jobs for us, but we'll use it to do our jobs more effectively. As such, GenAI won't replace the need for human attributes like creativity and problem-solving, but it will dramatically cut the amount of time we spend on repetitive or mundane tasks.

- Being adaptable: This includes being willing to walk away from what we know, even if we think it works, in order to try something new.

- Being curious: A trait that has driven every great inventor and explorer and is vital for success in our rapidly changing workplaces. Curiosity can be honed by training ourselves to listen actively, ask questions, and be open when we aren't sure about something. For me, curiosity and humility are two sides of the same coin. If we think of curiosity as "How can I/we do things better?", humility says "I don't know everything, but am willing to learn."

- Embracing a continuous approach to learning: Gone are the days when school and college set us up for a lifelong career. Keeping ahead today means constantly updating our skills and knowledge. We'll talk more about skills later in the chapter.

- Being willing to work collaboratively – with both humans and machines: Because, increasingly, this is how work will get done, by combining the best of human labor and machine labor.

- Being mindful of ethics: Most new technologies bring ethical challenges and the GenAI mindset doesn't shy away from this. Instead, it means continually questioning how things are done and the ethics of those decisions.

- Thinking critically: The GenAI mindset isn't about blindly following what machines tell us. Far from it. More than ever, we will need humans to think critically.

This is the same sort of mindset that's been adopted by those who have successfully harnessed other big waves of transformation, like the internet. Indeed, in his book, *The Geek Way*, MIT principal research scientist, Andrew McAfee, talks about the geek mindset, describing a geek as an "obsessive maverick" who is tenacious and unafraid to be unconventional. He sets out four characteristics that define "the geek way": speed, ownership, science, and openness. When I spoke to him, McAfee says this mindset is what has enabled geeks to inherit the earth (by which he's referring to the fact that one-third of all market capitalization gains made by US companies in the twenty-first century came out of Silicon Valley).[1]

McAfee's four qualities tie in nicely with what I think of as the GenAI mindset. Speed, for example, is about iterating quickly, failing when necessary, and using lessons learned to improve. Ownership means everyone is responsible for their own work and hitting their own goals (you might also refer to this as "autonomy"). Science means acting according to data, and making evidence-based decisions. And openness is the ability to accept criticism or new ideas.

All are essential elements for using GenAI successfully – and, I'd argue, all can be aided by GenAI, as well. GenAI will help us come up with new ideas, unearth insights in data to inform our decisions, complete our work in ways that best suit us, and experiment.

Of course, all of these qualities aren't just important in a work context – they're useful in everyday life, helping us navigate change and adversity, embrace new experiences, get along with others, and make ethical choices. Crucially, they are all qualities that anyone can develop and hone.

How this translates to organizational culture (and structure)

The ideas behind mindset are closely tied to the idea of organizational culture – which is also often either an aid or impediment to the successful adoption of new technologies. The GenAI mindset I've talked about has to start at the top and filter down across the organization, which means you need board awareness and buy-in for change. You need leaders that embody the GenAI mindset and foster a culture that embraces GenAI.

You may also need to look at your organizational structure. So many organizations still have rigid, hierarchical structures. Yet, the organizations that are most successful in this new, AI-driven world are more porous, flexible, and fluid. Why? Because they're set up in a way that can roll with change and innovate more quickly (as opposed to a hierarchical organization where decisions can often take an age to get approval).

Therefore, I believe the GenAI era will accelerate the need for more fluid and porous organizations. Where the business is organized according to teams, rather than a hierarchical structure, and where teams may be comprised of permanent employees in the office, employees who work from home, and freelancers – all collaborating seamlessly to get projects done. This means organizations will not only need to rethink traditional approaches to employment, but also prepare workers for a new way of working – project-based work, with cross-functional collaboration, using remote and digital tools.

We also need both business leaders and individuals to accept that the concept of a linear, lifelong career is dissolving. The future of work will be characterized by fluid career paths, driven by technological advancements, societal transformations, environmental challenges, and so on. Once again, the GenAI mindset – one that embodies a commitment to lifelong learning, adaptability, curiosity, etc. – will serve people well in this much more fluid working environment.

Requiring new roles within the organization

We've talked about how jobs will change in the GenAI era and the emergence of new roles, such as AI prompt engineer (Chapter 5). But one thing we haven't talked about is the requirement for new leadership roles.

In particular, I recommend organizations appoint a chief AI officer (CAIO) – a board-level position that promotes a better awareness of the technology across the business (and especially the leadership team), and ensures the technology is being used effectively. Basically, the CAIO takes oversight of the organization's AI strategy in order to align it with business goals. This includes identifying opportunities to deploy AI, ensuring the skills and people are in place to effectively execute the AI strategy, fostering an AI-driven culture, and dealing with issues around ethics, regulation, and compliance.

How is this different from a CDO (chief digital officer) or CTO (chief technology officer)? Much of what the CAIO does could be seen as a subset of what a CDO or CTO does, but their time is spent specifically on tasks that involve AI. If we consider that tasks and responsibilities involving AI are set to become such a big part of any organization (and therefore, the CDO or CTO's workload), it makes sense that you need a dedicated senior-level executive to manage it effectively.

What if appointing a CAIO isn't an option in your particular organization? Some organizations are appointing AI experts as non-executive directors to help the board understand AI technologies and how to implement them. In fact, this is a role I perform for a number of companies, and it's a great option if you don't have (or can't have) in-house knowledge.

Cultivating the Right Skills and Talent

The GenAI era will prompt a complete rethink of the skills needed to succeed in the workplace. This is yet another building block to think about when implementing GenAI.

The art of AI delegation

In the workplaces of the future, AI delegation will become a critical skill in its own right. What is AI delegation? It means working out what we still need to do for ourselves, and what's best left to machines. As GenAI becomes more powerful and more widely accessible, how proficient we become at putting it to work in order to drive efficiency and create value will increasingly become a driver of success.

For business leaders and managers, this means understanding the capabilities of GenAI, the tools that are available, and how they relate to your specific business function and/or industry. And for individuals, this means looking at your own workload and seeing how GenAI can reduce the time spent on repetitive tasks so you have more time for other, more important tasks.

AI delegation – whether by managers or individuals – can vastly increase efficiency by managing routine elements of work such as data entry, processing, and analysis, detecting errors, reviewing documents, scheduling, and time management. And as with any form of delegation, the value lies in what can be done with the time saved – more time for tasks that require original thought, strategic thinking, decision-making, and relationship building.

What about other skills for success? We essentially want people to cultivate complementary skills that help organizations get the best out of both machines and humans. Because, remember, we're not talking about total automation here – we're talking about job augmentation and making work better.

As a father of three, this is something I'm thinking about a lot lately. How will my children succeed in this future world? What skills can we equip them with at home to set them up for rapidly changing workplaces? It's something we should all be thinking about, not just for our own job, or the jobs of the people that we lead, but also the next generation joining the workforce.

For a thorough look at essential skills, you might like to pick up a copy of my book *Future Skills: The 20 skills and competencies everyone needs to succeed in a digital world*. It takes a practical look at essential skills for our future workplaces, with a particular emphasis on softer, human skills like empathy, complex decision-making, collaboration, and critical thinking – basically, the areas where humans have the edge over machines. Once again, it's the complementary skills that will become increasingly in demand.

Tapping into AI talent (via upskilling and partnerships)

Of course, you will also need to build AI knowledge and skills across the organization. This doesn't necessarily mean recruiting AI talent, though. The truth is, it will be hard for the average business to attract tech talent because competing with the likes of OpenAI and Google for talent is nearly impossible.

Therefore, the best thing you can do is invest in upskilling your existing people so they can understand the emerging technology, use GenAI in their work, and decide for themselves how it can be used to add value. This approach puts people in the driving seat, rather than make them feel like helpless passengers, having change *done to them*.

Talent development is different for each company, but the most obvious options include formal education and training programs, mentorship programs, and informal on-the-job learning opportunities. The good news is, there's never been a better time to be a lifelong learner, with a wealth of new courses coming onto the market to educate people in AI, GenAI, and data skills. What's more, many of these courses are free, and you can choose from courses that are specific to your needs (GenAI for video generation, for instance).

Online learning opportunities span the whole spectrum from massive online learning providers like Udemy and Coursera, to courses created by tech companies (and tech-specific educators). For example, IBM has launched an AI Academy, Microsoft and Amazon have created courses on GenAI, and Google has launched both free and paid-for GenAI training courses on its Cloud Skills Boost platform, including courses designed for non-technical roles (such as sales, marketing, HR, etc.).

May I also put in a good word for my own YouTube channel, which is a great (and free) resource for non-technical people grappling with technology changes. Just search my name on YouTube to subscribe to my channel.

Developing partnerships with start-up technology companies – and perhaps even university departments specializing in AI – is another great way to tap into technology expertise without hiring in-house talent. You may also want to consider acquiring businesses that have the in-house skills you need. Plus, there's the vast pool of freelance workers out there...

Retaining talent will become more important than ever

Competition for talent – especially AI-literate talent – is intense. So having put all that thought into essential skills, and equipping people with the skills for success, it makes sense that you really want talent to stick around. You need to create an environment that boosts employee retention.

This encompasses all the things you'd expect, like good pay, attractive benefits, flexible working arrangements, opportunities for career development, recognition for a job well done, a welcoming work environment, and so on. But again, it also comes down to the organizational culture and whether it supports attributes like curiosity, continual learning, and adaptability – or whether it squashes innovation.

In this era of rapid transformation, another good way to boost employee retention is to hire for culture fit and potential, not just skills – because when someone is a great fit for your organization, even if they aren't a perfect skills match, they're more likely to be happier in the company and stay longer. Remember, skills can be developed, but a cultural mismatch is hard to overcome.

Data as Another Key Building Block

AI is nothing without data. As such, data must be treated as one of today's most valuable business assets. (And crucially, as a shared asset, with data shared across the business. The last thing you want is to have lots of separate pockets of data that each team hoards.)

The first point to note is that your business should already have a data strategy in place. This is where you identify your business problems and unanswered questions, the data you need to solve those challenges, the technology you need to accomplish your goals, and how you will protect your data through good governance. If you haven't got a data strategy, I urge you to read my best-selling book *Data Strategy: How to Profit from a World of Big Data, Analytics and the Internet of Things*. And if you have got a data strategy in place, be sure to review and update it in light of what you've learned about GenAI.

There is so much data available in the world today. We have more data than ever before, and the amount of data is growing all the time. Yet, only a fraction of available data is used by organizations. A thorough, up-to-date data strategy will help you get the most out of this vast resource.

As well as having an up-to-date data strategy in place, you also need to consider the shelf-life of data. Because, like milk and reality TV stars, data can quickly go out of date.

The importance of real-time data

Timing is everything. It's useful to understand what happened in your business last week, last month, or last year. But even more important than that, is understanding what's happening in your business *right now*. Which is why one of the biggest trends in data and analytics is *real-time insights*. As you consider the data that will help you harness GenAI, be sure to think about how you can capture and act on information as it happens – or as close to that as possible.

The reason that real-time data is so valuable to businesses is that, in a world where we're creating 2.5 quintillion bytes of data every day, not only is it expensive to store old data, but the shelf-life of data is shrinking. The most valuable insights are always going to be in the most up-to-date data. As Naveen Peddamail, a Walmart senior analyst, told me, "If you can't get insights until you've analyzed your sales for a week or a month, then you've lost sales."[2]

The exact data you need will be specific to your business, but as a starting point (and this is something I talk about in my data strategy book), I always advise business leaders to focus on the data that will solve your biggest business problems and challenges, or help you answer your most pressing business questions.

Proprietary data will set you apart – but don't overlook external data

You can harness data from both internal sources (proprietary data from within the business) and external data from third-party sources. Proprietary data is obviously incredibly valuable because, by its very nature, only your business has that information. That is the information that will set you apart from your competitors.

That said, external data can be very useful. External data encompasses all the data out there that isn't owned by your business. Could be social media data. Could be weather data or satellite data. Could be demographic data. Could be internet search data. Wherever it comes from, you can glean valuable insights from third-party datasets. As an example, I know of one construction company that uses high-res satellite images which, combined with AI analytics, means they can monitor progress on competitors' construction sites.

Of course, there are challenges to working with external data. There may be a cost to access that data. You don't have direct control of the data (and you may find yourself overly reliant on the data provider). You could lose access to the data. And you'll need to be sure that the data you're buying or accessing has been collected and processed in a lawful, ethical way. But all things considered, external data has the potential to be extremely rewarding – and when combined with your precious internal data, allows you to build a wider picture of what's going on.

I'm aware that talk of data can make people seize up in anxiety, so to sum up my tips for finding the right data: make sure you have a thorough, up-to-date data strategy in place (one that's been updated to take account of GenAI); focus on the data that will solve your biggest business problems; think about the shelf-life of that data, and how you can get as close to real-time data as possible; and finally, start with your precious internal data, but also consider the value of external data.

Getting the Right Technology in Place

Finally, having considered culture, skills, and data, you can then begin to think about the technology you need to make all this happen. Again, every business will have different technology needs, but broadly speaking, you can think of technology requirements for GenAI in terms of two layers:

- The base layer is fast networks and connectivity, data infrastructure, and cybersecurity. These three are the foundational tech building blocks that will help you leverage GenAI (and other cutting-edge technologies) successfully.

- On top of this sits your GenAI tools.

The foundation: networks, data infrastructure, and security

Before making any decisions about GenAI technologies, it's really important to get your foundational technologies right. These technologies aren't nice-to-have options – they're absolute bedrock technologies. Must-haves, for any business, regardless of size or budget.

In terms of networks, you need fast, secure networks and easy connectivity, not just in your offices, but also on the go. The latest iteration in mobile network technology, 5G, will transform connectivity for many businesses, bringing swift connections and real-time collaborations, wherever your people are.

In terms of data management, we're not talking about collecting vast quantities of data – we're talking about collecting the right data, at the right time, and having the means to store, access, and use that data. There are lots of options for data storage but in my opinion, cloud storage is the best option for most businesses.

And in terms of cybersecurity, we're talking about technologies that keep your business safe from threats like ransomware, phishing, and breaches. Not only does this involve deploying advanced threat detection mechanisms, it also involves being aware of emerging threat landscapes, and training the workforce so they can detect potential threats.

These three foundational elements are essential to businesses of all sizes and budgets. A small company operating on a tight budget will obviously want to keep the foundations simple, but they're still necessary. If I were a small business, I'd focus on beefing up network connectivity to ensure seamless operations, getting a decent cloud-based data infrastructure in order, and ensuring the best cybersecurity possible. Those really are the three basic things you can do to prepare your business for next-level technologies like GenAI.

If you have more money to throw at your foundational technologies, you might consider leveling up your foundational elements. Choosing 5G for faster, more robust connections, for instance. Or integrating paid-for external datasets to enrich your insights. Or even dabbling in synthetic data to expand your repository.

Choosing GenAI tools

We've talked about GenAI tools throughout the book, and in the Appendix you'll find a handy list in one place. You can tap into readily available tools like ChatGPT or its underlying GPT-4 language model, but you'll have to consider the potential privacy implications. (At the very least, always be aware of whether the information you enter will be used for training language models.)

Lots of organizations that I work with choose to create their own secure version of GPT-4, but that may not be feasible depending on your budget and expertise. The great thing about GenAI is there are so many options, from companies on a shoestring to companies with deep, deep pockets. If you don't have the in-house knowledge to help you decide which tool or tools are right for your business, it's well worth consulting with an AI expert.

Remember to Take a Strategic Approach

Finally, to revisit what I said in Chapter 3, remember that GenAI has big implications for businesses. As such, you will need to review your overarching business strategy to ensure it's still relevant, and update it in line with the incredible possibilities of GenAI.

When I work with companies on their AI strategy, what often happens is they realize their existing business strategy is not fit for purpose. Because AI in general – and specifically GenAI – will change their business, for example, by rendering aspects of their service obsolete. So as a final reminder, please do take a thorough look at your business strategy and see whether it is still relevant in terms of where the world is heading.

When you're happy that your business strategy is up to date, then you can create an AI strategy, if you haven't done so already. (And, again, if you do have an existing AI strategy, it will also need to be reviewed and updated in line with GenAI.) As you might expect, I have a book to help with AI strategy, too. It's called *The Intelligence Revolution: Transforming Your Business With AI*, and it's designed to help businesses plan for and implement AI successfully.

But at heart, an AI strategy starts with two simple steps. First, you identify the potential applications of AI/GenAI in your business. These are your use cases. Then you whittle those potential use cases down to just a few (one to three) top-priority use cases, plus one or two "quick-win" uses. So, you're looking for a combination of high-value, long-term use cases that are key to long-term business success, plus a couple of quick-win projects that may not be as strategically important, but help you experiment with AI/GenAI, build confidence, and build buy-in. Having identified your use cases, you can then think about the data you need for those use cases, plus technology, and any governance issues.

While the allure of exciting new technologies is strong, it's really important to take a strategic approach. In terms of GenAI, this starts with understanding the impact of GenAI on your business operations, your products and services, and maybe even your business model – and then updating your business strategy accordingly, before you tackle an AI strategy and implementation.

Key Takeaways

We've covered a lot of ground in this chapter. To recap:

- Remember that GenAI is *a tool*. It won't do our jobs for us, but we'll use it to do our jobs more effectively.

- Adopting GenAI successfully requires a shift in culture and mindset. It requires a mindset that embraces curiosity, humility, adaptability, and collaboration. It requires an organizational culture where people continually challenge the status quo, are comfortable with change (and failure), are not afraid to experiment, and are open to learning new things. This culture and mindset must be modeled from the top down.

- To help with culture and mindset (and implementation in general), I strongly recommend organizations appoint a chief AI officer (CAIO) – a board-level position that promotes a better awareness of AI and ensures AI is being used effectively. As an alternative, you might appoint an AI expert as a non-executive director.

- In terms of skills and talent, AI delegation will become a crucial skill. For leaders, managers, and individuals, this means working out what we still need to do for ourselves, and what's best left to machines. Tapping into AI talent can be difficult for many businesses, so upskilling your existing people is likely to be the best approach.

- AI is nothing without data, so if you don't already have a data strategy in place, now is the time to create one. With so much data on offer, I recommend focusing on the data that will solve your biggest business problems. Also, think about the shelf-life of that data (real time or near–real time is best), and consider both internal and external data.

- In terms of technology, there are three fundamental elements that will help you leverage new technologies successfully: fast networks and connectivity, data infrastructure, and cybersecurity. Your GenAI tools then sit atop that bedrock. Turn to the Appendix for a list of GenAI tools.

- And finally, it's really important to take a strategic approach. You need to understand the impact of GenAI on your business operations, your products and services, and maybe even your business model – and then update your business strategy accordingly.

We're almost at the end of our journey. In the final chapter, we'll explore some predictions for the future of GenAI. Some of which may surprise you. . .

Notes

1. Generative AI: The Mindset Divide That Will Determine Your Success; *Forbes*; https://www.forbes.com/sites/bernardmarr/2023/11/13/generative-ai-the-mindset-divide-that-will-determine-your-success/
2. How to Use Real-Time Data: Key Examples and Use Cases; *Bernard Marr*; https://bernardmarr.com/how-to-use-real-time-data-key-examples-and-use-cases/

19

GLIMPSES OF THE FUTURE: PREDICTING THE TRAJECTORY OF GENERATIVE AI

Imagine a future where AI isn't just smart but also your creative sidekick. Generative AI could turn brainstorming sessions into a wild ride of endless ideas, design personalized virtual experiences, and maybe even help you write that novel you've been dreaming about. It's like having a super-smart, ultra-creative companion at your fingertips, making the future look pretty darn exciting!

That's what ChatGPT had to say when I asked it about the future of GenAI. As for me, I have a few predictions of my own on how GenAI will evolve. Let's get into them.

Are We Moving Closer to General AI?

All of the GenAI capabilities that we've talked about so far in this book fall under the umbrella of *narrow* or *applied AI* – meaning they simulate human thought in order to carry out a specific task or function (like drafting an email, or generating an image). We're not yet at the point of *general* or *generalized AI* – intelligent machines that can turn their attention to pretty much *any task*, just like the human brain can. In other words, while today's AIs do a good job of simulating human thought, creativity, simple decision-making, and conversation, they're not able to fully simulate everything the human brain does. But are we nearing that point?

Certainly, creativity (or the simulation of creativity) feels like a major milestone on that journey. Something that was previously considered uniquely human can now be done by machines to a pretty impressive standard. And they will only get better and better. There's no rolling back the clock on this intelligence revolution. From here, there is only forwards; forwards toward more intelligent machines.

Whether we'll achieve this vision of *truly* intelligent machines is still up for debate, but it does seem we're edging closer to that point. We now have machines that can see, hear, speak, read, write, and create. And increasingly, GenAIs are gaining the ability to do many of these things at once – such as being able to create text and images together. As an example, the third iteration of text-to-image tool Dall-E is able to generate high-quality text embedded in its images, putting it ahead of rival image-generator tools.[1] Imagine, for instance, an AI-generated image of a billboard sign with text on it, or a picture of a brick wall plastered with graffiti text. Creating images like these, with text in, has previously proven tricky for GenAIs. The most recent versions of GenAI tools can now see, hear, and speak, as well as write.[2]

So, one of my predictions is that GenAIs will continue this move toward multimodal AIs that can create in multiple ways – and in real time, just like the human brain. That will bring us another step closer toward general AI, or true machine intelligence.

According to DeepMind co-founder, Mustafa Suleyman, the next step beyond GenAI is "interactive AI" – by which he means bots that don't just chat, but can carry out all sorts of tasks by delegating to other software (and even people) to get stuff done for you.[3] In Chapter 16, we saw how GenAI can be used to write or review computer code, meaning you could use it to build, for example, a new recipe app designed around healthy eating. As AI becomes more interactive, you could, in theory, task an AI with the entire app-creation project – from writing and testing the code, to hiring nutritionists, food photographers, and recipe developers (some of whom may be bots), to liaising with beta testers, to releasing the app, and organizing the marketing campaign. In a simpler example, you could ask a bot, like ChatGPT, to book a night away for you and your partner – including finding and booking the hotel, choosing a restaurant for you, booking a table (and informing the restaurant of your partner's egg allergy), and booking a walking tour of the city. You could delegate the entire task to a bot.

This takes the notion of multi-model, real-time GenAIs to a whole new level, doesn't it? If Suleyman is right, AIs will become much more interactive and helpful – making our lives easier every day by taking on the burden of mundane tasks and allowing us to focus on . . . well, who knows what? Organizing our sock drawers, perhaps. The point is, it's another step on the journey toward generalized AI – intelligent machines that can do anything the human brain can do.

But how else can we expect GenAI to evolve? I have more predictions up my sleeve. . .

Combining Generative AI with Robots

If you've ever seen any of Boston Dynamic's videos, you'll know that robots are developing at an impressive rate. In the not-too-distant future, I believe we'll see robots being routinely equipped with GenAI capabilities – thereby vastly increasing the range of tasks that both robots and AIs can take on for us.

So far, GenAI enables us to automate and augment cognitive and creative jobs, including the work of doctors, designers, musicians, marketers, and more. Physical jobs such as building, assembly line work, cleaning, and so on are (by and large) unaffected by the wave of GenAI transformation. But combine GenAI with robots and that may change. We could see AIs working in all sorts of sectors. On factory floors, checking in on patients in hospital wards, on construction sites, in retail stores, in hotels, in restaurants, you name it. By embedding GenAI in robots, you have machines that can not only perform tasks but also generate new customer experiences. For instance, a hotel concierge robot could tailor travel itineraries in real time, based on the guests' preferences.

Looking further ahead, we may even live with intelligent robots in our homes. Imagine having an all-knowing robot companion in your home – a robot powered by GenAI that could answer any question you have, while also hoovering the floor, managing your schedule, planning what to have for dinner, helping you write that report for work, creating personalized learning plans for your children, and even suggesting what movie to watch in the evening based on your mood. It's like having an Alexa, Roomba, cleaner, personal chef, personal assistant, tutor, and babysitter all rolled into one.

NVIDIA is already working on combining GenAI with robotics. The company has updated its Jetson AI and robotics platform – which has long been adopted across industries including manufacturing and transportation – to facilitate the use of GenAI.[4] The main idea here is that GenAI brings advancements in computer vision (the ability for machines to "see"), by giving machines the ability to learn faster and become more accurate at identifying and reacting to the things around them. Traditionally, computer vision relies on systems being trained on vast amounts of data, with the machine learning to recognize specific objects and then react in specific ways. When a system comes across an object it doesn't recognize, it's stumped. Which is where GenAI comes in. GenAI offers greater generalization, because it can recognize and interact with elements it hasn't necessarily been trained on.

For industries that use robots relying on computer vision, GenAI could prove transformative. But it will also transform robots in other ways. For example, it could give machines the ability to communicate with colleagues around them.

In other words, although we may be some way away from intelligent home robots, in the very near future, GenAI will begin to impact robots in industrial and other work settings.

Brain–Computer Interfaces Will Allow for More Intuitive Interactions

At the moment, you need to go to an app or web page to interact with GenAI, but how about having an almost direct link to a GenAI system from your brain? You simply speak a question or request, and the GenAI responds. This could be achieved through smart glasses or smart contact lenses, or even through implants in the brain. Whatever the hardware looks like, the point is: the way in which we interact with GenAI may evolve to become much more intuitive and instant.

If it sounds like I've gone off the deep end, hold on. Because research is already well underway into the field of *brain–computer interfaces* (BCIs) – means for us to interact with machines or the internet through thoughts alone. Boston-based start-up, Neurable, is already working in this field, creating sensors that can decipher brain activity, understand the user's intention, and then translate that into virtual reality. Elsewhere, Elon Musk–founded Neuralink is developing implants that will allow two-way communication between the human brain and an app. Meta is also developing its own BCIs that can decode speech directly from the brain.

Developments in BCIs could end up transforming humans into practically a new species. To some extent this merging of humans and machines is already happening. People are being fitted with robotic arms and bionic eyes, for instance. So why not augment the human brain with the ability to tap directly into AI?

Nobody knows how the field of BCIs will develop, but I think it's a real possibility that we could, in future, be collaborating with machines in more and more intuitive ways.

Imagine the implications for human creativity and efficiency, if BCIs enable direct communication between the human brain and GenAI systems. Ideas could be generated, refined, and brought to fruition with unprecedented speed and precision. Decision-making and innovation would be vastly improved if we could combine human cognition and experience with the data-processing prowess of AI. It's a really interesting prospect, and – I admit – a somewhat wild prediction for the future. But with the speed at which AI and BCIs are developing? It's certainly not impossible.

Using Generative AI for a Better World

The final point I want to leave you with is this: as one of the most transformative technologies we've ever seen, GenAI can be a force for enormous good in this world.

GenAI can help us tackle some of the biggest problems on the planet. Yes, GenAI can be used to draft a funny speech for your friend's wedding, or come up with an idea for tonight's supper. But it can also be used to address issues like climate change, massive inequality, hunger, access to healthcare, and more. It can help us find new treatments for diseases. It can democratize access to mental health support. It can predict how infectious diseases will progress. It can address food security through crop yield optimization. It can do so much good. When you think about it, it's rather like giving humans superpowers.

Of course, on the flipside, GenAI can also be used to spread misinformation, create new biological weapons, or even build autonomous weapons that can identify and neutralize threats without any human oversight.

Which is why we need to ensure we use this super-potent technology for the right things. We will need regulations that will protect us and ensure GenAI is used for positive transformation – and not to create more polarization, meddle in elections, deliberately spread false information, and the like. We will need transparency around how these systems are used. We will need ethical guidelines and frameworks in place.

To some extent this is beginning to happen. Meta, for example, has announced that political ads running on Facebook and Instagram will be required to disclose if they contain AI-generated content and images.[5] It's an attempt to help voters make more informed decisions about the content they see online in the run-up to elections. Other tech companies are following suit. Google, for example, has a similar labeling policy, requiring political ads on YouTube and other Google Platforms to disclose the use of AI-altered voices or imagery.[6] Efforts like these will help to combat GenAI's ability to create realistic-looking (but entirely fake) videos, images, and audio.

We will also need technology companies (and organizations implementing GenAI tools) to address limitations around bias and hallucinations. Navigating a problem like hallucinations is tricky when it's still unclear *why* GenAIs occasionally say the wrong thing. But there are workarounds, such as running two GenAI models in parallel, with one model fact-checking the other. The good news is, a lot of work is going into this area, as it's in the interests of all major stakeholders in the industry to solve these problems.

So yes, there are challenges to overcome, and it would be naive to imagine GenAI will *only* be used for good. But my hope is GenAI will be *overwhelmingly* used for good, to tackle some of humanity's most pressing challenges and make our world better.

This is our opportunity. And what an opportunity it is.

Connect with Me

That brings us to the end of my predictions. But what do you think? Are you excited by the idea of GenAI or a little weirded out by it?

One of the things I love about writing books like this is it's a springboard for further discussion. So please do feel free to ask questions or share your thoughts. How are you beginning to use GenAI in your everyday life and work? How might GenAI help you solve your organization's biggest problems? How might your workplace be transformed by GenAI and other future technologies? What are your biggest implementation challenges? How do you see your own job role evolving?

And of course, you can always get in touch if you need help planning for this AI-driven revolution and implementing future technologies. I consult with businesses of all shapes and sizes.

You can connect with me on the following platforms:

LinkedIn: Bernard Marr

Twitter: @bernardmarr

YouTube: Bernard Marr

Instagram: @bernardmarr

Facebook: facebook.com/BernardWMarr

Or head to my website at **www.bernardmarr.com** for more content (including my podcast), and to join my weekly newsletter, in which I share the very latest information.

Notes

1. DALL-E 3 could take AI image generation to the next level; *Digital Trends*; https://www.digitaltrends.com/computing/dall-e-3-testing-leaked-revealing-interesting-new-text-features/
2. The New ChatGPT Can 'See' and 'Talk.' Here's What It's Like; *NY Times*; https://www.nytimes.com/2023/09/27/technology/new-chatgpt-can-see-hear.html
3. DeepMind's co-founder: Generative AI is just a phase. What's next is interactive AI; *Technology Review*; https://www.technologyreview.com/2023/09/15/1079624/deepmind-inflection-generative-ai-whats-next-mustafa-suleyman/
4. Generative AI Is Coming to Robots, Courtesy of NVIDIA; *eWeek*; https://www.eweek.com/artificial-intelligence/generative-ai-robots-nvidia/
5. To help 2024 voters, Meta says it will begin labeling political ads that use AI-generated imagery; *AP News*; https://apnews.com/article/meta-facebook-instagram-political-ads-deepfakes-2024-c4aec653d5043a09b1c78b4fb5dcd79b
6. To help 2024 voters, Meta says it will begin labeling political ads that use AI-generated imagery; *AP News*; https://apnews.com/article/meta-facebook-instagram-political-ads-deepfakes-2024-c4aec653d5043a09b1c78b4fb5dcd79b

APPENDIX: GENAI TOOLS

MULTIMODAL MODELS

ChatGPT

The application that kicked off the current generative AI craze, ChatGPT, has evolved since it emerged in 2022 and now includes multimodal capabilities, as well as access to GPT-4, the most powerful publicly available language model. It could fit into many of the categories in this list, so I'll just put it here!

https://chat.openai.com/

Google Bard

Bard is a multimodal chatbot much like ChatGPT but Google users might appreciate its extensive integration with tools like Gmail, Drive, and Maps.

Google Vertex AI

Multimodal search combining language and vision models aimed at enabling businesses to organize and analyze data.

https://cloud.google.com/blog/products/ai-machine-learning/multimodal-generative-ai-search

Meta Imagebind

Provides a multimodal platform based around six "sensory" datatypes – images, text, audio, depth, thermal, and inertial, enabling it to learn holistically, much like we do.

https://imagebind.metademolab.com/

Samsung Gauss

Samsung has created a multimodal suite of generative AI tools that will be integrated across its line of devices.

Writing/ Text Generation Tools

AI Writer

Writes content like blog posts while citing its sources, to help overcome issues of AI hallucination.

https://ai-writer.com

Anyword

Marketing-focused content generation tool with predictive performance scoring and audience analytics.

https://anyword.com

Copy.ai

Content creation tool aimed at businesses and enterprises, with built-in templates for common jobs.

https://www.copy.ai

Coursera

The online learning platform has created generative AI tools for students as well as teachers and course authors.

https://www.coursera.org/

DuoLingo

One of the most popular language-learning platforms, now with generative AI roleplay conversations and personalized feedback powered by GPT-4.

https://www.duolingo.com/

Jasper

Content creation tool aimed at marketers wanting to automate copywriting tasks like blogs, product descriptions, and social media posts.

https://www.jasper.ai/

Lex

An AI co-pilot for writers offering AI feedback on your work and tools for finding the right words or expressions, or generating ideas.

https://lex.page

Rytr

Generates blogs, emails, social media posts, SEO headlines, and ads.

https://rytr.me

Scribe

Automates the creation of documentation, step-by-step and how-to guides.

https://scribehow.com/tools/ai-text-generator

Wordtune

Generative writing assistant aimed at professionals.

https://www.wordtune.com/

WriteSonic

Geared toward creating SEO content and traffic-boosting copy.

https://writesonic.com

Education Tools

Cognii

Education platform offering personalized tutoring and student assessments generated by AI.

https://www.cognii.com/

Fetchy

Help with writing, planning, organizing, and lesson prep for teachers.

https://www.fetchy.com/

Gradescope

AI-augmented grading platform for educators; also enables peer evaluation of work.

https://www.gradescope.com/

Ivy

An AI framework for creating customer service chatbots, with a focus on helping institutions of higher learning.

https://ivy.ai/

Knowji

AI-powered language learning that creates customized lessons.

https://www.knowji.com/

Plaito

Generative text tool designed to help writers improve their skills with personalized feedback.

https://www.plaito.ai/

Querium

Personalized, step-by-step tutoring in STEM subjects.

https://www.querium.com/

Image, Art, and Design

Adobe Firefly

AI-powered graphic design for creating any kind of visuals; integrates with Adobe's creativity tools.

https://www.adobe.com/uk/sensei/generative-ai/firefly.html

Autodesk

This industry-standard design platform now provides generative tools aimed at improving users' skills and boosting creativity.

https://www.autodesk.com/

Canva

Generative design tools are now baked into the user-friendly graphic design platform.

https://www.canva.com/

Dall-E

Creates images based on text descriptions, now included in ChatGPT Plus.

https://openai.com/dall-e-2

Durable

Generate entire websites along with images and copy from language prompts.

https://durable.ai

Midjourney

Images from text; very powerful but currently only accessible over Discord.

https://www.midjourney.com/

Stable Diffusion

One of the most popular image generation models, unlike Dall-E it is open source.

https://stablediffusionweb.com/

Video

Colossyan

Generate synthetic content tailored for workplace learning.

https://www.colossyan.com/

Deepbrain

AI-generated virtual avatars and synthetic media aimed at corporate and business users.

https://www.deepbrain.io/

Descript

All-in-one AI video-editing platform with script-based editing and automated transcription.

https://www.descript.com/

Designs.AI

Generate graphics, videos, logos, and other design assets.

https://designs.ai/

Elai

Generative video tool geared toward designing training videos.

https://elai.io/

Filmora 13

Full AI-powered video-editing suite with chatbot co-pilot to help you out.

https://filmora.wondershare.com/

Fliki

Transform text into lifelike speech and videos, make videos in minutes.

https://fliki.ai/

HeyGen

Create talking photographs and other cool AI video tricks.

https://app.heygen.com/

Invideo

Create videos using a simple interface and pre-made templates.

https://invideo.io/

OpusClip

Automagically transform long-form videos into short, punchy viral clips.

https://www.opus.pro/

Peech

Create branded videos from your existing content library for podcasts, webinars, or social media.

https://www.peech-ai.com/

Pictory

AI video-editing platform that creates, edits, and narrates videos.

https://pictory.ai

Runway

Video generation for creatives with a focus on storytelling.

https://runwayml.com/

Synthesia

Turn text into video and create virtual video avatars that synthesize speech in multiple languages.

https://www.synthesia.io/home

Synthesys

Generate professional AI-powered avatars and voiceovers.

https://synthesys.io/

Type Studio

Create and edit videos simply by editing transcribed text.

https://topai.tools/t/type-studio

VEED:IO

Generative AI video creation and editing.

https://www.veed.io/

Sound, Music, and Voice Generators

Amadeus Code

Generative AI-powered songwriting assistant that allows users to pay per finished track.

https://amadeuscode.com/

AIVA

Great for those wanting to use AI to develop complex and emotional music pieces that sound like they were created by human composers.

https://www.aiva.ai/

Beatoven

Generate background music for online content (or any other type of music) in multiple styles, and edit with simple AI tools.

https://www.beatoven.ai/

Boomy

Create songs in seconds with a simple interface and a strong user community.

https://boomy.com/

Loudly

Music platform for creating AI-generated, royalty-free tracks, with AI-assisted recommendations.

https://www.loudly.com/

Mubert

Synthetic music generator that creates tunes to fit the mood of your content.

https://mubert.com/

Murf

AI voice studio with realistic and customizable text-to-speech.

https://murf.ai/

MusicLM

A Google AI Test Kitchen project that users can sign up to try out – Generative music creation from Google.

https://aitestkitchen.withgoogle.com/experiments/music-lm

Soundful

Generate unique tunes with the help of AI at the click of a button.

https://soundful.com/

Speechify

Text-to-speech tool for creating natural sounding synthetic voice.

https://speechify.com/

Soundraw

Create custom music tracks in many different styles and moods, for royalty-free use.

https://soundraw.io/

Splash

Create music based on text prompts, including vocals.

https://pro.splashmusic.com/

Wavtool

Music generator with user-friendly Conductor tool that guides even complete beginners through the process of creating AI music.

https://wavtool.com/

Coding Tools

AIXCoder

Augments programming abilities by providing intelligent code completion and optimization.

https://www.aixcoder.com/

Amazon CodeWhisperer

Automated code builder and assistant from Amazon, with real-time help using natural language prompts.

https://aws.amazon.com/codewhisperer/

Codacy

Automated code review and debugging.

https://www.codacy.com/

Codecomplete

Edit, analyze, and explain code in real time in order to streamline software creation.

https://codecomplete.ai/

Code Llama

Meta's AI coding assistant built on a tuned version of its Llama 2 language model, specializing in creating, analyzing, and interpreting code.

https://about.fb.com/news/2023/08/code-llama-ai-for-coding/

Hugging Face

Hugging Face is actually a community and collaborative platform, but it provides access to a large number of generative tools, models, and datasets.

https://huggingface.co/

Github Copilot

Provides contextually relevant code suggestions for programmers using OpenAI's Codex model, a version of its popular GPT-3 fine-tuned for coding tasks.

https://resources.github.com/copilot-for-business/

IBM WatsonX Code Assistant

Generative AI coding assistant from IBM powered by its Granite foundation model, with a focus on creating Enterprise-grade AI.

https://www.ibm.com/products/watsonx-code-assistant

Metabob

Automated code review that analyzes code for errors or bugs and suggests fixes.

https://metabob.com/

Mintlify

Automates the creation of programming documentation.

https://mintlify.com/

Mutable

AI-accelerated software development platform with automated test generation.

https://mutable.ai/

Replit

A cloud-based integrated development environment (IDE) augmented with generative functionality, and collaborative features.

https://replit.com/

Studio Bot

A generative AI tool from Google designed to help with software development for its Android platform.

https://developer.android.com/studio/preview/studio-bot

Tabnine AI Code Assistant

AI assistant for software development with a focus on security.

https://www.tabnine.com/ai-assistant-for-software-development-r

Warp

Not a code writer, but a terminal application that offers contextual autosuggestion, error correction, and suggestions on specific commands that a user might want to use.

https://www.warp.dev/

Data Analytics

Akkio

Generative BI platform that enables predictive modeling and insight generation.

https://www.akkio.com/

Alteryx

The Alteryx platform now incorporates a no-code AI Studio to let users create their own analytics apps, using custom business data.

https://www.alteryx.com

Microsoft Power BI

Microsoft has added generative analytics capabilities to Power BI, utilizing its Co-Pilot and Fabric AI platforms.

https://powerbi.microsoft.com/

Microstrategy

Generative AI assistant provides quick answers and insights into business data.

https://www.microstrategy.com

Qlik

Another established analytics and data platform that now lets users embed generative AI analytics content into their reports and dashboards.

https://www.qlik.com/

Tableau

Tableau Pulse helps users use generative AI to extract meaningful insights from data.

https://www.tableau.com/

Synthetic Data

BizData X

Simplifies data masking and anonymization with synthetic data generation for business.

https://bizdatax.com/

CTA Test Manager

Allows the creation of very technical and complex datasets.

https://www.broadcom.com/products/software/continuous-testing/test-data-manager

Cvedia

Computer vision and video analytics powered by synthetic data.

https://www.cvedia.com/

Datomize

Create datasets with dynamic validation tools to ensure they are as realistic as possible.

https://www.datomize.com/

Edgecase

Create labeled synthetic data as-a-service.

https://www.edgecase.ai/

GenRocket

Dynamic data generation with enterprise scalability, for creating data, to assist with software testing.

https://www.genrocket.com/

Gretel

Synthetic data platform targeted at software development.

https://gretel.ai/

Hazy

Generates synthetic data allowing customers to "mask" their real data, to solve security and privacy challenges.

https://hazy.com/

K2View

Generates data for the purpose of training machine-learning models.

https://www.k2view.com/solutions/synthetic-data-generation-tools/

KopiKat

No-code data augmentation designed to enhance privacy and improve performance of neural networks.

https://www.kopikat.co/

MDClone

Synthetic data aimed at healthcare professionals.

https://www.mdclone.com/

Mostly

Generate synthetic data that mimics real-world data.

https://mostly.ai/

Sogeti

Billed as a "data amplifier"; mimics real datasets by matching the characteristics and correlations of existing data.

https://www.sogeti.com/services/artificial-intelligence/artificial-data-amplifier/

Syntho

Self-service data generation for insights and decision-making.

https://www.syntho.ai/

Tonic

The "fake data company" provides a comprehensive platform for developing realistic, compliant, and secure synthetic data.

https://www.tonic.ai/

YData

Automated synthetic data generation to enhance productivity and AI model performance.

https://ydata.ai/

Productivity Tools

Airgram

Automatically record, transcribe, summarize, and share meeting transcripts and conversations.

https://www.airgram.io/

Beautiful

Transform ideas into fully realized slides and presentations with automated design features.

https://www.beautiful.ai/

ClickUp

Generative AI-driven workplace productivity suite with project management, time tracking, whiteboarding, agendas, and other features.

https://clickup.com/

Decktopus

Generate slide decks and presentations from natural language prompts.

https://www.decktopus.com/

Duet

Another Google service, this one is built into Workspace to provide a collaborative assistant for productivity tasks.

https://workspace.google.com/blog/product-announcements/duet-ai?ref=the-writesonic-blog-making-content-your-superpower

Fireflies

Transcribe, summarize, and search voice conversations.

https://fireflies.ai/

Notta

AI notetaking and audio transcription.

https://www.notta.ai/en

Cyber Security

Airgap

Comprehensive AI security-as-a-service that allows users to explore threats and analyze data with natural language processing.

https://airgap.io/

Crowdstrike Charlotte AI

Cloud security that you can talk to and question to get real-time, understandable insights.

https://www.crowdstrike.com/products/charlotte-ai/

Google Cloud Security Workbench

Google's comprehensive cloud security services include a powerful LLM-driven threat intelligence tool.

https://cloud.google.com/security/ai

Microsoft Security Co-Pilot

Summarizes threats and security signals with natural language generation.

https://www.microsoft.com/en-us/security/business/ai-machine-learning/microsoft-security-copilot

INDEX